TALES FROM THE TURF

TALES FROM THE TURF

REFLECTIONS FROM A LIFE IN HORSERACING

ROBIN OAKLEY

ICON

Published in the UK in 2013 by
Icon Books Ltd, Omnibus Business Centre,
39–41 North Road, London N7 9DP
email: info@iconbooks.net
www.iconbooks.net

Sold in the UK, Europe and Asia
by Faber & Faber Ltd, Bloomsbury House,
74–77 Great Russell Street,
London WC1B 3DA or their agents

Distributed in the UK, Europe and Asia
by TBS Ltd, TBS Distribution Centre, Colchester Road,
Frating Green, Colchester CO7 7DW

Distributed in Australia and New Zealand
by Allen & Unwin Pty Ltd,
PO Box 8500, 83 Alexander Street,
Crows Nest, NSW 2065

Distributed in South Africa by Book Promotions,
Office B4, The District, 41 Sir Lowry Road,
Woodstock 7925

Distributed in Canada by
Penguin Books Canada,
90 Eglinton Avenue East, Suite 700,
Toronto, Ontario M4P 2YE

ISBN: 978-190685-066-1

Typeset in New Baskerville by Marie Doherty

Printed and bound in the UK by
CPI Group (UK) Ltd, Croydon CR0 4YY

To Carolyn, who has always indulged my passion for racing despite not sharing it – the greatest gift a lifelong lover can give.

CONTENTS

CONTENTS

LIST OF
ILLUSTRATIONS

Images courtesy of the Press Association unless otherwise stated.

First plate section
Hurst Park when it was still a racecourse.
'Prince Monolulu'.
Sea The Stars and Michael Kinane triumph in the Derby.
Marcus Tregoning's Sir Percy taking the Derby from
    Dragon Dancer and Dylan Thomas.
Galileo: a top-class Derby winner.
Persian War winning his third Champion Hurdle in 1970.
Henrietta Knight with Best Mate.
The fairytale turrets of Goodwood.
Racegoers arriving at Windsor by boat. (racingpost.com/
    photos)
Ladies Day at Aintree.
Kempton, 1996: One Man heads for victory in the
    King George VI Chase.
Ouija Board takes the Nassau at Goodwood from
    Alexander Goldrun.
Giant's Causeway beats Kalanisi in the Coral-Eclipse.
Sir Michael Stoute on the receiving end of a smacker from
    Frankie Dettori following their St Leger win in 2008.

Second plate section
Richard Hughes.
Kieren Fallon.
Frankie Dettori.

Bookmaker Gary Wiltshire.
Tony McCoy.
Nicky Henderson's horses on the gallops at Seven Barrows.
Nicky Henderson at Seven Barrows with Gold Cup winner
    Long Run.
Trainer Barry Hills with 2,000 Guineas winner Haafhd, led
    up by Snowy Outen.
Henry Cecil supervising the morning routine.
    (racingpost.com/photos)
Paul Nicholls with Kauto Star and Denman.
Russian Rhythm winning the Lockinge Stakes with
    Kieren Fallon.
Mandarin poised in second to overtake Fortria and win
    his Cheltenham Gold Cup in 1962.
Singspiel at the Breeders' Cup: a tragic end to an
    illustrious globe-trotting career. (Getty images)
Sha Tin, Hong Kong. (Getty images)
Sheikh Mohammed bin Rashid al Maktoum.
World Cup day in Dubai.

ACKNOWLEDGEMENTS

My thanks to all the trainers and their wives, husbands, partners and staff who have allowed me into their yards over the years to share the magical world that training racehorses can be. Thanks too to the jockeys who have nipped out of the weighing room on busy afternoons to spare me a few minutes giving me their version of special moments on the track.

Thanks especially to the late and much-missed Frank Johnson who as editor of the *Spectator* brought me back into writing about racing when I had for too long been spending all my time with politicians, the people who tell lies to journalists and then believe what they read. Thanks also to all those *Spectator* readers who wrote in to protest after editor Boris Johnson dropped my Turf column to create more room for politics – and to Boris for then having the grace to reinstate me. Thanks to the *Spectator*'s understanding Arts Editor Liz Anderson and to the *Financial Times* for allowing me to recycle some of the material which has previously appeared in their publications, and to Racing Post Books for allowing me to reuse material first acquired in writing for them my biographies of Barry Hills and Clive Brittain. A very big thank you also to Peter Pugh and Duncan Heath of Icon Books for conceiving this volume of racing experiences and encouraging me to write it. I am grateful also to my friend Derek Sinclair for his good fellowship on the racecourse, even if he does have an irritating habit of backing far more winners than I do. And as always the deepest thanks of all to my long-suffering wife Carolyn who has spent a lifetime putting up with me and the havoc caused in our social life by my deadlines.

INTRODUCTION

You have to be there. With the BBC having chickened out of racing, Channel Four's team deliver well-informed and colourful coverage. But horseracing needs a broader canvas than the 28in screen. Even with a plate of tongue sandwiches, a ready supply of Budweisers from the fridge and the form book and telephone to hand, racing on TV can never quite compensate for not being present. You miss the buzz around the betting ring, the soft thud of hooves on wet turf, the instinctive intake of breath as a champion surges away from his field, the exhilaration of an air-punching jockey and his mount swaggering into the winner's enclosure. Racing has to be heard, smelled and absorbed as well as watched. And with a fiver on the nose you can even, for a moment, feel a sense of temporary ownership as your selection flashes first by the post.

That fine Australian writer Les Carlyon put it best in *True Grit*. Scoffing at the description of racing as an 'industry' he declared, 'So is packaging and tens of thousands don't stand around cheering a cardboard box that happens to be rather better than the other cardboard boxes.' Racing, he said, is 'an addiction, a romantic quest, a culture and a certain sense of humour. It is loaded with dangers, physical and financial and comes with a hint of conspiracy. In other words, racing is interesting.'

Buying a boat has been described as like standing under a shower and shredding £10 notes. Pessimists would tell you that racehorse ownership is like standing in a heap of stable manure burning twenties. The trainer of a horse in which I had a share told our jockey one day in the parade ring to 'Let him find himself'. 'Oh please,' I implored, 'Couldn't he just for once find the other horses in the race?'

But, win or lose, there is for me no sport with the same appeal. Jockey Mick Fitzgerald famously responded to interviewer Desmond Lynam's 'How did it feel?' inquiry after he had ridden Rough Quest to win the Grand National that it was 'better than sex', getting himself in trouble with his lady at the time, who apparently complained that he had rarely given her enjoyment for more than the nine minutes 45 seconds an Aintree winner can be expected to take to complete the race.

If Mick was overdoing it just a tad I would still go along with his fellow jockey who described going racing as 'the best fun you can have with your clothes on'. Racing is about speed, spectacle and athleticism. It is about colour, courage and character, about passion and the pursuit of perfection. For spectators it is simple: who passes the post first. To enjoy it you don't have to master the intricacies of rucks and mauls, the offside trap or when to take the new ball. It is the most instantly sociable sport of all. Your companion or client doesn't have to shut up for 90 minutes while the game is played; instead it is 'How did yours do in the last? What do you fancy for the next?'

Racing changes people's character: the tightest of bank managers splashes out on champagne after a win, the most decorous of ladies raises her hemline six inches or risks a crazy hat. No sport's appeal spans the classes better. Duchess and dustman unite in cheering home a winner.

The sheer beauty of the participants is enthralling. Watch the early summer sun glinting off the flanks of a perfectly toned Sea The Stars or the grace and power of Kauto Star taking a Gold Cup fence in his prime and you have no need of a picture gallery. As Clive Brittain's owner

Lady Beaverbrook once said, 'I have all the art I need but nothing makes my heart beat like a horse.'

Racing also appeals to that other basic instinct, the human love of a flutter. It carries a beguiling whiff of risk and uncertainty.

There was the famous story of the Dubliner at the Cheltenham Festival who won enough on Ireland's champion hurdler Istabraq to redeem his mortgage. He then lost the lot on Ireland's failing hope for the Gold Cup, only to retort, 'To be sure, it was only a small house anyway.'

Racing people are good to be with because they are optimists. The veteran US trainer Jim Ryan once declared that no man ever committed suicide or thought of retiring while he had a good two-year-old in his barn for the season ahead. The sport is full of character. Compare today's monosyllabic footballers with jockey Jack Leach, author of the marvellously titled autobiography *Sods I Have Cut on the Turf.* He spent his nights in the Turkish baths in Jermyn Street to keep to his riding weight: 'I used to take off ¾lb extra so that at the racecourse I could have a small sandwich and a glass of champagne before racing started. It made me feel a new man. If I had a few ounces to spare the new man got a glass too.'

Jack Leach was a Flat jockey. To me the jumping riders have an extra dimension: it is hard to underestimate the sheer courage it takes to drive half a ton of horse across a series of obstacles in cold, wet and biting wind for no more than £158 a time when they know that statistically they can expect a fall from every thirteen rides. When he quit the saddle to train, Brendan Powell reflected, 'Over the years I've been pretty lucky with injury.' There's lucky and lucky: he had endured two broken legs, two broken wrists, both collarbones shattered by repeated breaks and a ruptured stomach.

To me racing's appeal has much to do also with the bond between the rider in the saddle and the animal beneath. Jockeys need a clock in their head, sensitive hands and physical strength. But horses are individuals. Some like to force the pace in front, others are happier coming from behind. Some shrink from contact or stop the moment they have their head in front. Yet jockeys must divine their partner's character within minutes of meeting. Some have met their mounts on the gallops; often they have only the time from mounting in the parade ring to when the stalls open to get to know each other. The horse does not know how far away the winning post is and in that time a bond of trust must be established.

Frankie Dettori claims that within seconds of sitting on a horse he can divine its character, even its best distance. If ever I envied someone a gift that is it.

I was useless in the saddle, worse than a sack of potatoes, but that has never curbed my enjoyment from being with racing people. It is a little like the experience of the Parachute Regiment commander who was asked at his retirement party what it was that he enjoyed about jumping out of aeroplanes. 'I hate jumping out of aeroplanes,' he said. 'It makes me sick to the stomach every time I do it. But I just love being with the kind of people who *do* like jumping out of aeroplanes.'

For me too there is no place like the racecourse. I love being with racing people, who embrace all types, from royalty to the clergy. Though I have to admit there are some who don't share my pleasure. I was once at a Gimcrack racing dinner in York where a distinguished clergyman was invited to say grace. 'I won't, if you don't mind,' he replied. 'I would rather not draw the Almighty's attention to my presence here.' I've always been ready to take that risk.

A Zambian beginning

An early humiliation might have put me off horses for good. My father was a civil engineer and we lived from 1948 to 1951 in what was then Northern Rhodesia (now Zambia) while he was engaged in projects like Livingstone Airport and the Kafue Bridge. We almost led the colonial-style life and my mother had a horse, Pedro, a rangy chestnut with a white blaze. Although he was compliant with those of the female gender, the bad-tempered Pedro's main pleasure in life seemed to be attempting to maim with hooves or teeth any male human who came in contact with him. He was stabled close to what passed for the local racecourse in Lusaka, which is where, after a few lessons, I used to try to ride him.

Facing away from the stables, Pedro would not go a yard without maximum human effort. Turn his face for home, however, and he would become a tearaway enthusiast determined each time to break any Lusaka record for five furlongs. Naturally the first time he did it to me I came off. As I slowly sat up counting my bruises, an assured young lady of eleven or twelve rode up, leading another horse alongside hers. In total control she collected a self-satisfied looking Pedro (I swear he was as close to smirking as a horse can get) and inquired solicitously, 'Are you all right? Can I help you?' She was kindness personified but for a self-conscious ten-year-old boy there could be no greater humiliation.

Hurst Park memories

We returned from Africa to live in East Molesey, Surrey, a stone's throw away from the old Hurst Park racecourse

– well, if you had a smallish stone and a particularly good throwing arm. Sadly back in 1962 Hurst Park became a Wates housing estate but before then it had hooked me finally and irrevocably into racing. I used to ride my bike down the road, prop it against the fence and stand on the saddle or climb a tree as the jockeys rode by. There would first be the thunder of approaching hooves, then the blaze of multi-coloured silks as the riders flashed past: the likes of Gordon Richards, Eph Smith, Scobie Breasley, Charlie Smirke and Manny Mercer shouting at each other for room or cursing whoever was holding them in on the rail. They would disappear in a creak of leather and smacking of whips, the lighter divots they had kicked up floating back to earth behind them, to be greeted half a minute later by the roar of sound from the crowds in the stands as they fought out the finish.

Sometimes I would walk round to the entrance before racing, to watch the 'Find the Lady' three-card tricksters plying their trade on upturned orange boxes, one man warily on the watch for approaching constabulary as the other made his pitch. Equally cautious was a character they called the 'Watchman' who would open his coat to reveal 20 or 30 dangling timepieces available at bargain prices. Sometimes tipster Prince Monolulu would be there in his fake African Ostrich-feather plumes rasping out his familiar cry of 'I gotta horse', encouraging punters to part with a few shillings for a little slip of paper. The tips were mostly rubbish, I heard punters grumble, but he deserved the cash for his entertainment value as he told the crowds:

> God made the bees
> The bees make the honey
> You make a bet
> And the bookies take your money.

Peter Carl Mackay, Monololu's real name, wasn't any kind of prince in fact, although it didn't stop him from strolling nonchalantly among the royals at King George VI's funeral. Apparently Jeffrey Bernard, a fellow *Spectator* columnist, claimed that he was personally responsible for Monololu's demise. He visited the ailing tipster in hospital and gave him a box of chocolates. Monolulu chose a strawberry cream and promptly choked to death. There have to be better ways to go.

Once or twice at Hurst Park, after three or four races had gone, a friendly gateman would let me slip in for nothing, and from the start the subtle chemistry of the racing scene had me entranced. It was that extraordinary blend of the upright and the raffish, the social mix of shirts-off punters in the jellied eels inner ring peeling fivers off back-pocket wads, raucous bookies shouting the odds and elegant owners' wives in parade-ring silk dresses.

Hurst Park being a jumping course as well as a Flat racing venue, you would see both the emaciated white-faced pros from top yards and the pink-cheeked farmers' sons hoping to steal a novice chase on the family's pride and joy. Curly-haired young trainers in cavalry twills and velvet-collared coats blowing Aunt Honoria's patrimony in a couple of experimental seasons would mingle with weary-eyed ex-jockeys trying to make a go of it with a handful of cast-offs in a dilapidated yard.

Sometimes I would get a different view of the racing. Down by the seven-furlong start at the end of the straight, between the racecourse and the river Thames, was the 'Upper Deck' swimming pool. On the raised section which gave the venue its name you had the perfect view of the riders jostling at the tapes before the off, and more than once a jockey with a roving eye for the bikini-clad lovelies calling down to him would miss the break.

With nothing else left of old Hurst Park it is at least a consoling thought that when it died twenty acres of prime Thameside turf went into the laying of Ascot's new jumping track.

Liverpool days

The first opportunity I had to mix with and write about racing people came when I left Oxford and joined the *Liverpool Daily Post* as a graduate trainee. It was just after the Beatles had moved on from Merseyside to worldwide adulation and a friend insists he remembers a conversation one day which went:

Friend: 'Are you coming to the Iron Door this week to hear the Rolling Stones?'
Oakley: 'No, I heard them in Manchester a few weeks back: they're not going to make it.'

Just as well I wasn't trying to become a showbiz reporter.

We trainees were the dogsbodies of the two newspapers, the morning *Daily Post* and the evening *Liverpool Echo*, hired basically to be trained up to fill the perpetual shortage of sub-editors processing other people's copy. You began doing weather and temperatures, checking the Chicago Lard and Hogs prices on the City page, writing up local flower shows and painfully visiting incredibly courteous local families to borrow the mantelpiece picture of a beloved father or son to illustrate an accident report of a death in the docks.

Keen to gain experience and eager to supplement my starting pay of around £850 a year in the hope of being able to start a home with my wife-to-be Carolyn, I used to take on every role I could. Soon I was adding to my basic salary as a 'sub' by writing articles, leaders and reviews on a freelance basis under various pseudonyms, even some under the name of 'Susan Germaine' for the women's page. The key opportunity for me though was the discovery that the sports desk had no resident horseracing enthusiast and so 'Francis Leigh' (my two middle names) began a series for the *Echo* 'Around the Local Stables', shortly followed by a new racing columnist for the *Daily Post* who took upon himself the name of 'Mandarin', my all-time favourite horse (of whom more at an appropriate stage). When I was summoned one day to the management offices to meet Sir Alick Jeans, the *LDP* proprietor, I had imagined he might be planning to commend me for all my extra efforts, which nearly doubled both my hours and my salary. Instead all he had to say was, 'You are earning too much money for a young man of your age.'

The curmudgeonly attitude did not worry me because as well as making progress towards my aim of becoming a political correspondent I was enjoying the opportunity to begin imbibing racing lore from the likes of handicap specialist Eric Cousins, Neston trainer Colin Crossley and the experienced Ron Barnes. That required the purchase of my first car, a second-hand Mini with leopardskin seats. One day it was stolen in Liverpool. The police found it later in Bootle and when I went to collect it the thief had done me a favour: the only thing missing was the leopardskin seat covers!

Before that I used to travel regularly on special race-day coaches packed with shrewd Merseyside regulars to the local tracks of Aintree, Haydock Park and Chester. It was one of my coach companions who told me as we munched our way through cheese and onion baps en route to Haydock one day about a local unlicensed greyhound racing track on Merseyside. It sounded like a different night out and so a Liverpool housemate and I tried it one evening. As I remember, it was somewhere on the fringes of dockland and it made the expression 'run-down' sound like an accolade. The dogs were mangy, the handlers, even the female ones, even scruffier: they could have been extras auditioning for the 'before' role in dandruff shampoo advertisements. The ramshackle greyhound traps would have lowered the tone of an abandoned allotment and the hare looked like what was left of a well-used washing-up mop. No self-respecting hound would have chased it for more than ten yards. The crowd consisted almost entirely of whey-faced men with pronounced facial tics in long dirty macs.

We hadn't a clue what we were doing and conversation with scar-faced strangers seemed unwise. What puzzled us most was that most of them didn't seem to have a bet until 90 seconds before the off when there would be a sudden mini-stampede and clamour to get on two particular dogs which would rapidly be chalked up as first and second favourite. Usually they lost.

After three or four races we were emboldened to step forward while all were hanging back with a couple of £2 reverse forecasts on dogs two and three. Suddenly the place went berserk. As if we had given some secret signal, everyone else rushed in, emptying back pocket wads onto dogs two and three. Amazingly they came first and second, and after the result was confirmed three rather heavy-looking gents whose heads disappeared into their shoulders with no sign of any connecting neck suddenly become our close but silent companions, exuding an air of quiet menace. Whether we had inadvertently stumbled on or interrupted some code or signalling system I will never know, but having collected our winnings it seemed a sensible moment to slip away. As we walked through the gate I turned and waved at the shortest of our three shadows. He did not wave back.

By contrast the horse-watching on Merseyside was a joy. A beautiful sight that I enjoyed on a regular basis and still see in my mind's eye today was that of Colin Crossley's string at first light on a summer's morning cantering along the sands at West Kirby, silhouetted against the sea skyline as they kicked up the spray under stable jockey Eric Apter and colleagues. If they have beaches in the afterlife I will be happy to see any number of reruns.

At Sandy Brow, Tarporley, the former wartime fighter pilot Eric Cousins, who first took out his licence in 1954, proved himself one of the shrewdest placers of horses in the country, winning a couple of Lincoln handicaps, three Ayr Gold Cups, Kempton's Great Jubilee in four successive years, Ascot's Wokingham Stakes and the Portland at Doncaster. He did particularly well with cast-offs, as when he won the Cambridgeshire with Commander-in-Chief, formerly trained at Newmarket by Captain Sir Cecil Boyd Rochfort. It was Eric Cousins of course who introduced his neighbour Robert Sangster to horseracing and the pair brought off a fine coup with Chalk Stream in the 1961 Great Jubilee Handicap at Kempton. Because the horse was a tricky starter Cousins told Sangster to station himself by the bookies and not to have a bet until the trainer raised his hat to show the horse had got off with the others. From high up in the stands Cousins saw the start and doffed his hat. Sangster swung around and took a huge bet at 8-1. The horse got up in the last stride.

I was writing mostly tipping-oriented stable profiles and few of the local trainers' great thoughts have survived from my notebooks at the time. But I never forgot one experience with Eric Cousins. I began doing some short racing pieces for a BBC North sports programme. The very first time they sent me out with a bulky Uher recorder about the size of an accordion I duly recorded a talk with the Tarporley maestro, only to discover when I got back to the office that the material was completely unusable. Throughout the interview he had been gently rubbing a matchbox on his trousers and it came out on the recording as a noise like a buzz saw. Technology has never been my forte.

I didn't forget either my first talk with Ron Barnes. Having endured traffic troubles in the Mersey Tunnel I arrived an hour late for an interview at his Norley Bank stables. Quite rightly I was roundly bollocked by the substantial figure of the trainer, built on Sam Hall lines, who bore a fierce scar across his cheek from being grabbed by one of his stable inmates.

Just a few miles from industrial Liverpool we talked, looking down beyond his rock garden to wooded slopes with a mare nuzzling her foal in the paddocks and a two-year-old frisking on a lungeing rein. It was an idyllic scene but Mr Barnes, as the *Post* and *Echo* liked me to call trainers in those more deferential days, was going through a lean spell and he began my education in the downside of the trade. Training for Merseyside businessmen who were more likely to spend £500 than 5,000 guineas on their animals in 1965, he had sent out 28 winners. Then after being inoculated against the cough his horses had 'gone wrong' and the next season he had won only six races (with the four horses who hadn't been inoculated). He was the first of many to tell me over the next 40 years that it isn't training horses that is difficult – it is training the owners.

'If you can please racehorse owners,' he said, 'you can make chains out of sand. When you're getting winners it's fine. Everybody wants to buy you champagne and slap your back. Have a lean spell and even your friends don't want to know you – they're not interested in explanations. I wouldn't advise a young man to go into racing until he's made some money at something else [a policy he followed with his four sons]. There can't be more than four people in the country who make good money out of training horses. I know if I hadn't had a bit behind me I would have been finished last year.'

Ron Barnes's 'something' included a building company and a Warrington farm, not to mention 37 acres devoted to his brood mares, and our relations were sufficiently mended by the end of the interview for him to insist on me staying to watch his prize stallion perform. It was the first time I had seen a stallion in action and when the mare was brought into the yard I have never heard such a noise as the roaring he made, nearly kicking to pieces his stall in his eagerness to get out and get on with it.

Ron Barnes's maxim in preparing his horses was simple: 'Feed them well and work them to it.' And on one thing he was adamant: he didn't bet: 'If a trainer has to bet he's got bad owners.'

There were few giants of the training scene on my Merseyside patch in those days but I was given a good introduction to the practicalities at the lower end by the likes of Jack Mason, who had been beaten a neck on Melleray's Belle in the 1930 Grand National and by just a length in the Scottish version too. He never wanted more than around 20 horses and he told me, 'I wouldn't want 10,000 guinea yearlings in my boxes. I'd never get a moment's rest at the thought – I'd have to sleep with them for fear.'

One who did know what to do with quality though

was Rodney Bower, who trained in one of Merseyside's posher spots in Heswall, in a cobbled yard with an orchard and dovecots. His Border Stud Farm at the time I visited him had sent out Cool Alibi to win the County Hurdle at the Cheltenham Festival and had nearly brought off the double when Border Grace, already by then the winner of sixteen races, had finished second, anchored by an 8lb penalty, in the Mildmay of Flete Challenge Cup. That would have been an amazing achievement for a small yard essentially training just for a few friends – the kind of set-up which for so long provided the backbone of National Hunt racing. They were not a betting yard, but three members of the family did once find themselves picking up more than £1,000 for a fiver each way on the Tote on one of their horses. Very much an advocate of kindness in training horses, Rodney Bower told me, 'The whole art is discovering the idiosyncrasies of each animal – and they all have them. You don't want horses too clever – they are usually lazy – but you do want horses with courage. A good horse will strive to get to the front. That's the kind I like.'

After four years in Liverpool I achieved my aim of being promoted to political correspondent for the *Daily Post*, based at the House of Commons. Carolyn and I moved south, first to Surbiton and then, by strange coincidence, to Epsom, home of the Derby. It did not however bring to an end my racing articles for the paper. I merely began to interview and profile instead the trainers within easy reach of where we now lived. Even better, until the newspaper's accountants vetoed it, I had a wonderful perk. The *Daily Post* used to pay for me to have a ticket on the excursion train which in those days ran from London to Merseyside for the Grand National. I could enjoy a fine breakfast on board, watch the day's racing and have dinner on the way back while leisurely preparing my copy for the next day for Monday publication.

Grand National

The National has had a special place in my heart ever since my Liverpool days and early images still stick: in 1966 when Anglo won at 50-1 I had bought Mrs Oakley a gorgeous stop-the traffic pink trouser suit for the occasion. I am not sure which was the more agitated – the horses that passed her in it or my bank manager. An Irish priest whom I met at the Tote window (before an image-conscious church hierarchy forbade it they actually used to attend in their cloth) tipped me Rough Tweed, which was the first horse to fall. So much for divine inspiration.

There were raucous bookies tempting once-a-year punters to make it a fiver with calls of '1,000-1 the police horse', and as I gazed in wonder at the flesh-revealing ensembles adopted by most of female Merseyside I learned the definition of the 'Mersey tug', the characteristic gesture with which the heftier young ladies grasp both sides of their bras beneath their dresses to haul them up and rearrange their décolletage. In 1967 I remember I backed the blinkered Popham Down, the horse who brought down most of the field as he ran down the 23rd fence.

I had never experienced a sporting atmosphere like it. You could almost cut the tension in the air as white-faced young riders were swung up into their saddles by leathery-faced trainers in trilbies. You were not human if you were not swept up by the roar from the crowds as the tapes went up and the cavalry charged to the initial obstacle as if there was a stage prize for getting to that first as well. Then as the race unfolded, mini-drama after mini-drama: there would be retreats and advances, blunders and falls. Lumps of spruce would go flying into the air as horses dived through rather than over those big, forbidding fences, and jockeys would be left sitting on the ground beating their whips into the turf in frustration as the remaining field galloped on. Bechers ... the Canal Turn ... then Melling Road ... The Chair and what has became known as 'the Foinavon fence' imprinted themselves on the nation's memories.

It is early in this volume to tackle the downside of our sport but it was those early visits to Aintree which impressed on me so vividly that it involves tragedy as well as triumph, both for the horses who become casualties and their riders. Horses are so noble, so big, so commanding, so athletic in their upright prime that there are few sights in life quite so painfully shocking as when you first see one stricken, threshing on the ground with a broken limb, awaiting the humane despatch that is the only kind response to certain injuries.

It is the plight of the equine casualties that usually engages the media's attention but alas I will never forget either the sickening spectacle of Paddy Farrell being catapulted out of the saddle at The Chair in a fall in 1964 which was to leave him in a wheelchair for life. You somehow knew as he landed that this was a really bad one – the only good thing in the long run being that it was his injury along with that of Tim Brookshaw which led John Oaksey and others to found a proper compensation scheme for riders in the shape of the Injured Jockeys Fund.

The National today, of course, is not the National I first attended. Many things have changed: the prize money, the fences, the landing surfaces, the quality of horses running in the race, the distance covered to the first obstacle.

So am I now going to launch an old fogey's diatribe about things not being as they were? Am I hell.

I am a defender of the National and I will fight to the death for the race's retention in the sporting calendar against those who campaign for its abandonment (and who, should they ever achieve that objective, would move on smartly to demand the abolition of jump racing as a whole). But racing has to acknowledge that it lives in a wider world and that animal welfare concerns must be addressed. Those of us who thrill to a sport which inevitably involves casualties to both riders, who choose freely to participate, and horses, who don't have that luxury, have to be prepared to defend our involvement and to ensure that every possible safety precaution is taken.

Some years it becomes harder than others. After the mudlarks' benefit 2001 race which he won on Red Marauder, even jockey Richard Guest conceded, 'I am not sure we should have been out there.' It did not do much for the image of racing to have only seven horses set out on the second circuit and only two jump round the whole course without a fall. There was an outcry after the National of 1998 when again the race was run in atrocious conditions. Tragically three horses died and only six of the 37 runners finished the course. The *Daily Mail* in particular ran screaming headlines asking 'Did three horses really have to die for sport?' and an article insisting that the event had degenerated into a 'grisly farce'. 'This is surely not sport, this is closer to carnage,' cried the *Mail.* I was invited by the *Independent* to contribute to the debate and made the point that the three fatalities occurred at the first, fourth and fifth fences: 'It was not a cause of exhausted animals at the end of their tether being driven unwilling into the obstacles. They could have died the same way in any race anywhere.' Their deaths were not justification, I insisted, to ban the National but in what the *Racing Post* was kind enough to call a 'balanced analysis' I suggested that if it had been a midweek fixture in the sticks the card would have been called off, and added, 'What certainly can be said is that there were a number of horses in the field who were the equine equivalent of vanity publishing. Perhaps the authorities could look again at the race entry conditions to see if more stringent qualifications should be imposed.' That was a case I had been arguing since the 1970s.

Change for change's sake as a mere PR exercise I will always resist. It is the besetting sin of modern politics that beneath a media barrage governments insist on being seen to be doing something whether there is a quantifiable benefit or not. Racing is in danger of going the same way. But that does not mean we should resist carefully thought out changes that genuinely increase the safety of horses and riders.

The difficulty that racing faces is that the Grand National is watched by 600 million people in more than 300 countries. It brings in the punters who otherwise don't focus on a horse race all year and so it is both the sport's biggest shop window and its biggest potential PR disaster.

The animal rights activists were in full cry again in 2011 when two horses, Ornais and Dooney's Gate, perished and several horses finished temporarily distressed on an unusually warm day. It did not help racing's image that winning jockey Jason Maguire received a five-day ban for excessive use of the whip on winner Ballabriggs.

After that the one thing we racing lovers were praying for in the 2012 contest was an incident-free race with every horse coming home safe. That we were denied. Not only did According to Pete have to be put down after being brought down by another horse when running loose after a fall, so did Synchronised, the most high-profile horse in the race since he had won that year's Cheltenham Gold Cup, was ridden by the champion jockey Tony McCoy, was owned by the multi-millionaire punter J.P. McManus and trained by the National Hunt hero Jonjo O'Neill.

Phone-ins hummed for days with the opinions of the emotional and the ignorant, only every now and then including that rarity, the genuinely informed. Animal rights activists, ranging from those truly concerned with horse welfare to the crudest of class warriors, had their say and once again racing played on the back foot. The RSPCA, which had often in the past worked sensibly with racing's authorities to maximise safety, came out all guns blazing in 2012, labelling Becher's Brook a 'killer fence' and demanding its scrapping.

I entered the debate with a question: had anybody suggested because the Italian footballer Piermario Morosini had collapsed and died during an Italian Serie B football game or because Fabrice Muamba had suffered a cardiac arrest while playing for Bolton Wanderers that top-level football should therefore be abandoned?

I accept it had its limitations as a parallel. Footballers, those with brain cells anyway, make their own decisions; horses do not. But the key point is that we cannot eliminate risk from sport, or from life.

As for that year's Grand National, I tried to emphasise a few facts. Synchronised was not injured because he was driven beyond his limits: he was put down because he broke his leg, not in the fall where he lost his jockey, nor even jumping another fence when running loose; the accident happened, to the enormous regret of owner, trainer and jockey, on the Flat. He took a false step and shattered his leg.

It was at Becher's that According to Pete broke his off-fore when 'falling' but in fact he jumped the fence well: he simply had nowhere to go then because another horse, On His Own, had fallen ahead of him. The irony was that 'improvements' to Becher's following past protests probably did for According to Pete. What the professionals tell you is that easing Becher's in previous modifications has made jockeys less fearful of the fence. Instead of fanning out across the course to tackle it they now go faster and crowd in. That, it seems, is what unsighted On His Own and caused him to fall.

It is doubtful if changing any regulation could have prevented either death but on went the furore: scrap the National, scrap horseracing, let horses run free in fields, the animal rights campaigners were urging. But the week before, Great Endeavour, a quality chaser, was in a field owned by jockey Timmy Murphy, starting his summer holiday. No race was involved, there was no fence to jump, but he too broke a leg and died. Should we ban keeping horses in fields? Accidents happen and horses, because a broken leg in their case almost always means that life is unbearable or unsustainable, are especially vulnerable.

Fences are the problem, say the campaigners, for now. End jump racing. Keep it to the Flat. But three horses died in a night's racing at 2012's Dubai World Cup, where no horse has ever been asked to jump a single obstacle.

To listen to the campaigners, you would think there was constant carnage. Every death is sad, as those of us who spend time with jockeys, trainers or stable staff are especially aware. But that year horses participated in jumping races on 94,776 occasions. From that number, 181 horses received injuries which led to their deaths, a rate of 0.19 per cent. Not a bad comparison with your chances crossing the road.

It was little wonder that one racecourse chief told me before the 2013 contest, 'This year we'll all be watching from behind the sofa.' In fact, after the 2012 race three more 'drop' fences had their landing areas levelled out, and to calm the cavalry charge of 40 horses to the first fence the start was moved 90 yards closer to it, taking jockeys and horses away from the adrenalin-inducing hubbub from the stands. In the 2013 race, won by Aurora's Encore, that seemed to help, with jockeys taking the early stages less recklessly. Also since 2012, six-year-olds have not been allowed to run in the National and participants must previously have finished fourth or better in a three-mile chase.

I thoroughly approve of one change we saw in the 2013 race. Those big Aintree fences are now being built around plastic cores rather than timber posts, which can prove a fearsome obstacle on the second circuit when first-round fencers have kicked the spruce off them. That should probably have happened sooner and the fact is that serious, organised, well-informed campaigners have won some improvements over the years. Racing in the old days was too careless of the risks. But over recent years Aintree in particular and the horseracing authorities have responded to informed criticism with many changes designed to improve safety. We may even have gone too far: making the fences easier, some jockeys are warning, is making horses go faster and increasing, not diminishing, the injury risks. What we need now is a pause for the changes to bed in. What we seem to be forgetting, in an age when firemen are forbidden to wade into five-feet-deep ponds on health and safety grounds, is that the Grand National is not supposed to be like every other race: it is a unique sporting spectacle which engages the nation like no other and wins a TV audience far beyond any other race. It holds that position precisely because its fences are special, because at four miles plus it is longer than other races and because more horses take part than in other races.

We are now at a turning point. Yes, let us have careful statistical surveys and annual reviews. If practical steps can be taken to reduce falls and injuries by, for example, eliminating more drop fences where the landing point is lower than the take-off, let us implement them. But we cannot eliminate all risk or all casualties from a sport which involves half a ton of horse jumping obstacles at speed. Muck about much more with the Grand National and it won't any longer be grand or national, it will be just another lengthy steeplechase that there is no point in anybody tuning in to watch. And then how many of the horses who race over jumps today will even exist?

What many now forget is that in the 1970s the race did nearly die. Property developer Bill Davies had bought the course from Muriel Topham and tripled admission prices, with the result that when Red Rum beat L'Escargot in 1975 it was in front of the smallest crowd in living memory. So thank heavens for Ladbrokes who rescued the race in dark times before handing it on to the Jockey Club. Thank heavens too for handicapper Phil Smith who has set the weights for the National since 1999 and compressed the handicap to bring much better quality horses into the top end of the National field. For example he reduced the top weight from the crushing 12 stone to 11st 12lb

For many years large sections of the National field were running 'out of the handicap'. Because there is a minimum weight carried in the race of 10st 0lb (to ensure there are enough jockeys available) many horses which would have been given weights below 10 stone in terms of their ability were running carrying excess weight and with little chance. But with Martell and then John Smith's raising the prize money, better horses were attracted. Thanks to that and the higher achievement levels required from would-be participants, we do now get a better quality of race, even if the likes of Mon Mome at 100-1 and Aurora's Encore at 66-1 still give the bookies an occasional bonanza day in the biggest betting race of the year. Now almost every year the horses running in the National are doing so carrying the weight appropriate to their rating. It has become a proper handicap.

I talked to Phil Smith one year about how he made his assessments and he replied that he normally weighted horses on their form over three miles on tracks like Haydock or Kempton but he took into account the fact that Aintree was different and the race was much longer:

> For the higher weighted horses I try to reduce the amount of weight they carry, bearing in mind that the further they travel the more likely the weight is to have an effect. You and I might be able to run a hundred metres carrying a bag of sugar under each arm but if we have to run two hundred metres with the same burden we are going to notice it more.

Even handicappers can get things wrong of course. When Monty's Pass landed a huge £1 million-plus gamble by winning the National in 2003, Phil Smith was so confident of his handicapping that he had promised to jump off the roof of the stands if anything won by more than seven lengths. At the line there was twelve lengths between Monty's Pass and the second.

When Phil Smith took over, no horse carrying more than 11 stone had won since Jenny Pitman's Corbiere won in 1983. Not until 2005 when Hedgehunter won with 11st 1lb was that statistic overturned. By 2009 all the first four home carried 11 stone or more.

We all have Nationals we remember more vividly than others. I once worked on the *Sunday Express* alongside ex-jockey Dick Francis and like millions I have never forgotten his mount Devon Loch's collapse on the run-in in 1956, replayed so many times on grainy old newsreels. Nor will I ever forget the gallant effort by the top weight Crisp when Red Rum won for the first time in 1973. Crisp was carrying the maximum 12 stone, Red Rum 23lbs less and the only time Red Rum was in front was in the last ten yards. Crisp's rider Richard Pitman is one of the nicest guys on the National Hunt scene and unfairly blames himself for his mugging at the finish by Ginger McCain's charge. Trainer Fred Winter had intended Richard on Crisp to make the running and slow the pace from the front but there was no way the big black Crisp, an Australian import, was going to settle for that. The moment he had jumped one fence he wanted to attack the next and at one stage must have been forty lengths ahead of his field. Unfortunately he could not quite last home as Red Rum came after him but even coming second was for Richard, who had won races like the King George, the Hennessy and the Champion Hurdle, the most exhilarating ride of his life.

The greatest recovery I ever saw was Brendan Powell's success in 1988 on Rhyme n' Reason. Jumping Becher's the first time round, the horse lost his legs on landing and slithered many yards on his belly. By the time the pair set off again they were last of the 33 still standing. Gradually Brendan picked off the rest of the field and came with a great burst of speed after the last to beat Durham Edition and Monamore.

Others perhaps would choose the success by Josh Gifford's ex-invalid Aldaniti, ridden by cancer sufferer Bob Champion to win in 1981, as the ultimate fairy story turned into reality but for me Amberleigh House's success in 2004 was special. At Aintree I never missed the chance of a few words with Ginger McCain when I could get them, even if all he was in the mood for was the bluest of blue jokes, and I wrote that weekend:

> Beside the parade ring as the wind sent the petals from the flowering cherries swirling around Philip Blacker's bronze of Red Rum, three times the winner of the Grand National and twice second in the big race, groups congregated for family photos. Somebody had placed a bunch of red roses between the old boy's forelegs. Inside the track, hundreds passed Red Rum's daffodil-bedecked grave in the shadow of the winning post. Don't ever let anybody tell you that the Grand National has lost, or ever could lose, its magic.

> Trainer Ginger McCain, who won Saturday's race with Amberleigh House 27 years after his endeavours with Red Rum, does not forget it, declaring, 'You can have your Gold Cups at Ascot with those toffee-nosed people, you can have your Cheltenham Festival with all your county set types and tweeds. But this is the people's race.'

> He recalled when he first came to Aintree in 1938 or 1939 watching the race from the embankment on the canal: 'We never saw a horse. Heard the crack of the fences, saw some caps go by but it was all part and parcel of the magic of this game. The turf is torn, the spruce from the fences has been kicked all over the course ... in those days there would be three jockeys coming back on one horse or a jockey who'd pulled up coming back leading another faller.'

Winning owner John Halewood is a Merseysider too. These days he has his own box but he remembers coming with his father, who died soon afterwards, early in the 1980s. They went round to the Canal Turn because they could not afford the Members Enclosure and his father said to him, 'One day you might own a horse.'

As for Ginger, ruddy of face, forthright in his opinions, with a twinkle in his eye and so appreciative at 73 of the skimpily wrapped curves on offer at Aintree that he claimed to have been off looking for some little blue pills, he is part of what racing is all about. Trainer Mick O'Toole once declared, 'Racing is a game of make believe. If people didn't think they had horses that were better than they really were, National Hunt racing would collapse.'

You have to have that dream, as John Halewood did when he paid 90,000 punts for his National winner. But Ginger, now based in Cheshire, did have doubts when Amberleigh House arrived in his yard. 'It was three o'clock in the morning, teeming with rain and I was in dressing gown and slippers. The horsebox driver let down the ramp and there was this tiny horse shivering in the corner of the box, no rug, no head collar, and I said, "That's not him, that's not the Amberleigh House I saw win at Punchestown." You know how the Irish like to stitch up us English trainers. But what a grand little horse he's been.'

Many thought Ginger, who has been insisting for three years that he had another potential National winner even when the horse was so lowly handicapped that he could not get into the race, reckoned he was dreaming a dream too far. He thought his best chance might have gone when Amberleigh House was third last year. But he is happy to take older horses to Aintree, reckoning that while they may be beaten by younger animals round some of the easier park courses, the challenge of the big Aintree fences revives them by making them think where impetuous younger horses blunder their chances away.

I had in earlier days seen Ginger, who was by then based in Cheshire and enjoying the assistance of his canny and courteous son Donald [whose Ballabriggs was to continue family tradition by winning the 2011 National], exercising his horses on the Southport sands behind his used car salerooms. Ginger was old-school and proud of it in what we usually hoped was his tongue-in-cheek way: 'As for no French-bred horse winning the National since 1909 – everyone goes on about the French-breds. You'd think there was something magical about buying them. But Ryan Price bought them, Eric Cousins used to buy them. They talk about them being taught to jump when they are two years old and all that but they don't last. They're not like a big store-bred four-year-old that you get and break in with no mileage on the clock. Horses are like cars: you've only got so much mileage in them and when that's gone you've got nothing.'

Ginger, who was clearly no Lib Dem voter, goes on: 'They bring in this Yogi Breisner (the Scandinavian jumping guru much in demand with southern trainers and riders) – he's not a bleeding Englishman, he's not even an Irishman. Any trainer that has to bring in a foreigner to teach his horses how to jump should hand his bloody licence in because he's not entitled to it.'

That, I commented, should cause a few winces over Lambourn's breakfast tables. And if such opinions brought Ginger within dangerous reach of the Race Relations Act, he had the Equal Opportunities people gasping the next year when trainer's wife Carrie Ford, twice the leading woman jockey over jumps, was riding Forest Gunner in the National. She had been in the saddle for that horse's victory in the Foxhunters Chase just ten weeks after giving birth to daughter Hannah but Ginger dismissed her chance in the big race, declaring 'Carrie is a broodmare now and having kids doesn't get you fit to ride.'

But if Ginger was entitled to a little sounding-off after Amberleigh House's victory, others too had played a notable part, notably the horse himself who, said his jockey Graham Lee, was baulked so badly at Becher's that he took it virtually from a standing start. Lee too deserves enormous credit for his coolness. So often, races are given away by premature moves, particularly on such a highly charged occasion as a Grand National. Graham and Donald McCain, the trainer's son, had planned for him to ride a waiting race but the mayhem ahead of him had ensured that Amberleigh House was much further behind the leaders than they had hoped. When the horses came back into the straight with Amberleigh House still apparently out of contention, Lee did not rush to make up his ground as he felt a strong headwind. 'When I felt I should have been going for him I thought, well, I'll count to ten first because he's only got one run.' He let the others came back to him. As a result Amberleigh House's run came just as Clan Royal and Lord Atterbury, punch drunk, were beginning to roll all over the course. [Hedgehunter had fallen at the last.] That was a ten-second delay that probably won a National.

Whoever would have thought, as Graham Lee described the National victory as the best day of his life, that in 2012 he would return to the Flat racing career that had failed to take off before and ride a hundred winners that season.

Another National was special for me because it was won by the best jockey I will ever see over jumps, Tony McCoy. It was special for AP too, not just because he landed the race at his fifteenth attempt (it took Frankie Dettori the same number of attempts to win his first Derby) but because I believe it was the moment when the iron man of racing truly learned how much the racing public adored him.

Biblical scholars say five is the number of grace, three the number of perfection. 'Fifteen therefore relates to acts wrought by divine grace.' I don't know if Tony McCoy was saying his prayers as his mount Don't Push It cleared the last and headed round The Elbow for the Grand National finishing line but he deserved any divine intervention that was going.

So too did the punters who had backed Don't Push It all the way down from 25-1 to 10-1 favourite. That didn't happen because of anything in the horse's form. Only one horse in the previous 25 years had carried more than eleven stone to victory and Don't Push It carried 11st 5lb. Only seven of the previous 50 favourites had won and although he had a touch of class, Don't Push It was a quirky, unsociable individual who spent most of his time out in a field with sheep and never ran two races alike. The money was there for him simply because AP is a riding phenomenon, the champion for eighteen consecutive years in a sport in which simply keeping your body roughly in one piece for a full season is an achievement.

AP is utterly professional, totally dedicated to winning and afraid of nothing. At the Cheltenham Festival that year his body had taken a terrible battering in two crunching falls. But that didn't stop him riding the winner of the Champion Hurdle, bringing Denman home second in the Gold Cup and riding a race on Alberta's Run in the

Ryanair Chase which was both a masterpiece of tactical riding and a testament to his gritty determination.

For racing folk AP's victory at Aintree was all the sweeter because it was achieved in conjunction with two others who had also seemed to suffer a National hoodoo. Don't Push It's owner J.P. McManus, the greatest patron jump racing has ever had (and a man who looks after all his old horses after their racing days are done), had unsuccessfully run 44 horses before Don't Push It in his bid to win the race. Trainer Jonjo O'Neill, another great jockey in his time, never got round the National course as a rider and had yet to prepare a horse to win it.

When McCoy stood up in his stirrups after the line and waved his whip in triumph, the crowds erupted in one of the biggest public thank yous and instinctive salutes to greatness that I have witnessed. McCoy is famously unemotional. Tears, previously, had only been permitted in private, as when he sat alone in the weighing room shattered by the death of his young mount Gloria Victis at Cheltenham. This time they were out in the open as he acknowledged that many folk would have been unaware of his successes in Gold Cups and Champion Hurdles but that winning the people's race had wiped out what he saw as the negative on his CV: 'Everyone knows about the National so from a public point of view, to win the biggest race in the world means everything. At least now I can feel I've done all right.'

The nation followed up by voting AP BBC Sports Personality of the year, the first man from his sport ever to win that accolade, and if ever there was a people's champion in the people's race, he was it.

*   *   *

A question that has always intrigued me is whether there

is a 'National type' of racehorse that would make winner-spotting any easier. Certainly there are horses like Red Rum, L'Escargot, Hedgehunter and State of Play who have consistently run well at Aintree. I have talked about it with owners and jockeys over the years.

Bob Davies, who picked up a chance ride on Lucius in 1978 when Dave Goulding was injured and won the race, believes that the best sorts for the National were horses like him, two and a-half mile chasers that could just about get three miles. He put past winners Specify and Gay Trip in that category too. 'It depends on the going but normally in a dryish spring the ground is reasonable at Aintree and you need that bit of speed.' It is only when it is heavy at Aintree, he contended, that chances improved for the kind of dour stayers who would slog round soggy Chepstow to take a Welsh National. While most would think of Red Rum as an extreme stayer, Davies, long-time clerk of the course at Ludlow, pointed out that he contested five-furlong sprints as a two-year-old.

Josh Gifford, who came second to Foinavon in 1967 on Honey End after the 23rd fence fiasco, and later trained Aldaniti to win, didn't agree that there was any National 'type'. 'They come in all shapes and sizes and have been winning over every sort of trip,' he said. 'What you need above all is a horse with the right temperament who jumps the right way and a bloody lot of luck.' Aldaniti, he said, was a stayer and nothing else.

Jenny Pitman, who won with Corbiere in 1983 and Royal Athlete in 1995 as well as taking the void race in 1993 with Esha Ness agreed that Fred Winter favoured two-and-a-half mile horses for the National, but those were not the kind she won with in days when the fences were stiffer than now:

Corbiere was never the fastest but he was a brilliant jumper. He flew over them and gained a length or two at every fence. Royal Athlete jumped well too. What you need above all is a good jumper and a horse that is well balanced. There are a lot of fences to be jumped at Aintree and a horse needs to be confident. It's guts. I watched a television programme about the training of athletes the other day and the coach said that a number of athletes came to him with similar abilities but the ones who became champions were the ones with strong characters. Champions are the ones who will grind it down.

No wonder McCoy got his National victory in the end.

* * *

For their sheer fortitude I have come to admire the girls of Merseyside who year after year whoop it up at the National and on Ladies Day on the Friday. The year 2005 when Hedgehunter won and Carrie Ford rode Forest Gunner, prompting Ginger McCain's less than gallant comments, was typical. It was both wet and windy. Umbrellas turned inside out, racecards disintegrated into a sodden pulp and rain seeped down inside your collar. But everywhere you turned there were the she-packs in their wispy little fragments of silk and lace, enough sun-tanned bare mid-riffs on display to have risked a meltdown of the National Grid through the week before and heels so mountainous that you could have picked apples without a stepladder in them. Colour didn't seem to matter so long as it was vivid. I was myself wearing a rather natty pair of orange/ tan cords and when one young lady dressed in little more than a baby doll nightie declared 'Nice trousers. We could have them off of youse' I wasn't quite sure whether it was compliment or threat. Either way I fled. But the crucial thing was that while they were dressed more appropriately for a disco dance floor than an arctic blast, they never stopped enjoying themselves.

I like to think that if Carrie Ford had won that year the Merseyside girls would have cheered it as a great stride forward for womanhood. But, truth be told, most of them wouldn't have noticed if a Martian had been riding the winner, especially not the ones who were drinking their pink champagne from pint mugs.

Ginger, who had threatened to bare his backside to the elements if a woman won, hedged his bets by presenting Carrie Ford with a bunch of flowers earlier. But they may only have been on loan. The bunch that appeared later in the McCain family's name on Red Rum's grave beside the winning post looked remarkably similar.

I have got into the habit of paying my tribute to the old boy there each year before walking the course (Red Rum that is, not Ginger, though I guess he is now included) and if you have never been to a National I do advise arriving early enough to do so. They stoke the atmosphere up brilliantly at Aintree with bands and entertainers. One year recently I had to fling myself out of the way of a chap in a nun's outfit who flashed past playing boogie-woogie on a motorised piano. So I go out on to the course to remind myself that in the end it is all about jumping and to look once more at just how big the obstacles still are. Even the open ditches with their sloping spruce fronts require horse and jockey to clear an obstacle 5ft 6ins high and 10ft 6ins wide from the sighting board to the turf on the other side and I think of Mattie Batchelor's comment after his first round over the Aintree fences. 'People talk about Becher's,' he said, 'but The Chair is massive. I'm only a little guy and it looked like a block of flats to me.' But of course we all have our perspectives on danger.

John Oaksey did a memorable TV piece once flying over the Aintree fences in a helicopter to help illustrate how it felt to ride in the race. He kept urging the pilot to fly lower until finally the exasperated man told him, 'If one of your bloody horses hits an obstacle you'll be carried away in a nice comfortable ambulance. If we touch one they'll scrape us up with a trowel!'

I cannot look at Becher's without remembering Crisp, out on his own, soaring over it imperiously as if it was a child's toy, and thanks to historian Chris Pitt I will never pass the 23rd, the Foinavon fence as it has been known since the carnage in 1967, without thinking of Johnny Leech, who had remounted and carried on, and who suddenly asked himself, 'Am I on the right horse?'

There really is no race like it.

—————— Epsom days ——————

When I moved from Liverpool to London as my working base my horizons expanded from Merseyside trainers to the likes of Brian Swift, Jackie Sirett, Tommy Gosling, Cyril Mitchell, Harold Wallington and John Benstead, not to mention the Reigate veteran Jack O'Donoghue, who had trained Nickel Coin, a mare bought for just 55 guineas, to win the Grand National in 1951. I remember being horrified when he told me that he only had ten shillings each way on her.

The soft-voiced man from County Cork had a stable set among the poplars of Priory Park where jumpers and Flat horses shared the space with donkeys, ponies and three-day eventers, not to mention golden pheasants and a sheep called Sam who could jump a five-foot wall. Jack trained for, among others, Queen Elizabeth the Queen Mother.

An old-school horseman, he was insistent on the need for horses to be taught to jump properly and he put them over every kind of graduated obstacle. He didn't have that many stars but you didn't see O'Donoghue horses crashing down hurdles in those juvenile cavalry charges as if they were going ten-pin bowling.

It must have been after visiting him and one or two more of the old school that I wrote a rather grumpy piece I found in my cuttings from 1966. Flat owners were sending poor quality horses hurdling, I complained, without proper preparation in the hope of picking up some consolation prize money after failure on the Flat and it was ruining racing as a spectacle. Racecourse executives were conniving and not staging enough steeplechases.

> Poorly schooled novice hurdlers of doubtful quality, packed together in formless fields of twenty or more will not attract the public to racecourses: it's the chasers they want to see and it is the chasers who provide a far more satisfactory betting medium.
>
> Under the rules of National Hunt racing the course executives only have to provide two chases on a day's card and they can't be blamed for not exceeding their minimum. There is a dearth of good young chasers since owners are too concerned with a quick return and insist on sending young horses hurdling before they have developed their strength. Of course some make the transition at a later stage but many a young horse is ruined by premature hurdling and will not take to the bigger obstacles.
>
> It has reached the stage where it is ridiculous to describe National Hunt racing in general as 'jumping'. Fewer and fewer horses are actually jumping anything and hurdling has more in common with circus dodgems than with show ring equestrianism ...

What we want, and soon, is tougher hurdles, public
cautions for trainers sending out unschooled animals
(often permit holders with no experienced work riders to do the job) and financial incentives for owners to keep their horses for chasing. Half the money
awarded in prizes on a National Hunt course must be
for chases. I would suggest making this proportion
two thirds ...

A distinctive figure on the Epsom Downs when I was
jogging or dog-walking in the early morning was Reg
Akehurst, another like Eric Cousins who relished picking
up top handicaps. Understandably he didn't give much
away in casual conversation but when I visited him for a
stable feature I remember his delightful wife Sheila confiding a lesser ambition. As a jockey Reg had won the Royal
Worcester Porcelain Chase and the coffee service that went
to the winning rider. She now wanted him to train the winner of the same race so she got the tea service to match.

At that time – the late 1960s – Cyril Mitchell was training from the stables in the centre of the Downs and then
had in his care Peter O'Sullevan's wonderful sprinter Be
Friendly. It hadn't always been so easy. I remember him
telling me with a typical chuckle, 'I started with seven
horses and after a year's struggle I soon got that down to
two.' Appropriately after such an unpromising start, his
first winner was called Stitch In Time.

Cyril's son Philip was then the leading amateur rider,
prior to the commencement of his own training career.
Although there have been some rows along the way, he
pays tribute to his father's precious ability to rekindle
horses' enthusiasm. Cyril Mitchell, says Philip, planted
one essential silicon chip in his brain: 'Any fool can get
them fit but you must have them mentally happy and

enjoying their racing.' To me Cyril defined the trainer's task as 'not screwing up the good ones'.

Nearly 30 years later in July 1997 I was back at Downs House talking through the cycles of a trainer's life with the ever-amiable Philip. He then had a good one in the shape of Running Stag, whom he placed cleverly to win stacks of money racing abroad. The piece I wrote then started around the Mitchell family breakfast table overlooking the yard. 'Freddie was alarmed his stick insect might have died and had to be assured it was merely dormant, Jack had helped himself to enough breakfast cereal to feed both the family Alsatians ...' Racing is often dynastic: look at the Nicholson or Hills families. Now Philip has moved to train in Lambourn and both Jack and Freddie are upwardly mobile jockeys. It really is in the genes.

I always remember that day talking about Philip's Lincoln winner King's Glory. Bought like most of his at that time from Newmarket sales ('Go to Ireland and they see you coming and add a nought'), the horse had lost his confidence at racing's headquarters. A stable lass asked if she could go into the box to fetch him and it was, says Philip, love at first sight: 'They had an affair. The horse would call out to her every day when she came into the yard. It sounds silly but it was like a romance. The more they stayed together the more he blossomed.' Any logical person has to have his doubts about such anthropomorphism. But Henry Cecil used to say he talked to his horses and they were his best friends. If the trainer of 25 Classic winners says that, who are we mere scribblers to affect scepticism?

Sometimes I would gain an insight too into the jockeys who came down to ride the horses from those Epsom yards. I found a note from the 1970s of a conversation with John Benstead, a fine trainer of stayers. He regularly used Australian jockey Scobie Breasley who later came to train just up the road from us in Reg Akehurst's former yard. Benstead said he never gave Scobie orders after he had ridden a horse once, and he praised him for getting the utmost out of a horse without any apparent effort:

> Sometimes when it looks as though Scobie has won a race with an awful lot in hand the horse is at his last gasp. He's won races for me leading all the way when I would have preferred him to wait and the other way around. He may make it look easy but when Scobie has ridden a horse it has had a race.

Jockeys, of course, are not allowed to bet and many years later when I was for a while a member of Epsom's race committee helping to entertain connections after their successes on the course I was told of the colleague who approached Mrs May Breasley and congratulated her on a decent-priced winner from the yard. 'I expect your husband had a nice touch on that,' he said. 'Oh no,' she exclaimed, 'Scobie hasn't had a bet since he gave up riding!'

* * *

When I left the *Liverpool Post* to join the *Sunday Express* as 'Crossbencher' in the late 1960s my writing about racing came to a temporary end and it was not until 1995 when Frank Johnson as editor of the *Spectator* asked me to write the Turf column there that I began doing so on a regular basis again.

I was still based in Epsom and so was Reg Akehurst, now with 63 boxes full in Burgh Heath Road, a few hundred yards from where I lived. I used to love going up on the Downs in the early morning with the racing strings stark against the skyline as they passed along the ridge, and I was soon noting:

At the centre of Epsom Downs most days, at the top of the sandhill track you'll find the weathered figure of Reg Akehurst with his ever-attendant Alsatians Terry and Kally. As his experienced eye runs over the circling string, you'll be looking at probably the best trainer of handicappers in Britain, a man with the secret of rejuvenating horses which others have discarded. He is also a man not unknown to take a tilt at the bookies.

Reg is no lover of cold weather. He has taken a winter spell in Barbados for the past eighteen years and sometimes he does so with a little help from the ring. Just before his January holiday this year his Ballynakelly, a big ex-Irish import who had previously shown little on turf came out on the all-weather track at Lingfield. Backed down from 8-1 to 5-2 favourite he romped home, apprentice-ridden, by ten lengths. I asked Reg if that had paid the holiday expenses. 'It helped.'

He didn't win the Lincoln this year with the favourite Sharp Prospect but he's won it before. In the years since he gave up a 12-year career as a jump jockey he has sent out the winner of most other big handicaps too. He does well typically with older handicappers, well-bred types from Classic stables which he has bought at the Newmarket sales. Someone once described the unrelenting openness of the Newmarket landscape as 'miles and miles of bugger all' and although Reg Akehurst is a great admirer of Newmarket's facilities, he has a knack of taking Newmarket horses and rekindling their enthusiasm. 'Horses relax and do well here,' he says of Epsom.

'They like the downland gradients and the varied scenery.'

As for his reputation for cannily placing his horses when they do start improving, he insists, 'You don't have to cheat to win races. You know when a horse has come right and if you've got a horse you can win with, you want it to win. It's your calling card.'

Sometimes people read too much into the planning of an imagined coup. A summer ago his grey Silver Groom was running in the 'Hong Kong' at Sandown. They had been expecting a good run but jockey Jimmy Quinn found himself behind a wall of horses when he went to challenge. He reported back to the trainer, 'I had so much horse under me, but I just couldn't get through' so they aimed Silver Groom next for the William Hill Cup at Goodwood. By the time of the race the Akehursts had gone off with son Murray for his wedding in Barbados. They all piled into a Bridgetown betting shop, put some real money down and whooped home the winner. The bridegroom did so well, says Reg, that he even tipped the vicar.

What makes him cross though is the way the handicapper reacts to successes by his kind of stable. The Akehurst hurdler Bimsey won a good race at Aintree earlier this season and was raised 12 pounds for the William Hill Hurdle at Sandown. No complaint about that. But when fellow Epsom trainer Simon Dow's Chief's Song beat the highly regarded Putty Road at Cheltenham, his weight wasn't raised at all for Sandown. Bimsey meanwhile was raised another 4lb when a horse he had beaten into second won a race. Akehurst demanded a meeting with the handicapper to voice his complaint that what was going on was the handicapping of certain trainers rather than their horses. His point was sustained when Chief's Song duly won the William Hill with Bimsey in fourth.

The South Hatch trainer has even found that horses have had their handicap ratings dropped on leaving his yard and he complains, 'Why should we pay a penalty for showing we are better at the job? You become a victim of your own success.'

Reg argues that while three-year-olds may sometimes improve too fast for the handicapper to catch up with their progress, older horses only win when they are back to the rating at which they have done so before. With the figures available to all through the racing press, he argues, it is all there to be seen for punters who are prepared to do their homework.

The Epsom trainers were an intriguing mix. The hard-working Simon Dow, who has long deserved better horses than he gets, has put much effort into rebuilding Epsom as a training centre but for many years horse numbers remained low despite the easy accessibility of Epsom's training grounds for those plying their trade in the City of London.

A visit in August 1996 to a historic local landmark introduced me to a young trainer who then looked to be one of those who might help to bring a turnaround. It also reminded me of a little racing history.

When the future Liberal Prime Minister Lord Rosebery was told by the Oxford University authorities that owning racehorses was not consistent with undergraduate life he wrote home, 'Dear Mother, I have left Oxford. I have secured a house in Berkeley Square and I have bought a horse to win the Derby. Your affectionate Archie.' The horse was called Ladas and it finished last in the 1869 Derby.

But for Liberals, patience pays. Twenty-five years later, during his brief spell as Prime Minister, Lord Rosebery won the Derby with Ladas II. When critics then suggested that owning racehorses suggested a lack of seriousness the Prime Minister retorted that he had owned unsuccessful horses for years without anybody complaining. The first neat response, perhaps, to the politics of envy.

Lord Rosebery, who won three Derbies in all with horses he had bred, was passionate about the Turf and hosted magnificent parties in his red-brick Epsom mansion. Sadly though, the house and the stable complex at The Durdans were allowed over many years to fall into decay. The notoriously hard-to-please Rosebery, I wrote that August, would have been pleased to find a new breeze blowing through the place in the shape of the 32-year-old Joe Naughton, who had moved in to use it as his training base.

> Up on the Downs in his baseball cap and gaudy golf shirt, Joe Naughton is the epitome of racing's new generation. The son of a former managing director of Playboy Casinos, he is firmly aware of the need to market his product: 'You can't lay back, you've got to get out and meet people.' Back in the fast-expanding yard, standing amid clusters of new boxes in what used to be a huge nettle patch, he proudly reels off the modern facilities that would have made Lord Rosebery's eyes pop – the solarium, the treadmill, the magnotherapy rugs to massage a horse on the way to the races.

The once dilapidated indoor riding school had been refurbished as a sand area where the horses could come and have a roll and a kick to vary their routines and the trainer, who had been an assistant with Barry Hills through the maestro's highly successful four years as the master of Manton, had built up from five horses to 65 over five years, scoring early success with the speedy Hever Golf

Rose who won the Prix de l'Abbaye at Longchamp and took a course record at Goodwood. Bought for 6,000 guineas, the speedy filly collected £675,000 in prize money but sadly Joe Naughton's comet burned out quickly. He never had a horse as good and, plagued as many young handlers are by bad payers, he was forced to give up training in 2002. Even more sadly, Hever Gold Rose died in foaling.

One of my favourite Epsom characters was Terry Mills, a man who did it the opposite way round to Joe Naughton, coming into training having first made his fortune in the haulage business.

You know within a few minutes when you have walked into a well-run racing stable. It is not just neat tack rooms or a well-swept yard, it is organised bustle, the sense that everybody is moving somewhere with a purpose, the questions rapped out by a trainer and the answers from his staff. At Terry's Loretta Lodge on the Headley Road, the stable once owned by Brian Swift, I was struck by the seriousness of purpose and the teamwork between Terry, his son Robert and their long-time assistant Richard Ryan.

Terry didn't come from a racing dynasty. He began as a lorry driver when he left the army, built up the A.J. Bull haulage and demolition businesses and was at one stage running a fleet of 2,000 lorries. He began owning racehorses with an animal trained at Epsom by John Sutcliffe named As Dug, bought out of the proceeds from digging gravel inside the perimeter of the Kempton Park course. As Dug was second five times. Terry's next horse Swinging Trio won five times, and some twenty years on, Terry began training himself.

This was no rich man's indulgence. There was nothing amateur about it. The day I went to see him in August 2002 Terry was higher up the trainers' table than Henry Cecil or David Elsworth, his strike rate better than Mick

Channon, Richard Hannon or Barry Hills, and at that point his season's runners were showing a £62 profit to a £1 stake.

He paid top dollar for good staff and proudly showed me around a five-furlong Polytrack that had cost him six figures, the equine swimming pool, the £20,000-worth of blood-testing equipment on the premises. He was house-proud enough to stop the 4 x 4 at one stage to pick up a single scrap of plastic floating across a paddock. He wouldn't say how much he had sunk into racing but friends put it at more than £4 million, although he was usually willing to sell on his horses to Hong Kong and Singapore when he could take a profit.

When he put in his financial plan the powers-that-be exclaimed, 'But this shows you are going to lose money.' 'Of course it did,' he told me. 'Anybody who told them anything different would have been deluding himself.' But while he acknowledged he was subsidising the operation, Terry insisted, 'This is my pleasure rather than boats or houses in Spain, but it's got to be run as a business and it is coming right.' He added:

> Demolition and waste disposal were a kindergarten compared with this game. You go and spend £250,000 on a horse, gambling that it's got an engine. If it's no good you can't ring up and say 'Put a new gear-box in'. One minute you're up in the air with a winner, the next day two scope dirty and another pulls a muscle.

Terry Mills could be emotional. I was at Goodwood in August 2001 when Where Or When, the apple of Terry's eye, was backed down from 8-1 to 11-4 favourite for the Celebration Mile, a Group Two race. Coming down the finishing straight jockey Kevin Darley, sitting on the heels of the leaders, went for one gap after another only to find them all closing in his face. Finally he resigned himself to pulling out and coming the long way round the outside, only to be pinned in where he was by Richard Hughes, coming from even further behind on the eventual winner Tillerman, trained by Amanda Perrett for Khalid Abdullah.

The exuberant Hughes pointedly raised a single finger as soon as he had crossed the line with four horses in a line behind him. The gesture wasn't lost on the crowd who had seen him do the same at Ascot only to be judged second by the photo finish. But Terry and his son Robert, told by Darley that had he been able to get through on Where Or When 'we would have won a minute', were furious that their horse had not been allowed to run his race. Apart from turning the air blue about him Terry entered an official objection to Richard Hughes for holding in Where Or When. When it was rejected with no penalty for Hughes he protested furiously that there was one law for the Establishment and another for smaller yards like his – and it has to be said that there were one or two patronising Establishment smirks on view.

I am a huge admirer of Richard Hughes, not just for his tactical genius but for the searing honesty of his autobiography about how the strains on a young jockey can lead to alcoholism, but that day I had huge sympathy for Terry. There was no doubt that given a clear run Where Or When would have won. There were counter views. Mark Perrett, former jockey and husband to the winning trainer, insisted that Hughes, who admitted shutting the door on Where Or When, was only doing what he had been paid to do. When I argued that Tillerman's neck had been angled in towards Where Or When, preventing him from getting out while Hughes was supposed to be keeping a straight line, former champion jockey Willie Carson defended Tillerman's jockey, chiding me: 'He could hardly say "Oh, go on Kevin, after you, do please come out".' But trainer Philip Mitchell, one of the best amateur riders ever, had every sympathy with the Mills yard and their criticism of Hughes.

In fairness to Richard Hughes it had to be said that winning a race on Tillerman was a feat in itself. The horse, previously a disappointing favourite, has a mind of its own and had to be held up for a precision-timed final burst. If the pace was too slow while he was at the back he would fight for his head and lose interest. Where Or When too needed to be held up behind a good pace and for horses with that requirement there would always be the danger that gaps would not appear at the right moment. Kevin Darley had to take his share of the blame.

In the end, I concluded, it was a question of just how far the 'professional foul' should be allowed to go in our shirt-tugging age. Richard Hughes did not technically break the rules of racing. He did not maltreat a horse or endanger the safety of another rider. But the best horse on the day did not win and that could not be good for punters or for racing.

Fortunately there was a happy ending to that particular saga. Early that October I was able to tell *Spectator* readers that one of the pleasures and privileges of writing about racing was to rub up from time to time against success:

Sometimes you are there in the unsaddling enclosure when dreams are realised, when long-laid plans have come to fruition and when tears of joy are shed. Yes, I know it is only a sport but when Terry Mills declared, thumping his chest after his Where Or When, a 7-1 chance, had comprehensively beaten the odds-on favourite Hawk Wing in the Group One Queen Elizabeth Stakes, 'I can die a happy man now', it did not seem an exaggeration.

Terry, who had not slept for three nights, knew what his horse could do: 'He's been working like a dream for the past few weeks. He hasn't just got gears, he's got another gear after that. He is a monster.'

The horse Where Or When beat comprehensively that day was Aidan O'Brien's potentially great Hawk Wing. But as the one-eyed busker on the path to Ascot station told me later, 'He may be a hawk but he hasn't got wings.' When taken on by Where Or When, Hawk Wing's head went up and a supreme natural athlete was found lacking in the resolution department. I am not sure there was a miler in Europe who could have beaten Where Or When that day and jockey Kevin Darley told me, 'He has a terrific turn of foot. I tracked Hawk Wing because I knew we had only one horse to beat. When I went up to him and Mick Kinane asked him he went flat for a stride or two. Mine was a proper horse and he galloped to the line.' Victory was all the sweeter at Ascot that day because Tillerman was in the field and didn't make the frame. Big offers came in for Where Or When after that, but they were never taken.

Terry, who named many of his best horses after Frank Sinatra songs, was always good to talk to on the racecourse. He continued his quest to win a Derby with an Epsom-trained horse but tragically cancer took him before he ever did. However, he had great success with Where Or When, and Ascot winners too with Bobzao, Mitcham and Norton, the latter a 300,000-guinea son of Barathea named after Terry's old pal Bill Norton with whom he used to go dog-racing at New Cross in the days when neither of them had more than a few bob in their pockets. We miss him.

With another Epsom trainer I used to keep an eye not just on the condition of his horses but on the colour of the shirt he was wearing. It wasn't quite as familiar as Jack Berry's cherry-red shirts but Roger Ingram had a 'lucky' yellow shirt he would wear when he felt a winner coming on, he told me when we watched his string early on an October morning in 1998. As we watched Clonoe and Soviet Lady go through their not-very-fast paces, Roger swapped trainerly grumbles with John Benstead about the difficulty of finding races for moderate performers of the kind his owners could afford and about the excess of paperwork required by modern officialdom.

Roger had run Peaceful Sarah at Pontefract and fancied her enough to invest £100 in her chances. A top jockey who had not ridden his most distinguished race on her and failed to reach the frame came back to report that it was his opinion she didn't go in the soft ground. Next time out at Catterick, overnight rain had turned the course into a bog. Assuming that her chance had all but gone, Peaceful Sarah's trainer limited his investment on this occasion to a tenner, only for the filly to bolt in. 'Just imagine,' Roger reflected, 'the kind of trouble I would have been in if I had reported after Pontefract [as trainers are encouraged to do] that she didn't go in the soft. I could have been in really deep water.'

Roger Ingram's view is that he trains horses for their owners, not for the punting public. 'Unless you break the rules, the Jockey Club should leave you alone.' The best thing the authorities could do for smaller yards like his, he said, was to provide more 0–70 handicaps: 'If you've got a horse rated 48, half the time they can't get in a race. But they're too good for a seller.'

He started as a lad with Brian Swift. 'I had three rides as an apprentice. I like to think I got too heavy, but I was no blinking good.' Swift was one of the first British trainers to acquire Arab owners and he remembers how the lads used to jostle for the Sheikh of Bahrain's horses when the allocations were made. The £5 tips the Sheikh dispensed were much prized given that usually you were left with only around £2 a week after deductions.

In a typical racing biography Roger also had spells with Martin Tate, Michael Oliver (where he looked after National winner West Tip in his novice chasing days) and Frank Jordan. He was then private trainer to Terry Mellor at Southwell until the recession forced his patron to close down and he arrived to set up in Epsom with a single unplaced horse, Cheap Metal.

Roger insisted that he was as much the victim (well, nearly!) as the gainer from the gamble that made his name with the first winner he sent out while in Epsom. 'A friend had told me owners were crawling out of the woodwork here but they weren't.' Luckily one shrewd punter sent him Kinnegad Kid, who went on to win eight races, and an unknown quantity called Joe 'n Jack. Joe 'n Jack, it later transpired, had been banned from running in Ireland after his jockey never gave him a chance in a race there. Roger worked Joe 'n Jack for a few weeks and then, after being impressed by a trial gallop at Lingfield, reported him as ready to win. As the starting price drifted on course from 20-1 to 33-1 the owner and his friends backed him nationwide in small betting shops, leaving out the Big Three bookmakers.

After Joe 'n Jack bolted in there were investigations but no rules had been broken. It was a simple, old-fashioned betting coup. Surely Roger cashed in himself? 'I won a few bob. If I had really known what was going on I would have won a lot more. I was a bit naïve. He paid 80-1 on the Tote.'

The week after Joe 'n Jack's success, Cheap Metal won the first of his three hurdles at Plumpton and Roger Ingram was in business. At the time we talked there were fourteen in the yard, down from twenty at the start of the season (he doesn't carry on with no-hopers). With ten boxes let out to 'do-it-yourselfers' he reckoned he needed twenty horses to be comfortable at Wendover House, part of Walter Nightingall's and Scobie Breasley's old yard and home to Persian War in Arthur Pitt's time.

A miner's son from Tredegar, at 48 he still had the look of a cheeky pixie and somehow managed to catch more headlines than most small trainers. In 1997 he had wagered £500 with Bowman's at a useful price that he would train ten winners by the end of the year. They said payment was only due at the end of the calendar year – and then went bust before 31 December. He says he doesn't need to bet to survive but if you see a man in a yellow shirt walking the course before racing, as the careful Ingram likes to do when he fancies one, then it is probably worth taking a look at his entries that day.

* * *

Like many other Epsom residents in Derby run-up days, various trainers there will have suffered the experience of a scruffy-looking crew turning up on their doorstep and offering to tarmacadam the driveway for a bargain price that suddenly quintuples when the job has been completed. One racing figure I knew was once picked up by the throat by a seventeen-stone tar-spreader who threatened to kill him when he refused to pay more than the

£100 originally agreed. But one day on the edge of the Downs the scam merchants got their come-uppance.

The proprietor of a local livery yard agreed to let a tar gang patch a few holes. She came back from a West Country trip to find the whole yard asphalted, very poorly, and the driver of a scruffy van demanding several thousand pounds. Scared out of her wits, she was driven to the building society to get the funds but on a technicality withdrawal was refused. They drove her back to the yard to discuss the next steps, which were unlikely to have been pleasant.

What they didn't know was that the lady herself had a relative with a few unfortunate habits of his own. At the time he was on the run, thanks to a little misunderstanding when he had popped into the bank to inquire about an overdraft and just happened to be wearing a balaclava and carrying a shotgun. Just as she and the asphalter escorts arrived back, armed police in search of her cousin came swarming over the back wall. The asphalter team took one look, pushed her out of the door and screamed out of her yard in their van, never to be seen again.

* * *

Epsom racing's best asset has long been Simon Dow, training at Clear Height Stables just behind the grandstand. Nobody has worked harder to maintain Epsom as a vital training centre. Occasionally, as with Young Ern, the eternally youthful Dow gets a horse to match his abilities.

When a talented newspaper colleague of mine left to join a tabloid our then editor muttered that he would be 'playing the piano in a brothel'. Simon got much the same reaction from his banker father when at sixteen he said he was going to be making his future in racing but at 24 he was a fully-fledged dual-purpose trainer.

Plan A had involved a riding career. As he told me, 'At twenty I had visions of being John Francome, but then came maturity.' He obviously didn't lack courage: the matter-of-fact way he dismissed 32 shoulder dislocations was evidence of that. Nor would fitness have been the problem: Simon was Britain's schoolboy half-mile champion at fifteen. But soon he was recording in the *Directory of the Turf*, 'Riding career: Amateur 1983–85. Useless.'

Simon worked for Mick Haynes and Philip Mitchell before setting up on his own near Guildford with £1,000 worth of credit with the bank, a barnful of hay and two-and-a-half horses. He admitted later, 'There wasn't a horse in the yard that could raise a gallop but if you could talk, you could sell.' There were early winners and the numbers increased but soon he was down again to five horses. One morning two came back lame and a third was claimed by another trainer after Simon ran it in a selling race at Warwick, but he borrowed money, bought his Epsom yard and in four years had 50 winners on the board to launch his career. Since then it has been steady rather than spectacular, but the dreams are still alive and he has remained a fixture among Epsom's ever-shifting trainer population. It would be a much poorer place without him.

I worked alongside Simon for a while trying to help develop Epsom as a racing centre, and in particular to create affordable accommodation for stable staff in a suburb full of better-paid London commuters. Epsom Downs though are divided between the responsibilities of several different local authorities and they have not all been sympathetic to the needs of racing. In Newmarket and in Lambourn, local councils intervene actively to help the racing community and to prevent racing premises being closed down and converted into housing projects. Sadly over the years there has been little evidence of the same spirit among the local authorities with responsibilities abutting on Epsom Downs. In September 2001 I drafted a document for Simon and the Epsom Training and Development Fund which was a heartfelt appeal to local planners. I include some of it here because it typifies the problems faced by racing communities in many areas.

So many pleasures in life we take for granted. The glorious stand of beech trees at a beauty spot, the provincial theatre that lets you see London shows at half the price, the little delicatessen that always has your favourite cheese. Then one morning we wake up and they are no longer there. Blighted by benign neglect, no longer 'economically viable', squeezed out by bigger commercial interests, suddenly they have gone. It hasn't exactly been anybody's fault, but they will never be replaced and our lives are the poorer for it.

Do not please let that happen to one of the greatest glories which Epsom and the surrounding area enjoy. Epsom Downs and the horses trained there are a unique and precious part of our heritage. Go up on the Downs any morning and watch the training strings emerge from a woodland path, the riders chatting, the horses snorting recognition. Watch them power up the all-weather tracks, the lads crouched low on their backs, and see them swagger back after exercise, four-legged athletes revelling in their condition. It is a dull soul who is not cheered and enriched by such a spectacle.

It is not a sight you can see in any other suburban town, or almost anywhere else within a half-hour train ride from central London. But it is a sight which those living in or near Epsom have been able to enjoy for over two hundred years. Many people probably see their first horse on Epsom Downs and the horse gives Epsom something special.

In my business I have to travel a good deal. People ask me where I am from. When I simply reply with the word 'Epsom' alone it brings no more than a faint stirring of recognition. When I say 'Epsom – Epsom Downs where the Derby is run' you can watch the illumination light up people's faces. Epsom's horses and Epsom's trainers and Epsom's stable staff help give the area its identity. They add to the quality of life. But they and that quality of life are in peril if some of you in positions of authority cannot now make a leap of imagination and think what you can do to help.

Thanks to the tireless work of Simon Dow as chairman of the Epsom trainers, most of you know the basic facts and figures. In 1970 there were nineteen trainers and 520 horses in Epsom. In 1990 there were twelve trainers and 400 horses. Now there are eleven trainers and around 200 horses. Living in Epsom for 30 years I have watched yard after yard close and the premises go out of racing, sometimes turned over to housing estates, sometimes adapted for other uses.

Epsom has excellent training facilities and first-class, well-maintained gallops. It has talented trainers who can bring the best out of the animals in their charge. It has the advantage of closeness to London. An owner can watch his horse at work on the Downs and still be behind his City desk by 9.00am. It should be a thriving training centre to match, say, Lambourn or Middleham. Instead it is a training centre in decline. It needs new blood. It needs a way of encouraging stable staff to make their careers in Epsom rather than drifting off to Newmarket.

Those of us who work with the Epsom Training and Development Fund charity have had to settle for small beginnings. But we have a vision. First of all we want to work for the welfare of the racing community in Epsom, to improve conditions for stable staff and to help them when they fall on hard times. Secondly, for the sake of those staff, we want to make our contribution to rebuilding Epsom's status as a training centre. We want to initiate a virtuous circle with young trainers wanting to set up in Epsom because it has the right facilities, with good stable staff wanting to work in Epsom because it is a community which understands their needs and with both trainers and their staff encouraged by an influx of good horses brought in by owners because they are convinced that Epsom is on the up.

The first need we are trying to meet with the Fund is for more and better accommodation for those who work in Epsom stables. The long and awkward hours mean that stable staff must live near their work, but in an expensive commuting town affordable lodgings are hard to come by. Very young lads and lasses may settle for dingy bedsits or single rooms with landladies. But those at the end of their teenage years are not going to settle for that. They want and need some independence and a little space. If they do not find it in Epsom they will move to training centres elsewhere where they can find it, probably leaving just at the point when their skills have developed enough to make them truly valuable contributors to their yards. That is why a prime objective of the Fund is the development of a purpose-built hostel to house twenty or more stable staff in decent, though not luxurious style.

We want to be able to help stable staff with transport costs, maybe even with clothing at the very early stage when they go to the British Racing School to learn the basics. We want to be able to help with suitable leisure activities too to help build a spirit of camaraderie. Charity events run by the Fund have succeeded in raising tidy sums already and helping to form a social hub for the Epsom racing scene. But it will need a benevolent eye from planners if we are to take things further.

To help the staff there is a need to help the trainers too. And there the real need is for the development of starter yards. They need to be yards with access as directly as possible to the training grounds and with the minimum need for the horses to use public roads. That inevitably means development within green belt areas covered by the three separate councils. But what do we create green belts for if not to enhance the environment? And if training strings out on the Downs for all to see are not an enhancement of the environment I do not know what is.

Please, please do not stick with the mantras of well-worn sub-clauses in regulations which seemingly forbid the exercise of initiative. Please, please make that leap of imagination which is necessary if the Epsom Downs are to have a future. For if Epsom does not remain as a training centre, do not imagine that the Downs themselves will be as well maintained as they are today. Restoring Epsom's glory as a training centre is not just in the interests of racing folk – it is in the interests of anybody who wants Epsom to have an individual character, anybody who walks a dog or flies a kite on the Downs and anybody with the soul to thrill at the sight of horses and riders silhouetted on the morning skyline.

One of the key figures in the development of the Epsom fund was the famed crisis manager and company doctor David James, later Lord James of Blackheath, the man they called the City of London's Red Adair and the saviour of the Dome.

David when I knew him was one of the fearless punters in Ascot's Iron Stand Club, formed a century or so ago by the Prince of Wales so his chums could meet their mistresses and divorced friends in a convenient spot without having to leave the royal enclosure. Iron Stand members account for some 25 per cent of bookies takings' on some courses and you can see why.

Jilted at 26 by his then fiancée the young James, then earning £900 a year with the Ford Motor Company, decided that he would hazard on a horse the whole of the £600 he had saved for the deposit on their house. He was, he says, challenging the gods to dictate the pattern of his life on the outcome of a single race.

The very day he was wrestling with his marital misfortune, the weights came out for what was in those days (we are talking 1967) one of the best handicaps in the land, the *News of the World* Handicap on the last day of Glorious Goodwood. It was a 21lb limited handicap from 8st 0lb to 9st 7lb and Sucaryl, a horse trained by Noel Murless, had been allotted just 8st 6lb. Since Sucaryl, ridden by Bill Rickaby, that day ran a half-length second in the Irish Derby to a heavily fancied stable companion, Mr James decided that Sucaryl merely had to stay alive to win at Goodwood.

He invested the whole £600 on the nose, starting by getting 14-1 for the whole of his £75 credit line with Guntrips and carrying on with £100 at 8-1 with Ladbroke's and £100 at 7-1 with William Hill. The rest went on here and there at prices averaging 7-2. Overall his money was on at an average 6.5 to 1. But then came the courageous bit. Appalled by what the young man was doing, Lewes trainer Towser Gosden, a friend, counselled him against it and arranged with local bookies to buy up the bets at an average 3-1. David James would have been left with an impressive profit and no race to risk but he decided to stick with it.

I was not surprised to discover later that he was literally a man who had stared down the barrel of a gun and held his nerve. In 1986 he flew to Tripoli to negotiate the release of some British engineering company employees who had been taken hostage and was held himself while the Americans bombed the facility. It was also David who triggered the 'Iraqi supergun' affair by tipping off MI6 about some gun barrels he spotted when visiting a Midlands manufacturer.

That July David went through the first three days at Goodwood without having a single bet. *News of the World* day turned out to be a sticky, steamy one with the air thick with thunderflies. Sucaryl, by now the 5-6 odds-on favourite, came into the paddock totally stirred up, covered in foamy sweat as if he had just done three cycles in a washing machine. But still David James did not lay off, and just as well. In the race Sucaryl was never off the bridle, coming home in George Moore's hands a two-and-a-half-length winner. The gods had spoken. The intrepid punter had won several years' salary.

The money went into the bank. David James's business career took off and in the Epsom days when I knew him he was still unmarried. 'First I was too poor, then I was too busy and then I was too old.' Had he ever come close to it? 'My status has often been in danger, but I have always thought better of it in the morning.' However, for romantics, there was a happy ending. The iron-disciplined James, who works out every morning even earlier than Clive Brittain gets his horses on Newmarket Heath, overdid things on his rowing machine one day and suffered a stroke. Friends say he fell for one of the ladies who aided his recovery. Whatever the explanation for his change of heart, I espied him one evening at a Jeffrey Archer party to hear him say, 'Robin, meet my wife.'

The Derby

When the writer Bill Bryson went to Epsom for the first time he declared, 'The Derby is a little like your first experience of sex – hectic, strenuous, memorably pleasant and over before you know it.'

Having lived for some 30 years in Epsom I am of course a devotee of the Derby, although I have always been better for some reason at finding the winner of the Oaks. In earlier days we used to be able to buy a ticket as local residents which allowed us to take the car up to the course and park close to the rails about two furlongs out with a copious picnic and a few friends. Having the children jumping up and down on the car roof as the likes of Grundy, Empery and The Minstrel drove home to collect the Blue Riband didn't do much for the bodywork but since Mrs Oakley invariably backed Lester Piggott's mounts those last two were both Oakley family winners. I do remember too backing Morston when he won in 1973. Many years later I saw the action from a different viewpoint as I served for a while on the Epsom Race Committee.

Racing has had to branch out this century and a Race Committee colleague told me that we virtually doubled the gate on summer evenings with live music from tribute bands and the like after racing. One evening it turned out that the top performer engaged was a gay icon and some tentative ads were taken out in the gay media. An Epsom official responding to one booking call outlined the facilities, mentioning the Queen's Stand venues. 'Oh how delicious,' replied the caller, 'and what are we allowed to do *there*?'

Ascot may be grander, Goodwood prettier and Sandown Park somehow friendlier but Epsom on Derby Day has something truly special. The undulating mile and a half across the Downs with its tricky downhill bend, left-tipping camber down the straight and rising finish remains a supreme test of horse and rider. You need the temperament to cope with the hubbub, the speed to keep yourself out of trouble, the guts and control to remain balanced under pressure, the stamina to last out.

For years I have been battling those who say that Epsom has somehow lost its glory: for me it will never do so. It is true that we no longer see a quarter of a million streaming to the Downs on Derby Day to ride the roundabouts, stuff their faces with candyfloss and have their palms read between races by dark-eyed gypsy ladies. Nor does every leading owner these days seem to feel that his three-year-old will not have proved himself the best unless he is at Epsom on Derby Day. But Edward Gillespie, who used to run the show at Epsom before he became the embodiment of Cheltenham's charms, got it right when he told me back in 1996, 'The heritage is priceless. Take a horse over to win the Japan Cup and you are, what, the fifth to have your name inscribed. Win the Derby this year and you are on a roll of honour stretching back over 216 years before you.' He offered a comparison with tennis: 'Those stars who can't produce their game on grass like to pretend that the US Open or the French Open are just as important. But what is the championship everyone in their hearts still wants to win? It's Wimbledon.'

American John Galbreath may have been a little prejudiced when he declared in 1972, 'Anyone who doesn't consider the Epsom Derby one of the greatest sporting events in the world must be out of his mind', because his colt Roberto had just won the contest in one of the best finishes of all time. But the great Italian breeder Federico Tesio was no less of an enthusiast. He declared, 'The thoroughbred exists because its selection has depended not on experts, technicians or zoologists but on a piece of wood, the winning post of the Epsom Derby.' He was right because the horse that answers all the questions posed by the Derby has just what you need in a stallion – look at Galileo. That is why Coolmore's John Magnier and his team continue to support the Derby in days when the French have shortened their version to a mile and a quarter and the Americans allow geldings to run in theirs. As Magnier says, 'It is the race where all the qualities of a colt are tested.' That includes temperament: Sea The Stars trainer John Oxx puts it this way: 'You can't run any old horse in the Derby – you need an uncomplicated sort.'

First the horses climb uphill for four furlongs, streaming around a gradual right-hand bend. Then comes their only chance to settle as they switch left to the inner rail and head up to the top of Tattenham Hill. There follows a pell-mell dash down the slope to the sharp left-hand bend round Tattenham Corner.

Lester Piggott, who won the race an astonishing nine times, says of a potential Derby winner:

> Size is less important than the manner of racing. You need a horse that can lay up handy a few places behind the leaders: getting too far back at Epsom can be disastrous as there is no part of the course where you can rapidly make up ground forfeited early on. You have to get into a reasonable place and keep out of trouble as beaten horses fall back on the down-hill run.

Nobody wants to be pushed too far to the outside in a Derby field because the wider you are the more the

finishing straight camber works against you. Those on
the outside will be pressing to get closer to the rail. Those
on the rail will be fighting to hold their position. Not
only will their momentum down the hill take most horses
faster than they feel comfortable going, they need to be
prepared to co-operate with their riders in fighting for
position. There will be bumps and bangs along the way.
Winning a Derby takes a horse with courage as well as
ability.

Even when Tattenham Corner has been negotiated,
the horses face a further test in front of the stands. The
finishing straight is nearly four furlongs and as they reach
the final 200 yards, tired three-year-olds running through
a wall of noise face not just a further gut-busting rise to the
finishing post but that camber which tilts them in towards
the inside rail, making it hard for their riders to stop the
contestants hanging to their left and to keep them on a
true course to the line. As Richard Hughes points out, not
only do nine out of ten horses hang left at Epsom because
of the camber: nine out of ten jockeys are right-handed,
which makes the surge to the rail even greater.

I love not just the sight but the sound and smell of
Derby Day. Long before I ever got to watch the race I
adored the whole romantic sense of history surrounding it. Even before bank holidays were introduced in
the 1870s it was London's unofficial day out. Parliament
used to be adjourned for three days to accommodate the
Epsom meeting and of course the most sensational Derby
ever was in 1913 when the suffragette Emily Davison threw
herself in front of the King's horse Anmer as the field
rounded Tattenham corner, later dying from her injuries. Then the favourite Craganour, having passed the
post first, was disqualified for interference and the race
awarded to the 100-1 outsider Aboyeur. The only other

winner to be disqualified was the 1844 victor Running Rein who was later discovered to be a four-year-old. Although colts cannot run in the Oaks, fillies are allowed to contest the Derby: the last to do so and win was Fifinella in 1916 (when the wartime race was run at Newmarket). She took the Oaks as well, two days later.

Among those I did see were the ill-fated Shergar, whose winning margin was a majestic ten lengths in 1981, and the unbeaten Lammtarra, who only ran four races in his life, although they included the 1995 Derby, King George VI and Queen Elizabeth Stakes and Prix de l'Arc de Triomphe.

Amid the Derby jockeys Lester Piggott reigns supreme, having scored the last of his nine successes on Teenoso in 1983 and the first on Never Say Die in 1954 at only eighteen. There were no celebrations: he went home that night and mowed his parents' lawn, although he did sneak into a cinema for a private showing of the race newsreel the following week.

The great Sir Gordon Richards only won the Derby on Pinza at his 28th and final attempt in the Coronation year of 1953. The most remarkable of Steve Donoghue's six Derby victories was the one on Humorist in 1921. After losing several races by faltering in the last hundred yards the horse had a rogue's reputation. Although his mount was distressed afterwards, Donoghue won by a neck without using his whip, saying he would rather have cut off his arm than done so. A few weeks later Humorist died in his box after a massive blood loss. Post-mortems revealed that all his life he had been consumptive and his only remaining lung had finally collapsed.

We all have to explain away our losers and the winners that got away. The best example of that I ever came across was from Peter O'Sullevan, the man whose distinctive honeyed gravel voice provides the soundtrack for so many favourite racing memories. In 1961 Psidium had been so far out of sight in the 2,000 Guineas his jockey would have needed binoculars to pick up the field. Consequently few gave him a chance at Epsom, where Roger Poincelet dropped him out at the back and he came with a rattle at the end of the race. Who says French jockeys can't negotiate Epsom? Psidium only passed Dicta Drake 50 yards out but so fast was he travelling that by the post he was two lengths up. The 66-1 shot made his way to the winner's enclosure amid a stunned silence. Peter O'Sullevan had written in the *Daily Express* before the race, 'If Psidium wins I'll be very psurprised.' Taxed about that by Psidium's owners after the race, he replied with typical O'Sullevan panache: 'Consider me in psackcloth.'

Which then are the Derbies that stick in my mind? I would have to include Shergar's triumph under Walter Swinburn: I would never have believed a horse could win the Derby by such a margin. Kris Kin was not perhaps a great horse but he is in my mental scrapbook because of Kieren Fallon's sublime ride the day he won in 2003.

Sir Percy gets in too because of the incredibly exciting finish when he triumphed in 2006 and because his trainer Marcus Tregoning is one of the nice guys of the sport. Sea The Stars I would include not because his Derby was a particularly exciting one but because l believe John Oxx's handling of him in his championship year was one of the finest sustained training feats I have ever witnessed. For a horse to win six Group Ones in six months – the 2,000 Guineas, the Derby, the Eclipse, the Juddmonte International, the Irish Champion Stakes and the Prix de l'Arc de Triomphe – over a range of distances and against the experts at each one is quite phenomenal.

Aidan O'Brien's victory with Galileo has to be in there

too and for sheer nerve I must include the victory by Pour Moi for André Fabre and the precocious jockey talent of Mickael Barzalona.

To me Kieren Fallon is the best Derby jockey we have seen since Piggott. Never mind the long series of head-lines earned for the wrong reasons: the drink, the per-sonal relationships, the court cases, the severed retainers and that horrific injury in a fall at Ascot which almost lost him his arm; at Epsom it seems the Force is with him. In 2003 at 38 he had been champion for five of the previous six seasons. His mount was the inexperienced Kris Kin, trained by Sir Michael Stoute and owned by Saeed Suhail who had at one stage during Kieren's drinking troubles taken him off his horses. At Stoute's instigation, Suhail had gambled £90,000 by putting Kris Kin back in the race at the last possible forfeit stage, days before it was run. Punters took the hint and on the day backed him down from 14-1 to 6-1 third favourite.

The chestnut, a notable sluggard on the gallops, was having only his fourth race and Fallon, by now teetotal, had never ridden him before. They did not quite jump off with the early leaders The Great Gatsby and Dutch Gold but Kieren, aware of the need for a good position, quickly sent Kris Kin after them up the early rise. Crucially then, finding his mount short of room as they reached the top of the hill and a little uncertain about scrapping for it, Kieren did not drive him hard but let the horse do what he was comfortable with and regain his confidence. He said afterwards, 'I was a bit worried there but I let him find himself. He came through it in a stride or two and was man enough to hold his own. Coming down the hill into the home straight I knew when I dug deep he was going to answer.'

So Kris Kin did. Three furlongs out you would not have

said Stoute's contender was among those going the best but Fallon balanced him, moved out enough to get a clear run and then began demanding of the horse beneath him with all the power he can generate. He conjured up a tremendous surge through the last furlong, caught The Great Gatsby ten strides from the line and won going away by a clear length. Said Sir Michael Stoute, who had won the race previously with Shergar and Shahrastani and who does not waste words, 'That was one of the greatest rides you will ever see at Epsom.'

Sir Percy's triumph in the 2006 Derby was heartwarming because for once the race did not go to the big battalions able to pay millions for a horse. Victoria and Anthony Pakenham had paid just 16,000 guineas for the son of 2,000 Guineas winner Mark of Esteem. It was thanks to the Guineas that Sir Percy's participation in the Derby remained in question until close to the race: they had not watered at Newmarket that year and he became jarred up in finishing second to George Washington and had to have intensive physiotherapy throughout his Epsom preparation.

Jockey Martin Dwyer was briefly in doubt too. Riding at Bath the day before, he was thrown in the paddock, cracked a rib and hurt his back. Worried whether his jockey was fit enough, even trainer Marcus Tregoning had his problems on the way to Epsom: he was picked up for speeding on his way from Lambourn and given a ticket even though he sought mitigation as the trainer of the third favourite in the Derby. Some policemen have no soul.

The race itself was as exciting as any ever seen. For some reason, I think I had been caught in conversation until too late, I watched from close to the finishing post and I could not have called the winner of the first photo finish since 1997.

It had been a rough race with plenty of scrimmaging coming to Tattenham Corner. At that point Dragon Dancer, ridden by Darryll Holland, joined Dylan Thomas and Johnny Murtagh in the lead with the maiden Hala Bek (Philip Robinson) and the Aga Khan's Visindar, the favourite, closing on the leading pair under Christophe Soumillon. Sir Percy was only ninth or tenth at that point.

Coming up the cambered straight experience and balance became crucial. Although the first two were not stopping, Hala Bek, who looked full of running, was beginning to look as though he might catch them and compensate his popular trainer Michael Jarvis, whose Coshocton had broken a leg close to the finish four years before. But as Visindar fell away and Robinson urged Hala Bek to go for it he veered violently to his right under the pressure.

The lightly raced Dragon Dancer had never won a race and when urged by Darryll Holland to challenge Dylan Thomas seemed momentarily uncertain what was expected of him. Hala Bek's swerve and Dragon Dancer's hesitation cost them both because Martin Dwyer had taken a gamble. Despite the likelihood of the horses ahead of him lugging left with the Epsom camber he spied a gap along the rail and went for it late with what they reckoned was Sir Percy's single burst of speed. It was one of those daring manoeuvres that makes a jockey look a genius when it comes off and a dumbo when it doesn't. The compact Sir Percy was a well-balanced horse with more experience than his rivals and he had the courage to respond. Just as Holland had made Dragon Dancer's mind up for him and he got by Dylan Thomas, Sir Percy flashed past them both to win by a short head.

So convinced was Darryll that he had won that he looked down at his own number cloth in disbelief when the photo result was called. Second and third were separated by a head and third and fourth by another short head.

Sir Percy, who had been unbeaten as a two-year-old, never seemed quite the same horse afterwards and did not win again but as Marcus Tregoning has said since, 'How could they ever say it wasn't a good Derby? Of course it was, and one of the most memorable.'

Among English-based trainers, I have been happy to celebrate Derby success too for Luca Cumani, for William Haggas and for Michael Bell, all of them men with that precious gift of sharing their pleasures and involving the racing world in them. But in recent years betting calculations have often involved the Coolmore contingent trained by Aidan O'Brien.

After O'Brien succeeded with Galileo in 2001 I wrote:

> Not so long ago, after Golan's burst of speed took him from last to first in the 2,000 Guineas we were talking of him as a potential world-beater. The only question was whether a horse with that much speed could last the Derby distance. Golan did last the distance and lasted it well. But he was beaten out of sight by Galileo who truly could be one of the horses of the decade.

I had written in advance in my *Spectator* column that there was a case to be made for Galileo:

> I only wish I could have had a whisper beforehand of what the 31-year-old Aidan O'Brien was willing to tell us after the Derby. In that soft-spoken, hesitant voice of his, he declared that when he gave Galileo his first canter as a two-year-old the horse was already good enough to win any six-furlong maiden race you cared to put him in. After his last run, Galileo had

improved in his next piece of work by an incredible 15–18 lengths, said the young master of Ballydoyle. 'It was very hard to believe that he was doing what he was doing. I have never seen a horse do that and show that kind of speed.' So good was Galileo at home that they thought the other horses must be wrong. Although there now seems to have been a change of heart from the Coolmore team, who have decided to go for the Irish Derby after all, O'Brien even suggested initially after the Derby victory that we might see Galileo running over a mile or a mile and a quarter in future rather than the Derby distance of a mile and a half. He explained, 'Speed is his thing. He just finds it very easy to go very fast.'

Clearly he does. Derby-winning Jockey Mick Kinane complained that the early pace of the race was slow and Galileo was unchallenged at the end of the race, and yet this year's winner ran the second fastest Derby time ever. 'You wouldn't want to pick him up,' said Kinane. 'He just took off.' When we asked Aidan, with an American campaign in mind, if Galileo would handle a dirt track he replied, 'This one could gallop on water.' (They always did say that the Irish definition of soft going approximated to the Grand Canal in Venice.) No wonder that co-owner Michael Tabor, asked if he had had a bit on the horse, replied, 'Several times, at prices from 7-1 down.' And when he talks about 'a bit' it probably means he won enough to buy a lump of Mayfair.

He and I deal in different numbers, but I understood exactly what Michael Tabor meant when he told us once after he had won £200,000 at 5-1 on Danetime, 'I back horses because it has been a way of life for a long time. It's not the money, it's being right that is important.'

I could have listened to Aidan and the Coolmore

team for hours and the most striking thing about the brilliant young trainer who has now taken the Irish 1,000 and 2,000 Guineas this season plus the Oaks and Derby double is his incredible and quite genuine modesty. Ask him how he does it and he immediately gives all the credit to a 'wonderful' stable staff who 'look after the horses and don't let me interfere too much'. Is there no contribution from him, he was pressed. No, not really, it is just that he is lucky enough to get some well-bred horses, he said. Believe that and the moon really is made of blue cheese.

Maybe in that way he does have the luck of the Irish. But that is not why he trains so many winners. Just watch him with his horses in the parade ring, talking gently to them, brushing over their quarters, sponging out their mouths. You can see that this is a magical man with some special kind of affinity with the animals in his charge …

As for the Coolmore operation, they go from strength to strength. Last year they had the brave and consistent Giant's Causeway. Now their great sire Sadler's Wells has produced a long-overdue Derby winner too. Said John Magnier, sounding a little miffed that anybody had ever doubted the prospect: 'He's had five Oaks winners and five seconds to go with the five seconds in the Derby. I don't know what they'll do when they start acting around here.'

O'Brien performed even better the next year. He trained the first two home in the 2,000 Guineas at Newmarket, Rock of Gibraltar and Hawk Wing, and then he came on to Epsom and repeated the 1, 2 feat in the Derby with High Chaparral and Hawk Wing twelve lengths clear of the field. It was the first time any trainer had done that for 50 years. It meant that in just five years O'Brien had trained the winners of sixteen European Classics. As an

Irish voice inquired loudly at the entrance to Epsom's surprisingly poky little winner's enclosure, 'What on earth
is he going to do when he grows up?' One more year of
success like that, I ventured, and we would all be cheering
on Godolphin's petro-dollar-fuelled battalions as plucky
underdogs. And how does O'Brien know when a horse
is ready? He told the media one day, 'You know by his
behaviour, the expression on his face, how he carries on
with himself.' Simple really. If only we punters could share
the language which Aidan and his horses speak.

The most recent Derby that remains vivid in my memory was the one that introduced us to a precocious new
riding talent and laid the foundations for the break-up
of Frankie Dettori's long and profitable association with
Sheikh Mohammed and Godolphin.

As André Fabre walked off the Derby course following the success of Pour Moi in 2011 I watched one of the
horse's connections embrace him and declare, 'I'll tell
you one thing. He's a cocky little bastard, isn't he?' It
wasn't the horse the hugger had in mind: jockey Mickael
Barzalona, despite winning by just a head after coming
from further behind to win than any Derby jockey most
of us can remember, had stood bolt upright in the stirrups and waved his whip in exultation a couple of strides
before reaching the post.

A jockey who had done that for an old-school trainer
like Barry Hills might well have had a crack of the whip
across his own backside the next morning on the gallops.
Never mind whether it was 'not quite British' as I heard
some say; showmanship of that kind is unprofessional
because it could unbalance the horse and bring the risk
of injury. When we sought to winkle an opinion out of
M. Fabre, however, he contented himself with noting that
the rider is only nineteen. Not for nothing is France's best

trainer, champion for 22 of the previous 24 years, the son of a diplomat.

It was a day when the racing community had hoped for the Queen to have her first Derby victory with Carlton House but the French had waited 35 years for a Derby victory and when it came it came in extraordinary style. Mickael Barzalona's ride showed us not just an instinctive genius in the saddle but a jockey with astonishingly cool nerves for any age.

Disregarding the Lester Piggott maxim on how to ride the Derby, he and André Fabre had planned to run the race the way Pour Moi did, letting most of the field coast ahead of him then picking them all off from the rear. As Fabre confessed, when planning such a tactic it was a relief to find there were only thirteen horses in the Derby field. But setting out to win from the rear is one thing, actually carrying out such a precarious manoeuvre in your first Derby is quite another. Barzalona is a precious talent and he should delight us for decades.

We already knew there was something special about the youngster whom Fabre had nurtured since he was sixteen. Sheikh Mohammed's Godolphin team had swiftly begun using him as an understudy to Frankie Dettori and Barzalona had impressed when he had popped over to Newmarket earlier that season and rode a couple of winners on his first day there. I hoped at the time that his talent would not become distracted: one mature lady of my acquaintance after seeing the dark-haired young jockey (who could easily pass for fourteen) expressed immediately her willingness to take him home and tuck him up in bed. I don't think it was reading him bedtime stories she had in mind.

I had in fact backed Pour Moi because I felt instinctively that he was the business. I believe horses have to stay to win the Derby and there was no question in Pour Moi's pedigree, since he is by Montjeu out of a Darshaan mare. In his previous race he had shown formidable finishing speed, always a key asset in a Classic, and crucially an unusually assertive André Fabre had for the first time ever brought a Derby candidate to Epsom for a trial run around Tattenham Corner.

When Carlton House, trained by Sir Michael Stoute, had suffered a minor injury during Derby week I had doubled my bet. When you talk to great trainers and read their memoirs it becomes clear what fine-tuning is involved in preparing a horse for big races, on the Flat or over jumps. The smallest setback can frustrate calculations. In 1987 when Jimmy Fitzgerald's Forgive 'n Forget was favourite for the Gold Cup the race was delayed for more than an hour by snow. Asked afterwards why he had failed to win, Fitzgerald declared, not totally tongue-in-cheek: 'My horse was trained to the minute and by the time they finally set off he was over the top.'

The real puzzle was why it had taken those 35 years since Empery's victory in 1976 for the French to win another Derby. I believe there were several contributing factors: France has no track resembling Epsom, few French races are contested pell-mell the way the Derby is, consequently few French jockeys excel at Epsom. Finally, in recent years with the 'French Derby' – the Prix du Jockey Club – taking place the same weekend, French entries for Epsom have been dwindling. When Pour Moi and young Barzalona rewrote the statistics manual the only sadness is that it was at the expense of Carlton House.

But what about the future of the Derby itself? Of one change in recent years I do approve: long may the race be run on Saturdays. Like the Grand National, the Derby is the people's race, not just for the racing elite, and should be run on a day when most can get to it, even if most of what used to be called the working class nowadays prefers to take the family car to the garden centre. Switch it back to the Wednesday and it would become like so many other sporting events these days: the preserve of the corporate sponsors and their lucky guests. Crucially, let us leave alone the race conditions.

Not everybody, I have to concede, is an Epsom fan. I have engaged in amiable debate for example with Mick Channon, who insists that the authorities ought to blow up the Epsom course and start all over again. But on this issue I am a Rocker, not a Mod. Indeed I sometimes fear that what I call the sun-dried tomato syndrome, the craze for modernisation for modernisation's sake, is taking over the whole of life. Why cannot a chef these days give you a Caesar salad without a sprinkling of beetroot crisps or a crème brûlée without chucking candied cherries on the bottom? Even in a Botswana game reserve one day my steak came with an unordered orange sauce. Classics should be left alone, and that applies to the Derby too. Nobody thinks of training ivy up Nelson's column or swapping Big Ben for something sponsored and digital; so the modernisers should keep their hands off the Derby. Run it later in the year, urge the experimentalists. Cut back the distance as the French have done from a mile and a half to a mile and a quarter. Transfer it from Epsom's switchback to a flatter course like York or Ascot. Phooey. The true test of the Derby is that it is an extraordinary race in the full sense of that word – and it is still the race that everybody wants to win.

When Ruler of the World triumphed in the 2013 Derby it was yet another sign of the Coolmore empire's domination. Standing on the winner's rostrum in their dark morning suits, John Magnier, Michael Tabor and

Derrick Smith looked like three wise old crows who have collected not just the early worm but a whole lawn-full. This was their third successive Derby victory. The first, third and fourth horses were sired by their star stallion Galileo and the second by his son New Approach. In five years, twelve of the twenty horses who had come home in the first four in the Derby had been owned by Coolmore, all but one of them trained by Aidan O'Brien.

Does their domination matter? Not to me, I wrote at the time. The dream they dream is of winning the Derby. Not the 'Epsom Derby', note. There is no such thing. All the others, the Kentucky Derby for example, need the geographic prefix. They are imitations, quite good ones in some cases, but imitations. The Epsom race is *the* Derby. What is good for British racing is that Coolmore, owning and breeding the best horses, see it that way too and want to bring their potential stars, lots of them, to Epsom for their ultimate test. As Aidan O'Brien put it, 'The whole throughbred breed hinges on the Derby. It's what racing is about for everyone working in stables and on studs.'

Cheltenham

To everything there is a season. Shortly before the swankier Russian yachts slip into their South of France moorings for the summer, the seafront bistros suddenly attract a cluster of young ladies with underworked fingernails and minimal bikinis. When the waterholes dry up, vast herds of wildebeest sniff the African air and trundle off to pastures new. As the leaves begin to turn in Britain, swallows seize on the excuse to fly south from the so-called English summer. My favourite seasonal signal is the first big autumn meeting at Cheltenham, the moment when after lavishing attention through the summer on sleek equine whippets I turn my attention to the more substantial figures of the winter jumping game. From then on everything becomes a prelude to the Cheltenham Festival itself. The cars are muddier, the suits less sleek and breast-pocket handkerchiefs are second-generation. These are days that smell of wet Labrador: the churned turf sucks at your shoes and sometimes you buy a coffee simply to thaw out your fingers to turn the racecard pages, but it is all a part of the glorious build-up to the Festival itself.

One of my best racing moments wasn't on a race-course at all. It was having Jonjo O'Neill at his Jackdaw's Castle yard in the Cotswolds talk me through every yard of Dawn Run's triumph in the 1986 Gold Cup. She wasn't a handsome mare, certainly not a friendly one, but she was grittiness personified, filling her lungs and roaring back to win after being passed by three horses. The word Jonjo kept using about the whole Cheltenham experience was 'magical', and so it is.

I have been a Cheltenham regular since my student days at Oxford (when I could cadge a lift) and if I knew I had just four days left on earth I would probably choose to spend them at the Festival. There is no spectacle quite like the armada of horses thundering downhill towards the last obstacle in the Triumph Hurdle or two well-matched speed steeplechasers and their riders eyeballing each other throughout the final gut-busting climb to the winning post in the Queen Mother Champion Chase, the gladiators enveloped in a wall of sound as the crowd cheer on their fancies.

Somehow at Cheltenham you feel part of the history, a history which includes days like the one in 1990 when farmer-trainer Sirrell Griffiths won the Gold Cup with the 100-1 shot Norton's Coin having milked a herd of cows before setting off for the course. The great steeplechaser Golden Miller was owned by the eccentric Dorothy Paget, who slept by day and lived by night and was allowed by bookmakers to bet on races after they had been run. Golden Miller won five Gold Cups in a row and was second in the next. In 1983 Michael Dickinson performed the extraordinary feat of training the first five home in the Gold Cup.

Vincent O'Brien, perhaps the greatest trainer ever, warmed up his career winning a string of Champion Hurdles and Gold Cups before he turned his attention to the Flat. But before he and amateur jockey Aubrey Brabazon won the first of them they went into the bar for a couple of stiffening port and brandies. Not quite how it is done these days.

Horses who became national favourites like the greys Desert Orchid and One Man earned a special cheer for their successes at Cheltenham and the course has a unique added attraction – the hordes of Irishmen and women who pour into this quiet corner of Gloucestershire to support the band of Irish horses who come to do friendly but desperate battle with the best of England. Ryanair boss Michael O'Leary was asked one year recently what he liked about horseracing and he replied simply, 'I'm Irish.' He went on to add, 'We Irish love girls, drink and racing, although we sometimes get the order wrong' and I have to admit that among my Cheltenham recollections are the three young ladies known as the 'Sisters of Murphy' who arrived by orange helicopter to promote a popular stout in 1998. Lisa B, Nina and Philippa, clad in various combinations of slinky black leather trousers, hot pants and minimal tops were a walking tribute to female fortitude, not to mention the tenacity of the zip industry. With the amount of flesh exposed they clearly risked what my grandmother used to refer to as 'a nasty chill on the umby'. Was Lisa betting on the next race, I asked (a correspondent's life is sometimes awfully hard). 'In my costume,' she replied accurately, 'there's no room for money.'

The Irish add a special zest to the massive gambling which goes on, in the past aided by the punting priest Father Sean Breen. He used to hold special services for the shamrock brigade, seeking the Almighty's blessing on the Irish hopes, adding, 'Though we do appreciate it's difficult for you, Lord, with so many Irish runners.'

Geneva-based financier J.P. McManus has been known to wager more than £500,000 on a race. Indeed, if he were to back every one of his horses that runs for £1,000, that alone would cost a fortune. I asked him at Cheltenham one year how many horses he had in training. He would not say, replying only that 'There are too many slow ones'. He added, however, with his gentle smile, 'But I'd know if any were missing.' Friends say he has more than 200 in training at 40 different yards, costing him at least £4 million a year.

When the fearless bookmaker Freddie Williams was still with us McManus had £100,000 each way with him on Lingo, which won at 13-2. When he asked Williams, who also ran a Scottish water bottling plant, for £500,000 on another race, the layer inquired wryly if McManus knew that it was water, not whisky, he bottled, but still accommodated him to a further £100,000.

The late David Johnson, another big owner, took at least £500,000 off the bookies when his Well Chief won the Arkle Trophy. 'Everyone was on big time,' he said. 'We backed him down from 33-1 to 12-1 and then we ran out of money.'

The turnover is colossal. The on-course Tote alone takes upwards of £2.5 million a day through Cheltenham

and with off-course and on-course bookies and betting exchanges it is reckoned that some £400 million
is gambled over the four days. Some even come just to
watch the more fearless punters, says Edward Gillespie,
Cheltenham's long-time managing director: 'When
people come for the first time they say they've never physically seen so much money change hands. In our daily lives
we don't often see such handfuls of notes. It's the sheer
strength of the market. Put on several thousand pounds
at Cheltenham and a bookie doesn't flinch.'

But the Cheltenham Festival, the annual Olympics of
jump racing, is about far more than the betting. There
is nothing quite like that moment in early March when
the crowd opens its lungs to roar off the start of the first
race. The helicopters of the rich will have clattered in over
Cleeve Hill. Numb fingers will have wrestled with car park
hamper chicken legs and currant cake (surely only the
British could picnic in March). The first few thousand
of the 170,000 pints of Guinness which will be drained
at the four-day Festival will have been sunk and revved-
up younger jockeys, struggling into the tights they wear
beneath their breeches and striding out into the parade
ring with the intensity of fighter pilots on a mission, will
be dreaming the dream that this year they will ride their
first Festival winner.

More than 55,000 people a day will be about to participate in the first true rite of the British spring, confident that this is some of the best fun you can have with
your clothes on. That first race roar encompasses a whole
range of emotions. From racing's professionals – the trainers, jockeys and stable staff – there is excitement that their
highest hopes, fine-tuned to the peak of fitness, are about
to be put to the test. For the spectators, the Cheltenham
roar is a moment of sheer exhilaration at the thought of

the four days of effort, drama, heartbreak, achievement and excess that lie ahead, testing both wallets and livers.

At Cheltenham, the temple of the jumping horse, the spectators don't just crowd around the parade ring to take a look at the equine stars, they pack ten deep around the pre-parade ring too, watching the competitors being saddled, the lads and lasses who know their charges by shorter, more familiar names than their racecard titles giving their burnished coats a final brush down. Other courses have thrilling races too. What makes Cheltenham special, and brings greater risk to the horses and jockeys participating, is that everything happens that much faster. Nor is it any coincidence that Edward Gillespie, for so long Cheltenham's guiding hand, is also a theatre-lover and amateur actor: set against the Cleeve Hill background, Cheltenham is a natural amphitheatre, an effect accentuated by the steep banking around the winner's enclosure and the long walk back through the stands from the finishing straight where the crowd can applaud both the victors and unlucky losers. A day out at the Festival is pure theatre.

The Cheltenham crowd has a camaraderie which comes partly from habit, and partly from an acknowledged passion for the efforts of horse and rider and a willingness to support its judgement with hard cash. Most who watch will have their own precious memory of a favourite contest, a winner heftily backed, a moment of glory etched on the inner eye for ever more. Perhaps the older ones were there for the epic Gold Cup contests in the 1960s between the incomparable Arkle and the brave Mill House, others for the popular grey Desert Orchid's triumph in 1989 or for the third of Best Mate's big race victories in 2004 when he showed that he wasn't just an athlete blessed with a high cruising speed but a doughty battler too.

Extending the Festival in recent years from three days to four has taken away nothing from the intensity of the experience. But if the racing is little changed there are significant differences among the audience either out on the terraces or jammed in busy bars where you can hardly lift your elbow to drown your sorrows over a loser. For some, the rites and sights of Cheltenham are a welcome reassurance that the vision of the English countryside which they fear each year is about to disappear has survived another twelve months. If ever they need a preservation park for the trilby and the Barbour, Cheltenham will provide it. There is no shortage still of tweedy ladies who appear to socialise, shop and probably even sleep in their sheepskins. But these days the crowd is getting younger. There are stretch limos rolling up alongside the four-wheel drives, sharper-suited young men from the City sporting this month's hair gel and the latest iPads cutting deals in the hospitality boxes.

What brings all sorts to Cheltenham is the assurance of quality, the knowledge that they will see the best in competition with each other. 'It *is* the Olympics of racing,' Michael O'Leary told me. 'The best jumps horses from England, Ireland and France. You know that every owner, trainer and jockey is busting a gut to win. That and a very challenging course and the whole carnival atmosphere.' Unlike some grand Flat meetings, he says, Cheltenham is for everybody. 'It's culturally different, there's none of the pomposity of Ascot.' One ex-military owner with a traditional trainer calls the Festival 'the best all ranks event around'.

If you grow up in a family with an interest in racing, Michael O'Leary says, 'There are two races you remember, the Grand National and the Cheltenham Gold Cup. To win either is a dream come true. Why? Because it's so bloody difficult.' His War of Attrition won the Cheltenham Gold Cup in 2006 and he told us then, 'I've died and gone to Heaven.' Even now he says, 'When I look back on life as a doddering old man it is something I will remember, along with my marriage and the birth of my children.'

* * *

One race that remains particularly vivid in my memory is the contest between The Dikler and Pendil in the Gold Cup of 1973. In their time there was no sharper rivalry in the racing village of Lambourn than that between the adjacent yards of Fulke Walwyn and Fred Winter. Walwyn was the established big name in National Hunt training when the former champion jockey, who had ridden for him, set up shop at Uplands next door and there was nothing Winter's lads liked more than to win a race against what they referred to as 'Over the wall' and have the chance to brag over a pint in the Malt Shovel about doing so. After Walwyn had won the 1964 Grand National with Team Spirit the Winter yard got off to a great start with two early Grand Nationals, Jay Trump (1965) and Anglo (1966). The stable was full of stars like Bula, Pendil, Killiney and Crisp, most of whom occupied boxes in the part of the yard that came to be known as 'Millionaire's Row'.

In 1973 there was huge stable confidence behind the spring-heeled Pendil, one of the most naturally talented chasers seen for years. The odds-on favourite for the Gold Cup at 4-6, he simply exuded class and was unbeaten in eleven races over fences. The Dikler, by contrast, was a big, brave but rather unorganised horse who pulled hard and was never an easy ride.

On board The Dikler that day was the tough northern jockey Ron Barry, who was nursing a secret. He had broken a collarbone only ten days before (which had not stopped him winning a big hurdle race at Chepstow the Saturday before the Festival) and he was worried that if The Dikler fought him on the way to the start he might not be able to stop him running away with him because of the pain.

They got to the start without incident but because of his injury Barry could not fight his wilful mount and he said afterwards that he reckoned this allowed the Dikler to 'go to sleep' and relax on the first circuit, though others put that down to his horsemanship.

Pendil, ridden by Richard Pitman, hit the front two out and looked to be about to justify his short price. At the last he was a good three lengths clear of his pursuers. But as the crowd cheered him up the finishing hill in anticipation of emptying the bookies' satchels, Pendil began to falter. Ron Barry, driving his mount with every ounce of his considerable strength, began reeling him in. About 50 yards from the line he got The Dikler's white nose in front and kept it there. Poor Richard Pitman, later a much-admired TV commentator, suffered the worst day of his riding life, only to have another in that year's Grand National when the top weight Crisp too was collared on the line by Red Rum.

Much has been written about Desert Orchid's Gold Cup victory in 1989 and I am not alone in having it as a special memory. When readers of the *Racing Post* were asked to vote on the 100 greatest races years later, this was the one that finished on top. Not, the paper pointed out, because it was won by a hugely popular horse, but because it was a great contest too.

The conditions on 16 March 1989 were foul. It was a day of heavy rain, sleet and snow. Only after a midday inspection was the ground ruled fit to race. Many worried that the spectacular grey Desert Orchid, who never seemed to like the Cheltenham track anyway, would be pulled out. Trainer David Elsworth was made of sterner stuff. He declared him to run, saying, 'The ground is horrible and conditions are all against him, but he is the best horse.' 'Elzee' even increased his bet as Desert Orchid drifted to 3-1.

Team Dessie went for boldness in the race too, rider Simon Sherwood taking him out into the lead, his easy jumping helping to conserve his energy. On the second circuit he was joined by Elsworth's other runner Cavvie's Clown, second the previous year, and Fulke Walwyn's talented Ten Plus, who passed Desert Orchid at the fourteenth of the 22 obstacles. Tragically, three out, Ten Plus fell, fatally injured. Approaching the second last the tough, mud-loving Yahoo came through on the inside to take the lead. But Desert Orchid was ready for battle and set out after him.

By the last they were almost level and somehow Desert Orchid and a jockey who admits he was 'knackered' summoned up what was, in the dire conditions, the equivalent of a burst. Simon Sherwood said afterwards, 'I have never sat on a horse that showed such courage. By hook or by crook he was going to win.' With Desert Orchid drifting left to eyeball Yahoo, the mud-spattered pair's surge took them clear to win by one and a half lengths, eight lengths clear of Charter Party, the previous year's winner. Horse and jockey were applauded every step to the winner's enclosure.

Sherwood had a remarkable understanding with Desert Orchid. He lost only one of the ten races he rode on him, and titled his autobiography *Nine Out of Ten*. Ironically the horse who won when Dessie fell in the tenth of them was Yahoo. As for Desert Orchid, the winner of

Hurst Park when it was still a racecourse: the winning jockey here, on Lord Derby's Peter Pan, beating Lester Piggott, is apprentice Barry Hills, whose biography I was later to write.

Top of the tipsters? 'Prince Monolulu', who I used to watch with fascination as a boy, drums up business outside the racecourse.

Sea The Stars and Michael Kinane triumph in the Derby – just look at the rise and the camber horses have to cope with at Epsom.

Marcus Tregoning's Sir Percy taking the Derby from Dragon Dancer and Dylan Thomas, one of the best finishes ever.

Galileo: a top-class Derby winner
who has been a formidable performer as a sire.

The much patched-up Persian War, a horse who epitomised courage, winning his third Champion Hurdle in 1970.

Henrietta Knight with Best Mate, whose three consecutive Gold Cup victories were a great training feat.

(opposite) The fairytale turrets of Goodwood – 'a garden party with racing tacked on'.

Racegoers arriving at Windsor by boat. The Monday nights there in summer are a relaxed racing experience unlike any other.

Ladies Day at Aintree: they add to the glamour but how much do they see of the horses?

Kempton, 1996: One Man heads for victory in the King George VI Chase.

Ouija Board takes the Nassau at Goodwood from Alexander Goldrun
– one of the great duels.

Giant's Causeway beats Kalanisi in the Coral-Eclipse
– another battle never to be forgotten.

Sir Michael Stoute on the receiving end of a smacker
from Frankie Dettori following their St Leger win in 2008.

four King George VI Chases and a Whitbread and of 27 of his 50 races over fences was the most popular jumper for decades. His exhilarating jumping and front-running gave him equine charisma, and though he retired in 1992 he continued to be cheered to the echo when he appeared in racecourse parades.

One of my favourite spectacles at the Festival is the Queen Mother Champion Chase, when the best two-mile jumpers take each other on over the minimum distance. In the millennium year of 2000 Edredon Bleu and Direct Route gave us one of the most thrilling finishes I have ever seen. Few races for the two-mile crown fail to excite. The speed at which the horses jump the downhill fences is terrifying, magnifying the results of any error. Usually the race is fought out between well-established stars who have clashed with little quarter given or received in races like the Tingle Creek Chase at Sandown. Owners, trainers and jockeys often tell you that this is the race they dream of winning and Tony McCoy wanted this prize above all else. On Edredon Bleu in 2000 he secured it.

Edredon Bleu, in the Aston Villa stripes of Jim Lewis made famous by Best Mate, had run second to Call Equiname in the previous year's race. But the quick conditions this time were ideal for Henrietta Knight's charge, of whom McCoy said, 'I didn't worry coming down the hill at Cheltenham flat out at 38 miles an hour – it never occurred to me that this fella might not take off.' Direct Route, trained by Howard Johnson and ridden by Norman Williamson, had been put under pressure by Edredon Bleu's jumping earlier on but as the two began to shake off Flagship Uberalles at the last, Williamson came upsides. Fifty yards later Direct Route was a head in front. Both riders and horses really went for it, heads down, locked together up the hill in the ultimate nostril-to-nostril duel.

With 70 yards left, the knot in Williamson's reins came undone. But nothing made any difference, says McCoy, whose television replay button gets more use than any in the country. Neither horse ever changed its stride pattern and at the line McCoy and Edredon Bleu had it by a short head.

Deputising for his regular paddock companion Best Mate, Edredon Bleu went on to win the 2003 King George over three miles. But for me that Champion Chase was his finest hour.

It was the Cheltenham Festival too which provided for me the classiest ride I have ever seen. Lester Piggott's short head victory in the Derby on Roberto, Paul Carberry's success on Monbeg Dude in the 2012 Welsh Grand National and Frankie Dettori's efforts on Grandera in the 2002 Irish Champion Stakes all come into the reckoning for such an accolade, but Tony McCoy's extraordinary victory on Wichita Lineman in the William Hill Chase at the 2009 Cheltenham Festival tops my personal list.

McCoy and Wichita Lineman were made for each other. AP likes tough, genuine horses who are prepared to give their all for a rider and he described Wichita Lineman as being like one of those boxers who would never go down however hard you hit him. He wasn't very big, he wasn't particularly fast, he wasn't the perfect build for jumping fences, but he was a trier.

At the 2009 Cheltenham Festival trainer Jonjo O'Neill didn't aim J.P. McManus's novice chaser at one of the youngsters' races; instead he chose to take on older, more experienced horses with him in the William Hill Handicap Chase, reckoning that he was well enough handicapped to win it. AP wasn't quite so convinced, fearing that the small Wichita Lineman might find Cheltenham a bit intimidating in his first handicap with 23 others lined up against him.

He kicked off in a nice position, on the inside about halfway down the field, but even passing the stands for the first time the horse wasn't finding it easy and his jockey had to nudge him along. While some of his more experienced rivals seemed to be gliding effortlessly over the obstacles Wichita Lineman was obviously finding jumping the fences a real effort. At the second last fence on the first circuit, Lacdoudal jumped slightly across Wichita Lineman, almost pushing him into the side of the fence, and McCoy's mount pecked on landing. The mistake affected the horse's confidence and he jumped the next fence slowly and deliberately.

Setting out on the second circuit the pair were only in fifteenth place and Wichita Lineman made another mistake at the last fence before turning down the hill. At that point Tony McCoy, hoping to set off after the leaders, gave him a couple of smacks with the whip. With three to jump, Wichita Lineman was some fifteen lengths off the pace with at least ten horses in front of him. From the stands his prospects looked somewhere between hopeless and bleak. But McCoy saw things differently. When he pulled out to get Wichita Lineman running he felt the horse pick up and reckoned they might still be in with a chance.

There was another mistake at the third last. That would have had most jockeys abandoning the struggle and waiting for another day, but not McCoy. When he pulled Wichita Lineman to the outside his mount picked up again – and then came the boldest move of all. Anxious to save a little in the tank for the gut-busting climb up the final hill, McCoy at that point let his mount drift in again behind horses. That was probably crucial.

They jumped the second last well and coming round the home turn were in sixth place with one to jump. As soon as they straightened up McCoy took his mount to the outside again so Wichita Lineman would have a good view of the last fence. Daryl Jacob had kicked clear on Maljimar and for a moment McCoy wondered if he was too far gone for them to reach him. As he later described:

> I wasn't sure we could catch him but I concentrated on getting him running up the hill, about clawing back the five or six lengths the other horse had on us. It looked like a tough ask but I knew Wichita Lineman would give everything he had. We didn't start gaining on Maljimar until about 100 yards from the winning post but when we did, we closed quickly.

First AP had to pass Choc Thornton on Nenuphar Collonges to take second place. Once they had managed that, seemingly taking an age, Wichita Lineman could see his target and could see too that he could catch the leader. McCoy asked for everything and drove with all his strength. Nobody could sum it up better than he did: 'Stride, stride, stride, one, two, three. Gotcha! There's the winning post. Yes!' Only at that moment, he says, did he become aware of the din from the Cheltenham crowd cheering home the favourite.

Even McCoy, rather more given to ruthless self-criticism than to the faintest of toots on his own trumpet, declared, 'It was probably one of the better rides that I have given any horse. In fact I'd say in my own little head I thought it was probably the best ride I have ever given a horse.' From the ecstatic reception for horse and rider, there were few there that day who didn't agree and the professionals took the same view. At the ensuing Lester

awards for outstanding performances in the saddle Tony
McCoy collected the prize for the jumps ride of the year.
Tragically Wichita Lineman wasn't around to join the
celebrations. A month after Cheltenham, at the very first
fence in the Irish Grand National he clipped the top and
fell. Just as the horse was getting up another horse tried
to jump over him and broke his back. McCoy walked away
in tears.

* * *

When in recent years I wrote my book on the Cheltenham
Festival, my research led me to happy historical discov-
eries like the group of horsemen who used to patronise
the King's Arms in Prestbury, close to the course, in the
1850s and 1860s. George Stevens, Black Tom Olliver and
Thomas Pickernell had between them ridden eleven
Grand National winners, their fellow drinker William
Holman trained three of them and landlord William
Archer rode another. Pickernell used to ride under the
name of Mr Thomas because his family were clerics
and didn't approve; in later years he was known to take
a stiff drink before competing at Aintree, to the extent
that he once inquired of a fellow jockey which way the
horses should be facing. Later I came across characters
like George Duller, the specialist hurdles rider known as
'The Croucher', who was virtually impossible to dislodge
from a horse. He flew his own plane and later became a
racing driver.

I had not realised until I began my researches that the
Champion Hurdle was not run until 1927. The Gold Cup
was first run three years before that but until the Second
World War it was seen by many owners and trainers more
as a prep race for the Grand National than a contest worth
winning in its own right.

One of my early racing heroes – although of course I never saw him – was Golden Miller, five times winner of the Gold Cup and once of the Grand National, despite the fact that he had a marked aversion to the Aintree obstacles. It is at least arguable that Golden Miller's fourth Gold Cup victory, against Thomond in 1935, was one of the greatest races ever seen. Billy Speck, who rode Thomond, died after breaking his back in a Cheltenham seller at the next meeting: it is a measure of the popularity racing enjoyed in those days that his funeral procession in the town was two miles long. His saddle, whip and colours were buried with him.

My favourite Cheltenham period was the golden age of hurdling from 1968 to 1981. Through those four-teen years the Champion Hurdler's crown was won in some enthralling contests by just seven outstanding horses: Persian War, Bula, Comedy of Errors, Lanzarote, Night Nurse, Monksfield and Sea Pigeon. Of those only Lanzarote failed to win the title more than once.

The Cheltenham crowds loved the battered, coura-geous Persian War for his honesty and courage. Time after time he was patched up from injury to come back and triumph at a course he made his own.

Having won in 1968 and 1969, Persian War had not won a race since the previous Easter when he ran in the 1970 Champion Hurdle. He still managed to beat off Major Rose and win again: afterwards the horse had an operation on a 'soft palate' condition, which revealed that he had a broken wolf tooth that must have been causing him severe pain for months.

In 1971 he beat his old rival Major Rose once again, but the then unbeaten Bula came with a wet sail under Paul Kelleway at the last and left Persian War four lengths behind. It was Bula's thirteenth consecutive victory, and

Fred Winter's star scored again in the next Champion Hurdle by eight lengths, despite a three month lay-off with a leg injury.

In 1973 it was the turn of Comedy of Errors, trained by Fred Rimell. Peter Easterby's Easby Abbey made the running and still led at the last, where he was joined by the held-up Captain Christy. But the Rimells' stable jockey Bill Smith had Comedy of Errors really motoring at that point and he swept past them like a motor launch overtaking dinghies. In 1974 though, Comedy of Errors was beaten by Winter's Lanzarote.

In 1975 Comedy of Errors cruised up to Lanzarote when he wanted, swung wide for better ground round the bend and stormed up the stands-side rail to win convincingly. It was the first time a deposed Champion Hurdler had taken back his crown, but he was only to hold it for a year.

In 1976 it was Peter Easterby's Night Nurse, only a five-year-old, who made all the running under Paddy Broderick to win the Champion Hurdle. Night Nurse was a brave horse who made the running not because he was a tearaway but because he was comfortable out in front, a natural jumper. He skimmed his hurdles and got away fast from the obstacles.

The next year, on very heavy ground, Night Nurse faced not only his regular and consistent rival Bird's Nest but two more outstanding hurdlers who were to become adored by the Festival crowd: Sea Pigeon and Monksfield. Despite the appalling conditions, Ron Barry opted to make the pace as usual on Night Nurse, hoping that way to find the best ground. At the hurdle at the bottom of the hill, Monksfield hit it hard; Night Nurse jumped cleanly and was off up the rise to the winning post to record an authoritative win by two lengths. Dramatist was third and

Sea Pigeon fourth. Monksfield rallied but could not get to the leader.

The tough little 'Monkey', trained in Ireland by Des McDonagh, had already performed in 52 races over four years by the time he came to the 1978 Champion Hurdle. That season Monksfield, who had a taste for Granny Smith apples and kept other stable inmates awake with his snoring, was two months off the course in the autumn with a leg infection. Maybe the unaccustomed rest helped bring him to a peak.

This time Night Nurse was in trouble, not skating over his hurdles with the usual facility. On Monksfield, Tommy Kinane, aware of the need to draw the finish from speedsters like Sea Pigeon, committed for home early. Approaching the last, Frank Berry, who was deputising on Sea Pigeon for the injured Jonjo O'Neill, brought his mount up to challenge. It was too soon, and Monksfield, who always responded when the gauntlet was thrown down, drew away again up the hill to win by two lengths.

The same two dominated the finish the next year. This time Jonjo O'Neill was back on Sea Pigeon and Dessie Hughes was riding Monksfield. But Jonjo too got it wrong. He attacked Monksfield on the final bend and jumped the last in the lead, confident that he was going to win. Both took the last obstacle perfectly, but halfway up the run-in Sea Pigeon began to 'empty' on the sticky going. Monksfield clawed his way back. Sea Pigeon's stride shortened and, in clinging mud, Monksfield, his head lowered almost to his knees as he thrust forward, passed him 50 yards out to win by three-quarters of a length. 'It's a pity pigeons can't swim,' observed Easterby.

If racegoers thrill to the front-runners who set sail for home and defy the others to catch them, they thrill even more to the 'hold-up' horse who swoops like a predator with a well-timed burst of speed at the death, and in 1980 Sea Pigeon, who had once finished seventh in the Derby, produced just that kind of finish.

Sea Pigeon had had an interrupted preparation after an injury and was only 90 per cent fit. At the top of the hill, his jockey related afterwards, he was wheezing and gasping. So Jonjo switched him off, gave him time to get his second wind, and jumped the last this time a length down on Monksfield. They landed level and Sea Pigeon produced such a surge of power that they were clear half-way up the run-in, sooner than the jockey had intended. They went on to win by seven lengths to the roars of an ecstatic crowd.

The Cheltenham crowd loved the classy, quirky Sea Pigeon and they loved Jonjo, whose cherubic grin and twinkling eyes were accompanied by a steely determination in the saddle. Sadly, when Sea Pigeon came back to defend his crown in 1981 it was without his usual part-ner. Jonjo's leg had been shattered in 36 places in a fall at Bangor and his efforts to get back in time to ride Sea Pigeon exacerbated the injury, requiring a further opera-tion. This time it was John Francome who provided a silk-smooth ride, delivering Sea Pigeon halfway up the run-in to pip Pollardstown and Daring Run. 'Pure class,' said Francome, who also declared that he had never ridden a jumper with such acceleration.

Sea Pigeon and Night Nurse, who won 70 races between them, are buried side by side at the Easterby yard of Habton Grange with a plaque that reads 'Legends in their Lifetime'. As they were.

The same can be said of two trainers with an incred-ible record at Cheltenham: Nicky Henderson and the now retired Martin Pipe. Writing my Cheltenham book gave me the chance to enjoy extended talks with both of them about some of their Festival winners.

Martin Pipe

Martin Pipe first came to notice on the Festival scene with Baron Blakeney, the winner of the Triumph Hurdle at 66-1 in 1981. In fact it was his first winner at the course, let alone the Festival. With typical self-deprecation he says:

> We really fancied it. If it had been trained by a proper trainer like Fred Winter it would have been about 14-1. It had won its last couple of races and had reasonable form. Baron Blakeney was about sixth or seventh on ratings but because it was trained by an idiot, an unknown, it was such a big price. We told everybody to back it. All the owners' kids had £10 each way on it and all won nearly £1,000.
>
> Paul Leach rode it, beating a horse of David Nicholson's ridden by Peter Scudamore. We always had a picture of Baron Blakeney beating Broadsword in the hall and so when he came to work here Scu had to walk past it every day as soon as he came in the house. He didn't appreciate it.

Martin Pipe had to wait another eight years for his next Festival winner, Sondrio in the Supreme Novices Hurdle. Sondrio had been sent for stud duties in the USA but was then gelded and came to Martin to be trained.

> He had won nearly $450,000 in America but he hadn't raced for some considerable time and he was a gross horse, he was very fat when we ran him at Hereford. I remember apologising to the owner. Of course he won, didn't he, and was aimed at the

Festival. Two weeks before that he ran at Ascot. He was a certainty. He couldn't possibly get beat. Scu rode him, and he *was* beaten. He never jumped a hurdle and did get beat. Scu didn't want to ride him at Cheltenham, he'd been offered another ride in the race and so Jonathan Lower, who was our second jockey at the time, came in and we schooled him every day, two or three times a day trying to get him to jump. He was a big strong horse; he probably didn't respect the hurdles and could go straight through them, but you can't do that in championship races. So Jonathan was schooling him morning noon and night and he rode him.

Scu rode this other horse and fell early on and he was lying on the ground listening to the commentary. Jonathan made all and as he was going past the post and it was announced that Sondrio was the winner Scu was beating his whip on the ground in frustration. The ambulanceman ran across and said 'You're obviously in great pain'. And he was saying 'Go away, go away, leave me alone'.

When he took out his first training licence in 1977 Martin Pipe was not an overnight sensation. He had never worked in anybody else's yard and he learned his business by trial and error, starting with the cheapest of horses at the lowliest tracks. For ten years he averaged no more than a dozen winners a year. But the results by the end of his 29-year career were phenomenal. He trained the winners of 4,182 races, 3,926 of those over jumps. He was champion National Hunt trainer fifteen times and appointment as his stable jockey virtually guaranteed the chosen rider a jockey's championship too. He took Peter Scudamore, Richard Dunwoody and, many times, Tony McCoy to the title. He rewrote the record books: the fastest 100 winners in a season, the fastest 200 winners, the most prize money won, the most winners trained in a lifetime (achieved after just 25 years). His record total of 243 winners in the 1999/2000 season will probably never be beaten and he won the Grand National with Minniehoma.

Although he never trained a Gold Cup winner, Martin Pipe twice trained the winner of the Champion Hurdle; Nicky Henderson is the only man living who has trained more Cheltenham Festival winners than Martin Pipe's 34. Pipe revolutionised the training of jumpers.

With his interval training up steep slopes and a ruthless eye for the opportunities offered by race conditions, Pipe sent his horses to contest the right races hard and leathery fit. Peter Scudamore would make the running on them as often as not and leave fields strung out behind him.

Punters owe Pipe a vote of gratitude because since his day most horses from other yards too have been sent to the races ready to run. French bloodstock agents too should bless him – Pipe was one of the first to spot the possibilities of importing early-maturing and early-schooled young horses from France who could exploit the significant pull four- and five-year-old novice chasers enjoyed in the weights. He was the first to have his own laboratory on site to analyse blood samples rapidly and monitor the health of his horses. Until he began, no trainer had been quite so meticulously organised or so ruthlessly efficient in his planning.

Self-taught he may be, but the lessons were still painful:

> We used to buy only cheap horses, the cheapest we could buy. The first horse we bought was £300. I got it home from Ascot sales and didn't realise until

then it only had three legs. It had a bowed tendon. That was how much I knew. From that came all my involvement in veterinary matters, I loved it so much. We had to get the vets to treat the tendon and give the horse a year off. Once you start paying through your pocket it makes you learn so much quicker. The horse was called Bobo's Boy and we got it to win a point-to-point about eighteen months later. It was a very valuable lesson.

I wanted to win sellers. I managed to win with cheap horses. I thought that if I could win sellers, since there's one every day, I could get 50 winners a year, wouldn't that be fun? I wanted to start at the bottom. The first time I had 50 winners they were all hurdlers. I couldn't afford to buy a chaser.

Working in his father's bookmaking business wasn't such a bad preparation for training, says Martin. It taught him method and a respect for figures and for information. He learned to handle paperwork and organise systems. That is why son David now has a sheet with all the horses on, listing all the work they do. Says Martin:

All our jockeys have to give written reports on their rides. We have a written report every day on every horse in the stables. The head lad does one, all the assistants do. So David can look and see this one has a cut on his knee, its been treated with ointment, it's OK or he can't run for four days ...

It's just having all the facts that are available. Facts and figures, that's what life's all about. You must have your finger on the pulse and know everything. All their temperatures are taken every day. By 7.30 every morning David knows the temperature of the horse, whether he's eaten up, everything, and he says 'Ah that one will have to have an easy day' or whatever.

Martin's father's experience also explained his 'no excuses' approach.

> He had horses in training with other people and he used to have, say, £100 on when they said the horse was fancied. The horse would get beat and the trainer would say, 'Ah, I thought he'd get beat, he didn't eat up last night.' There would be all these excuses after the race: 'They didn't go fast enough for him' … Why didn't we make the pace then? You can only do that if you jump well. So you've got to teach your horse to jump well. When I first started training my horse would jump one hurdle: 'That's it. He's good. He's jumped it well, take him to the races.' But of course racing's different and they didn't jump so you had to do it properly. You have to school them loads of times.

He was worried at first that too much work would crock his horses and they would be unable to race.

> But that's a risk you've got to take. You've got to have practice at what you're doing. Jumping is all about jumping. If you don't jump you don't win. That's why Make A Stand was a Champion Hurdler. I remember seeing it loads and loads of times: Group horses coming out to run over hurdles and they couldn't jump and got beaten.

His first Champion Hurdle winner was Granville Again in 1993:

> He was very laid back. He had a lot of problems and Michael Dickinson came across and helped me with them. I am very friendly still with Michael.

He gave me advice on what to do with him and how
to train him and that has helped me train many more
winners.

It is appropriate that the two should be friends. Both are
totally imbued with the work ethic and with a voracious
thirst for knowledge. If he isn't watching the horseracing
monitor screens Martin Pipe will have his head in some
obscure veterinary volume.

The second Champion Hurdle winner was Make A
Stand, whom he plucked from Henry Candy in a seller
at Leicester.

We sent out a letter to all our owners offering a half
share for £4,000 and my wife told me off saying no
one else would buy the other half. Lo and behold we
couldn't sell it and we retained the half share. I am
very glad we did because over the next year the horse
won £250,000.

Make A Stand was a real athlete. It took him a
while to get going, he wasn't a natural early on, but
once he had the hang of it he could really jump. AP
got on very well with him but loads of jockeys won on
him. Jockeys who got on him just had to understand
the pace, to allow him to dictate and just conserve
his energy. He was really exuberant, he really enjoyed
it. He really enjoyed his racing. In the Champion
Hurdle we were really anxious but it was great that
he went on and kept going up the hill.

Suffering a number of health problems, Martin Pipe
handed over to his son David in 2005, but an ankle operation has very much improved his mobility. He is still very
much in evidence at Pond House and full of relish at what
they do.

He loves to see the youngsters being taught their job:

> There's nothing better than watching youngsters, three-year-olds, going round in a loose school. They're only playing, enjoying themselves, but you see them jumping, you see them having to think for themselves: 'There's a jump coming up here, I've got to shorten or to lengthen', and they learn. Conditional jockeys would see them in the loose school and think 'I want to ride this one, this one is super, he just goes there and pings it – all you've got to do is to point him at the jump and he'll jump it, so the horse is full of confidence.'

And if he likes to see horses being taught to think for themselves, the same goes for jockeys at Pond House. It is, says Martin Pipe, a much more professional era:

> Everything is much more professional now in every field, in every walk of life. With television, with videos, with everything, we can now see all the replays and see what went wrong. AP didn't like it at first when we had all the slow-motion replays, although he does it all the time … You have to learn by your mistakes. We have tutors now and mechanical horses. We've always had one of those. We don't allow our jockeys or the lads to carry whips on the gallops so they can go and practise on the mechanical horses and learn how to use their whips there and be instructed how to use it correctly, how to change their whip hands.

How appropriate it is that Cheltenham named a race on the Festival programme after Martin and chose the conditional jockeys race as the one.

Nicky Henderson

It can only be a matter of time before they name a Cheltenham Festival race after Nicky Henderson. Nobody has ever succeeded there more often. Of course, some comebacks take longer than others. George Foreman, the Punching Preacher, won the world heavyweight boxing title for the first time in 1973, lost it to Muhammad Ali (then Cassius Clay) in 1974 and did not regain it until 1994 at the age of 45. When Nicky Henderson became champion jumps trainer in the 2012/13 season it was not for the first time. But it had been a while. The previous seasons in which he had been champion were 1985/86 and 1986/87. Throughout the intervening period the championship had largely been divided between Martin Pipe (fifteen times the winner) and Paul Nicholls (seven times).

Nicky Henderson's Cheltenham Festival record is quite incredible. It took David Nicholson, 'The Duke', eighteen years to train his first Cheltenham winner. Noel Meade bent, Pope-style, to kiss the turf when he had his first Festival success after 21 years of trying. Nicky Henderson has proved himself a master of fine-tuning with no fewer than 50 Festival winners, taking the Champion Hurdle five times and the Gold Cup twice, most recently with Bobs Worth, a £20,000 purchase.

Nicky has been kind enough to give me time when I have been engaged in a number of writing projects and I have never forgotten my first visit to his Seven Barrows stables in January 1999. At 7.30am the neat black and white yard with its big chestnut tree in the middle was a hive of activity with the clatter of buckets, the swish of brushes and the wisecracking of stable staff tacking up the horses under the watchful eye of head lad Corky Browne, a weathered figure in a khaki coat. He had started his feeding routine two hours before.

In the office, secretary Rowie Rhys-Jones sat imperturbably fielding endless phone calls. The walls were stacked with form books and Timeform annuals going back years. A set of sit-on jockey's scales stood in the corner festooned with sticky labels recording stable staff weights. Next to it was a hoover, which clearly didn't get much exercise, and in a corner basket lolled a Dalmatian and a rough-coated terrier.

A marker-board recorded the handicap ratings of the 100-plus horses at Seven Barrows, with red for chase form, black for hurdles and green for the Flat. There were pictures around the walls of previous stable stars like See You Then, Remittance Man, Classified and Zongalero. Nicky himself was constantly on the phone. He was appalled that day to discover that Martin Pipe had ten entries in the Stakis Casinos Handicap Hurdle at Warwick, all with jockeys declared, to qualify them for a Cheltenham final.

Soon we charged across the yard (no other word would do) to the covered ride where Henderson buzzed around calling out questions to stable lads and lasses, assessing the progress of horses due to run soon. Blessed with eternally youthful looks, he is a man of natural authority, confident in his status and radiating intensity. Photographer Ed Byrne, who was there on a separate assignment, commented wryly, 'He probably takes some of the nuts himself.' There was the creaking of boots and saddles, the chewing of bits as some horses trotted on their toes while others loped around with a more relaxed 'seen it all before' air.

Words were not needed to see where the life force of the whole operation came from. Just occasionally you get the chance to glimpse such a phenomenon – Graeme Hick rattling the boundary boards with a flick of the wrist, Michael Schumacher getting the line right through a tricky bend, Tina Turner strutting exultantly across the stage to lift the crowd with a twitch of the hips. With Nicky Henderson in the centre of the indoor school at Seven Barrows you had that same sense of a person in their element, doing what they were ordained by nature to do and doing it con brio.

Accompanied by black Labrador Wanda we moved on at an Olympic walker's pace to the schooling grounds behind the stable. There Mick Fitzgerald and fellow jockey John Kavanagh were involved in some serious education, constantly slipping off one horse and mounting another to put it through its paces. Two of their charges had had an indoor session with jumps coach Yogi Breisner three days before. The stable's conditional jockeys, said Nicky, loved those sessions because they learned as much as the horses.

With Wanda scurrying about eagerly retrieving leg bandages, Nicky dashed from fence to fence calling out comments and seeking the riders' opinions as they were legged up on other horses. The hard work jockeys put in on these occasions is the forgotten side of the job and you can injure yourself just as easily on the schooling grounds as on the racecourse. That day Stormyfairweather, a Cheltenham winner to come, nearly deposited Mick on the damp grass. When he first joined the yard on finishing his claim at Jackie Retter's, some owners would insist on having Richard Dunwoody or Jamie Osborne on their horses. 'Now some don't want to run their horses unless they have Mick. He's really good at talking to owners too.' Indeed. Introducing a hurdling demonstration at Lambourn's Open Day, trainer Richard Phillips explained a delay by commenting, 'They would have been here five minutes ago – but Mick Fitz had just begun a sentence.'

On my visit Nicky said that he was basically an old-fashioned trainer, making full use of his 400 acres of grass gallops including a stiff mile and a half. 'But we do use the all-weather too. Philip's Woody [a fine old stable servant then at eleven] doesn't set foot on grass from one year's end to the next but he comes out and wins his four every year.'

What did he remember from his days as assistant to Fred Winter? Mostly, he said, the regimentation and the routine. It was the end of the 'old school' era. Winter's and Fulke Walwyn's horses would be out on their appointed days. 'Fred would always say "For God's sake don't go swopping things about". Nothing was ever really changed at Uplands.' Since then there had been enormous change, particularly in the use of interval training. 'In the old days, on Saturday mornings for example there would be a huge rush to get your team first up on Mandown. Now you hardly see a horse up there. They're all going up and down a precipice somewhere.'

The competitive element hadn't changed though. For a long while Winter battled Walwyn to be Lambourn's top dog. When Henderson became the new challenger for space on the honours board, 'Fred took us to Stratford on the last day, fighting for every pound'.

Nicky does not buy much of his talent ready made. Although he has some ex-Flat horses, he still likes to buy jumping-bred three- and four-year-olds and educate them steadily into mature performers. But although he likes to see his horses get a break, especially the older ones, he did wonder aloud about the logic of giving jumpers a couple of months off at grass:

We must all be crackers. Nobody says to an Olympic athlete, 'OK, you've won your race. Now go off for eight weeks, go to the pub every night and be sure you smoke plenty of cigarettes.' We do 90 per cent of the damage when we're getting them back to fitness after the summer break.

A full works breakfast with the fresh-faced assistant trainers Harry Dunlop and Iona Craig was still not relaxation time for the trainer as he made phone calls, scanned the paper and fired out questions. Then it was back to the office to speak to Rowie, who was asked to ring a couple of trainers and find out if they were running their charges in a particular race. By now it was sheeting down on the indoor ride with a gale blowing. The third lot of mostly younger horses were spared the misery of battling with the elements that day on the gallops; instead they were to trot seven times around the indoor ride, giving them about a mile.

Other days at Seven Barrows (named after the Saxon burial mounds) I have been aboard the 4 x 4 as Nicky has roared and slithered up muddy tracks to the top of the all-weather gallop, steering with one hand while the other clasps his mobile to his ear. It is a not a mode of travel recommended for those of a nervous disposition.

Having begun at Windsor House in Lambourn village in 1978, Nicky swopped premises in 1993 with Peter Walwyn. He was expanding despite the recession and by January 2000 had notched up his first thousand winners over jumps. The 2,000 mark was passed in January 2011. He told me at the time, 'It's nice to get it out of the way. But I've a friend down the road, B.W. Hills, and he's on 3,000. You can think again if you think I'm going after him.' It seems unlikely that Nicky will seek to emulate

Martin Pipe, who stacked up 3,930 jumps winners before retiring at 60. That is partially because the focus at Seven Barrows has been more on quality than quantity and especially on those Cheltenham winners.

Nicky's Cheltenham experiences started in his days as assistant to Fred Winter at a time when he was also a leading amateur rider. His first Festival ride was on a horse owned by his mother and trained by Winter, which was, he says, 'a sure ticket to the hospital. I think we'd managed to negotiate five fences before the ambulance picked me up.' The year Winter won the Gold Cup with Midnight Court Nicky rode Humdoleila to win the last race on the card for Barry Hills: 'Barry said "Don't have one behind you at the top of the hill" and I thought I had better obey instructions. It won. We had a very good night.'

Does he treat Cheltenham candidates differently in the yard?

You try to say to yourself 'Don't do anything different'. Workwise you don't. But you just try and put that little extra on them. I don't say that you give them a little bit extra because if you really thought that was going to work you'd do it to every horse every day. It's silly to say we do anything special and yet we do. You probably start a month before. They just get a little bit of extra help. I think it's probably just to keep the trainer feeling he's doing something to make a difference rather than the fact that he knows it's going to do any bloody good. Nowadays the build-up is more and more and Cheltenham have got the art of promoting to an absolute T. On the Flat you've got several bites at the cherry. You've got the Guineas meeting, you've got the Derby meeting, you've got Royal Ascot, Chester, York, Goodwood, the July meeting, Doncaster, the Newmarket Champions

meeting ... if you miss Royal Ascot you've got
Goodwood, if you miss Goodwood you've got York
... you've got several cracks. We finish up with the
whole year hingeing around a section of four days ...
they've pushed this four-day event into a completely
different stratosphere at which the Irish input is
phenomenal.

A bad Cheltenham is a horrible feeling. It's an
empty year, however good the rest of the year has
been. With the younger horses we don't over-race
them. In January we consciously back off them,
especially those we know are going to Cheltenham;
once we've got the Christmas festivals out of the
way you've a pretty good idea of the 'A' team. The
handicappers kind of fill themselves in a little bit but
you know where your novices are, you know where
your championship horses are. So they suddenly
become in Cheltenham prep from there. You're
backing off them consciously, starting again knowing what your prep race is going to be and it is geared
to that.

The night before that discussion he had been making
plans with J.P. McManus about his champion hurdler
Binocular and when he was to come back in after a summer break:

When I said 'Where do you want to start?' he said
'There is only one objective. How you get there is
entirely your own business, but just get there.' That
has to be the attitude with a horse like him. We're
in the nice situation that there might be a couple of
others like him as well so they've got to fiddle around
each other. But horses like that, you know exactly
what you'll be doing before the season starts. It all
comes down to one date.

Then you've got to make sure that one or two horses get into the handicaps you want to get them into. So you've got to start planning on those. Am I high enough to get into the Jewson? Will I get into the Coral? I've got to get a third run into that one to get into the Fred Winter … you are planning away all the time. You've got a horse you want to run in the Coral that you realise might be two or three pounds too low to get in so you've got to try and push it up. The novices handicaps, you've got to get three runs into them to be able to run.

Is there a problem with owners pressuring him to go to Cheltenham with a horse that isn't up to it, or too soon?

There is, because I don't think there's anyone who goes out to buy a horse who doesn't start asking, mentally at least, 'Have we got a Cheltenham horse here?' I'll be saying, 'We haven't broken it yet, but I hope so.' Every time you buy a horse you start with a dream. The owner who doesn't think of his horse as a potential Cheltenham Festival horse is rare indeed.

The only time one tries to assert one's influence is when there is a young horse who is not ready, he's a year away from Cheltenham. Then I will try and persuade them to wait a year. They know as well as I do the pitfalls that befall racehorses. They know as well as I do that the chances of it's being 100 per cent in a year's time are pretty hard. The story on that score was River Ceiriog.

He was owned by Bobby McAlpine and had come to me from Barry Hills. He was still a maiden coming into Cheltenham and though we did think he was good I hadn't won a race with him and his jumping hadn't exactly been natural. Bobby McAlpine was chairman of Aintree. I'd stayed with him for Aintree and my plan was to run River Ceiriog on the Friday after Cheltenham in a maiden at Wolverhampton in order to lead him into the novice hurdle at Aintree. I spent the whole of Sunday morning trying to persuade Bobby that it would be more sensible to go to Wolverhampton, win the maiden and then go on to Aintree. Bobby being Bobby, he won the argument and we pitched up at Cheltenham.

I was just getting the saddle off Steve Smith-Eccles for the first race when in comes Peter O'Sullevan asking 'Nicky, how do I pronounce this horse's name?'

I said, 'Don't worry Peter, you won't have to mention it' – and River Ceiriog came in one of the easiest winners of the Supreme Novices Hurdle we've seen in many years; I think it was twelve lengths he won by. Sometimes you have to bow to owners' wishes and there you are. It was a wonderful day and it wouldn't have happened if he hadn't persuaded me to do it.

The race I'm not so keen on with young horses is the Champion Bumper. You've got to be very certain that you've got a very good horse for that bumper. That is a race I'm nervous of. I've messed up a couple of good horses in that over the years ... In the average novice hurdle there's always a pack of horses you can go round with that anybody can keep up with. At Cheltenham if you're not in that first half-dozen coming down the hill you are flat to the boards, off the bridle, invariably tired and everything's happening too quickly. You can do a lot of damage to a horse that isn't ready for it and I think that's what happens in that bumper. If you're in that half-dozen and you're travelling, it's great. But once you start coming down that hill off the bridle and struggling then it is very easy to damage young horses mentally and physically.

One of the enjoyable things about spending time with Nicky Henderson is to hear him talk about those Festival winners, something he does with affection and with humour.

The horse who won Nicky three of his five Champion Hurdles was See You Then, who had legs like glass and could be raced so rarely that the racing press nicknamed him 'See you When?'. He was typical of Nicky's attention to detail. Steve Smith-Eccles, who rode him to all three victories, believes that See You Then's second success in 1968, a year when much racing was frosted off, was achieved only because his trainer drove a tractor at intervals through the night to keep the all-weather strip at his stables useable when many trainers were unable to work their horses. He said of Henderson's feat: 'Winning two Champion Hurdles with such a horse would have been an outstanding training achievement. To win three was a horse-racing miracle.'

What I learned talking to his trainer was that See You Then was not only a permanent potential invalid but a savage too.

We put a 'Yorkshire boot' on him one day because we thought he was knocking a leg. It took us four days to get it off him. He was a wonderful horse outside but inside the box he was a brute. He would eat people. Glyn Foster looked after him all his life and got bitten and kicked to ribbons over the years. [Head lad] Corky Browne and I couldn't go in the box without him. Nor could vet Frank Mahon …

We ran See You Then just once in the last year before Cheltenham. He went to Haydock and it was obviously going to be a tense night waiting to see what was going to happen to his legs. I woke up in the early hours and thought, 'I'm going to go into that box and take those bandages off and see what they are like', knowing full well that I couldn't really go into the box without Glyn – and it was a Sunday morning; he probably wasn't going to be coming in until about 8.00. I got up and went downstairs and went to his box and, oh my God, the door was open … there was Frank Mahon sat on the manger. I said, 'What are you doing?' and he replied, 'I couldn't sleep. I thought I'd come and take those bandages off and see how he was.' 'So why are you up there?' He said, 'He won't let me out!'

Then there was the two-mile chaser Remittance Man:

He was a terrible worrier, he used to go round and round his box, so we put a sheep in with him. The first sheep was nicknamed 'Alan Lamb' and then we had 'Ridley Lamb' and 'Nobby Lamb' – the sheep came from Dad's flock. When Nobby went home for the summer and joined his mates, another sheep was sent. Remittance Man flung it out, literally. He picked it up and chucked it out of the door. We put it back in. There was a lot of fur flying and then out it came again. I thought, 'We can't do this to the poor sheep', so I had to go back to Dad's flock and look for the right one, not easy with 400 of them. Amazingly we sent in a horse and 399 of the sheep went one way and one came out, and that was Nobby. From then on we used to put a blue blob on his backside – the sheep – when he went home for his summer holidays!

There are many and varied secrets to a trainer's success.

───Races and courses───

There is something about life on the racetrack that
encourages people to let themselves go and to have a
good time. Sometimes though a little caution is required.
'Chaps don't make passes at girls who wear glasses' goes
the old refrain. But at Kempton Park in October 1999 I
discovered that that doesn't necessarily stop the girls in
glasses. As I was queuing for a drink, a lady in a smart suit
with a hefty pearl bracelet and red bag turned from the
bar and declared, 'I could drown in those beautiful eyes.
You must let me tell your fortune.'

As I looked behind me to see if Cary Grant or Paul
Newman had joined the queue, she said, 'No, I mean
you.' A Turf columnist at that moment short of copy, it
seemed to me, could do no less than accept her offer, with
the proviso that the fortune-telling included her selection
for the next race.

Pausing only to exploit the gap at the bar with
envious dropped jaws to either side still watching her
self-confident exit, I seized a fortifying whisky and
joined my new friend, to discover she was slightly less
discriminatory than I had imagined. Another fifty-
something, heavier than me and in a leather jacket,
had been selected for the fortune-telling treatment too.
She obviously always backed each way. Feeling my jacket
lapels, Violet, as I shall call her after her chosen colour
of eyeshade (and there was a lot of it), declared, 'I have
you down for a successful businessman. Well, reason-
ably successful anyway, though perhaps a bit of a fly-by-
night.' I would have to look again, I decided at that point,
at my second-best racing suit. Until that moment I had
always seen it as a tasteful compromise between the hairy
tweed set and the sort of thing you wear when you are

not quite sure how formal an out-of-London occasion might be.

As the analysis continued it became apparent that Violet had no idea what was even running in the next race and that she was less inclined to predict the long term than to attempt to influence my immediate future. As she claimed that she had connections with the on-course medical team Leather Jacket muttered ungallantly into my ear, 'I think she's into mouth-to-mouth resuscitation too.' So, explaining that I was a happily married man of 33 years and pleading the need to get my bet on for the Cesarewitch, I left them to it. As I did so I heard Violet telling Leather Jacket, 'Well now, *you* look to me like a boy who likes a bit of fun ...'

Normally, to Mrs Oakley's relief, my racecourse focus is on the horses and the races, and over the years I have developed my favourites. Epsom and Aintree I have already discussed but here are some of the other tracks associated with my most vivid racing memories.

Kempton Park on Boxing Day – King George Day

Kempton Park for me is not the most atmospheric of tracks, although it has sometimes been a profitable one. You can't go far wrong, for example, backing Nicky Henderson's horses there between December and March. But one day at Kempton is very special: the Boxing Day card including the King George VI Chase, which is always won by a classy horse. Some potential Gold Cup candidates don't always show their best over Cheltenham's undulations and extra two furlongs but excel at the sharper, flatter Thameside track.

My film director son Alex and I go to the King George together every year that his filming schedule and our wives' diaries permit, but arriving there amid the boisterous crowds on the day after Christmas brings mixed memories. Scenes of Kauto Star's five victories and Desert Orchid's four float back along with the heroics of Silver Buck and Wayward Lad in the Michael Dickinson heyday. Unfortunately there is also engraved on my memory the year the infield churned to mud and even leaving before the last race, along with dozens of others I got stuck in the car park. I turned up three hours late for my brother-in-law's Christmas dinner (he thought I had done so deliberately) and was banned by the family from Boxing Day racing for two years.

In 1996, when One Man won the King George for the second time they were trying to keep the party spirit going with an Irish band, a pantomime horse, a man on stilts and a hung-over fairy of uncertain years who had gone rather heavier on the lipstick and mascara than is customary for Tinkerbell. As she muttered and gesticulated about the lack of Christmas spirit around her she was in danger of being done by the stewards for a whip offence with her wand. One does have sympathy though for someone forced to pirouette in the biting cold in tights and several yards of net curtain. Perhaps she should have stationed herself by the champagne bar entrance. Put a match to the fumes wafting out of there and you could have incinerated the nation's entire stock of Christmas puddings.

It had long been a maxim of mine never to ignore a horse which French maestro Francois Doumen sent over at Christmas time. He had won four King Georges. But this time it was Djeddah in the Feltham Novices Chase who did the business at 9-2 (11-2 for us early birds).

It was of course the King George VI Chase that we had all come to watch. Any owner/trainer combination prepared to take on Gordon Richards' selected in any of that season's big chases, especially anyone prepared to take on the redoubtable One Man at Kempton on good ground or better, deserved a salute.

When the British boxing champion Don Cockell was due to fight Rocky Marciano, negotiations were proceeding about the size of the ring and the great Jack Dempsey's advice was sought. 'If I were Cockell,' he said, 'I'd go for a five-acre field, heavily wooded.' The right terrain counts for a lot and it was hard to see what was going to beat One Man over Kempton's flat right-handed three miles.

The talented but inexperienced Strong Promise was never going well. The handsome Mr Mulligan led them at a good pace but was cooked when he fell at the last and Rough Quest was totally unsuited to the conditions. I didn't know whether to praise the United Racecourses chairman Andrew Wates for the sense of duty he felt towards the Christmas crowd in running his Grand National winner or to castigate him for risking a horse we all loved on the frosty Kempton turf. I suspect he felt the same. But the important thing was that Rough Quest came home safe and sound and did so within twelve lengths of the winner with everything favouring One Man.

I wrote at the time:

> One Man is a fine horse, a spectacular jumper and a real crowd-puller. The way he moved up to Mr Mulligan when he chose had the stamp of real class but many better judges than me believe he does not get a yard over three miles, certainly not 3m 2f around the Cheltenham gradients. Nor is the course lucky for him: he has been beaten there 30 lengths in a hurdle, he was injured in the Sun Alliance and he flopped in last year's Gold Cup. I suspect he will not

run in the Gold Cup, so don't take any of that 10-1 the bookies are offering.

For once I was prescient: One Man was again beaten out of sight at Cheltenham in 1997. But the next year Gordon Richards took the bold step of aiming his 'little bouncing ball', as he called him, at the two-mile Queen Mother Champion Chase, in which he scotched his Cheltenham hoodoo with a famous victory.

Glorious Goodwood

What memory of England do expatriates call to mind when they dream of home? Tower of London Beefeaters? Thatched cottages with roses round the door? My vision if transported for a tour of duty alongside the grey, green, greasy Limpopo or in the Kalahari would be of sunny days at Glorious Goodwood with a light breeze blowing above the world's loveliest racing backdrop.

They have been racing over this patch of the Sussex Downs since 1802. King Edward VII, who popularised there both the panama and the linen suit, called it 'a garden party with racing tacked on'. For me it is Ascot without the excess.

Goodwood's stands with their floating canopies don't look like a concrete imposition on the countryside, more an *Arabian Nights* children's book fantasy, dream castles which could be wafted away to a never-never land where the Pimms flows forever and punters back nothing but winners …

Certainly it is quality sport. You won't see horses running faster than they do in the Goodwood Stewards' Cup when the sprinters breast a rise and thunder down towards the grandstands. Famous middle-distance horses like Ouija Board and Giants Causeway have burnished their reputations here and racegoers don't forget battling stayers like Double Trigger and Persian Punch who have slugged it out over the undulations for two miles and more in the Goodwood Cup.

Other courses have beautiful surroundings, so what makes Goodwood 'Glorious'? Former managing director Rod Fabricius told me one year, 'One of the joys of Goodwood is the active participation of the family of the Dukes of Richmond', amid whose estate the course lies. All the sports practised on the estate, he said, from cricket to motorsport, had followed the passion of one or another family member. They move with the times, but draw the line at tribute bands: 'Goodwood is first and foremost a racecourse. We are trying to be contemporary but not to lose sight of the heritage.'

Amid the stately home business, the golf courses, the hotel, the farm shop, the Goodwood Festival of Speed involving two wings and four wheels, the racecourse, occupying just 500 of the estate's 12,500 acres, has to contribute a profit. The racecourse chairman, the Earl of March, said, 'We've been racing here for 200 years and there's nothing else to support it except the estate, so it's got to work.'

The innovative management of Fabricius and clerk of the course Seamus Buckley, Goodwood stalwarts for as long as most can remember, has been crucial. Racecourse commentaries for the crowd were first introduced here. Goodwood ran the first-ever 'enterprise meeting' without Levy Board backing, setting the tone for racecourses being able to open up for business on the days they wanted.

Crucial to racing quality has been their turf husbandry. One year I walked the course with Rod and Seamus at 6.00am, their sticks prodding the dew-damp turf to test the going. At 700 feet in drying winds, maintaining the course in trim to keep quality horses coming for five days is an art. Fields of horses weighing up to half a ton means plenty of depredation. Thirty tons of topsoil will be brought in to repair the racing surface after Glorious Goodwood. Intriguingly, during the winter season deer graze happily on the track surface. Then as soon as the ground staff put the fertiliser down on the course in March, the animals move off to the woods.

Walking the track it looks so much wider than on TV. You also see how steeply some of the ground rises, how sharply the camber falls away down at Oaktree Corner where a horse running too wide would be in danger of losing its back legs.

Many horses are trained these days not on turf but on 'all weather' synthetic tracks and are unused to galloping on the firm. Seamus makes sure therefore that there is always some juice in the ground. But that has made a significant difference. The horses of 1802 wouldn't recognise the racing surface. 'Once you water, you lose the downland turf. The profile changes. There is no going back.'

Those old horses would still recognise though the stables built on a grand scale in 1793 by the 3rd Duke. At other racecourses the runners are stabled on site; at Goodwood they are bussed over in horseboxes from a palatial knapped-flintstone yard one and a half miles away. En route they pass the equally palatial kennels where central heating was laid on for the prized hounds many decades before it was available to the grandees living in Goodwood House.

Looking after the animals is as traditionally British as it gets. And over an equally traditional afternoon tea the Earl of March put his finger on Goodwood's appeal:

'It's the epitome of England in summer. It's not trying to be pretentious. It's about meeting friends and quality racing. It's glamour coming to the country – very English.'

Goodwood always produces quality racing as well as quality races. It isn't just the good prize money, though that helps, but also the buzz of expectancy which the course somehow creates and the need for intelligent as well as strong riding. The year 2003 was typical. I noted that it wasn't the pretty girls in pastels who put the gloss on Goodwood that season, nor even the steel bands which the *Observer* was crustily demanding be silenced. It certainly hadn't been the weather. What made it was the character of two wonderful horses who didn't just have ability but also the will not to be beaten – the veteran Persian Punch and the flying filly Russian Rhythm.

'Keep a diary, honey, and one day it will keep you,' advised Mae West (perhaps forgetting that only good girls keep a diary – bad girls don't have the time). If ever there was a horse whose diary I would have wanted to read, Persian Punch was the one. Jockeys who rode him say that the then ten-year-old knew more about racing than they did. After he had become the oldest winner of the 191-year-old Goodwood Cup, Martin Dwyer declared, 'I think he's taking the mickey out of me. He knows where the winning post is and towards the end when I was tiring he went "Right, come on, let's go and win".' With Persian Punch jockeys knew they had been in a scrap. He took a lot of stoking up. When Dwyer became Persian Punch's regular rider, jockeys who had ridden him before advised him to take an oxygen tank out with him.

That day it was as if Persian Punch deliberately allowed Jardine's Lookout, another brave battler, to get close to him: he then produced one final heave to let him know who was boss. You could see he positively enjoyed milking the crowd's emotion afterwards.

In the winner's enclosure, delighted owner Jeff Smith said, 'He's a war horse. You could see someone in armour on him charging the enemy.' With the massive Persian Punch you could mount a gun turret between his ears and another atop his quarters and send him into the desert heading a column. He was that comparative rarity, a character Flat horse who stayed around long enough to earn the same affection as the longer-competing stars of jump racing. With Persian Punch there was always a sense of drama too. So often he won by fighting back, as if galvanised by other horses having the effrontery to pass him, and his victories were scored not by a sudden burst of speed but by eyeballing his opponents in a dour struggle for mastery through the last couple of furlongs.

In the Addleshaw Goddard Stakes at Sandown that year the four-years-younger Cover Up passed Persian Punch but foolishly did so too soon. The old boy rattled back to catch him just before the line and win by a short head. Persian Punch won the Lonsdale Stakes at York in 1998 by the same margin from another grand stayer, Celeric. And it was only by a head that he beat his Goodwood rival Jardines Lookout in the 2001 version of the York race. In the 1998 Henry II Stakes at Sandown he was passed in an epic struggle by Samraan but once more came again to win by a head.

As a gelding, Persian Punch, who sadly died in a race at Ascot, provoking probably the biggest public display of emotion ever seen on a racecourse, never had a future anyway in breeding. But Russian Rhythm, winner that Goodwood week of the Nassau Stakes, made sure that she would be a highly sought-after mare, not just because she was a fine big, handsome filly with an athletic walk and a high cruising speed in her races. It was the attitude she showed in races like the Nassau victory that made her such a prospect. She showed herself to be brave as well as beautiful.

In the Nassau, Kieren Fallon tried to keep the Michael Stoute-trained filly, running over two furlongs further than she had tackled before, on the better ground close to the rail. As the two in front of him slowed and two attackers moved past on his outside he lost crucial momentum. But that was where class told. Other jockeys might have panicked: Fallon moved out and crucially waited for his filly to collect herself before launching his drive after the long-gone Richard Hughes on Ana Marie.

Russian Rhythm, on ground she did not enjoy, stuck her head down and went for it, responding to every urging from her jockey and prevailing in the end by a neck. Said Fallon, 'She has a big heart and is very game.' It was a gameness rewarded by victory in five of her six races to that point, including three Group Ones.

It was the same in 2010 when Barry Hills trained his 50th winner on the course and Henry Cecil was running previous winner Midday in the Nassau Stakes.

Midday, both saucy madam and serious racehorse, could as easily have lined up with the naughty-eyed, hip-swinging chorus girls performing in the members' enclosure as on the track. In the race she cruised into the lead a furlong out and then slowed. As a rival stormed past she slipped into gear again under Tom Queally, regained the lead and won going away as the ambulance men looked around nervously to see where the resuscitators were needed. That second burst of acceleration, which only the best can produce, was Midday's way of saying 'Look, I can do it any way I like'.

In beating Stacelita and Antara, the filly twice came

off a true line but she survived the first-ever televised stewards' inquiry that followed and kept the race. So she should have done. She was clearly the best in the race and her showboating didn't deny others their chance. It was fortunate that the race was under English rules. As former Tote chairman Peter Jones noted watching beside me, 'In France she would probably have lost it.' Just as well that English interpretations prevailed. Her trainer insisted, 'They went very slow and she had to sprint, and then she thought she had done enough.'

I sometimes meet non-racegoers who insist that the very act of racing horses represents cruelty. But horses are competitive animals and you could have no clearer demonstration of that than Midday's reaction when, having almost pulled herself up, she eyeballed Stacelita coming alongside her. 'She has so much raw ability that she rallied again,' said her jockey. It was the same that day with Barry Hills' Critical Moment. When challenged for the lead early in the straight he reacted, and when Desert Myth came at him in the dying stages he found even more for jockey Michael Hills.

If that wasn't enough to celebrate, we had two more winners from jockey Richard Hughes, taking him to a record nine at the meeting, beating the record previously shared by Lester Piggott, Kieren Fallon and Johnny Murtagh. Approachable and articulate, Richard is just the sort of personality racing needs. Race-riding is all about confidence and that day confidence was oozing out of every pore in his body. Yes he was well-placed in having the pick of rides from his father-in-law Richard Hannon in an annus mirabilis for an always successful yard, but on his then current form he could drive home a winner with a donkey draped across his shoulders.

Richard Hughes is famous for coming from behind in

last-gasp finishes. Before the Glorious meeting the *Racing Post* had interviewed him on how to ride the course – stayers' contests, mile races and sprints – and it proved to be a masterclass from a real thinker in the saddle. Every young jockey, I suggested, should tear out the page, have it laminated and pack it with their saddle for next year's Goodwood meetings.

Break too fast from an outside draw trying to get to the rail, says Richard, and you can use up too much horse too early in the race. In any Goodwood contest over 1m 4f or more, the best place to be is in the first four, so you can get breathers into your horse. Don't come wide in the Goodwood straight, you will cover too much ground. As for those heart-stopping swoops from behind:

> If you are coming from off the pace you are actually better off coming from right out the back. People complain about me and Jamie Spencer sitting last but if you sit last you can see everything that's going on. You can go left, right or straight on. If you are two lengths closer you will almost certainly be snookered.

That day he did it every way, including an all-the-way win on the juvenile Libranno. And the course celebrations after that record ninth victory? There weren't any. He was off to Lingfield to ride in the 6.25. This is a jockey with the work ethic too.

Another man who is invariably worth listening to on racing matters is Middleham trainer Mark Johnston, whose Goodwood raiders have a remarkable strike rate. Asked after his fourth success at Glorious Goodwood in 2006 how he seemingly tutored his horses in tenacity (two had scored on their second run at the meeting) and how they always seemed to battle, he replied:

It's simple physics. The effort required for half a ton of horse to accelerate is huge. It often looks as though a horse is coming to catch ours, but ours is staying on again. What is really happening is that when a horse accelerates it is bound to slow down again. If the post doesn't come soon enough it looks as though our horse is going away again when it is only maintaining a level speed. The way to win a race is to cover the distance in the fastest time. The best way to do that is to run at an even pace.

His stable motto of 'always trying' could not be more apt.

The historic course always seems to provide lively betting markets too but one of my favourite Goodwood stories is of a gamble which came unstuck. I think it was Clive Brittain who told me of the day when Sir Noel Murless and one of his owners had a horse they believed was a certainty for a Goodwood handicap. It was early days, before Murless became one of the leading trainers, and they put an apprentice on the horse to help them obtain a good price. Both owner and trainer invested enough to win themselves a new car. It was a hold-up horse and the only instructions to the young rider were 'Stay in fourth place until you pass a little red hut about a furlong and a half out. Then you can go on and win as you like. But don't do anything before you see the red hut.' Nobody ignored instructions from Noel Murless, but unfortunately for all concerned, since they were last on the course the hut had been painted green. The apprentice did as he was told, kept looking for the red hut, and passed the winning post in fourth with a double handful.

One of the greatest races I ever saw in my life was at Goodwood: the contest for the Nassau Stakes in 2006 between Ouija Board and Alexander Goldrun. Ouija

Board, so brilliantly handled by Ed Dunlop as she stacked up her air miles around the world's leading tracks, wrung every last drop of emotion from a faithful crowd as she took on Jim Bolger's well-travelled mare who also boasted a string of Group Ones on her CV.

Both mares looked glorious in the paddock, coats gleaming, ears pricked, intelligent eyes reflecting the experience of 35 world-class races between them. In the race Frankie Dettori was back on Ouija Board after she had suffered a nightmare run under Christophe Soumillon in the Eclipse. Unusually, Frankie had her in the van from the start because he was determined not to be beaten in a sprint finish by specialist milers. He told us afterwards, 'She was the class horse in the race. I know she stays twelve furlongs and we took it to them. I am just glad that it worked out and I didn't mess up.'

Lord Derby's mare though was not the only class horse in the race. Frankie opened up a gap when he committed fully three furlongs from home. But at that point Alexander Goldrun, ridden by Kevin Manning, pulled out from last place and flew after the leader, her white blaze prominent as she ate up the ground. Two furlongs out, the hope of Ireland was in front and looking likely to stay there. But with Dettori and Manning throwing everything into it, both mares stuck their heads down and battled furiously to the line. Both had pace, neither lacked courage. The classic duel had the crowd on tiptoe and strong men spent of emotion afterwards.

Ouija Board, applauded past the stands on her way to the start, was given three cheers when she came back. But so was Alexander Goldrun. As Jim Bolger said with that contemplative, quiet smile of his, 'I've never heard such applause for a runner-up.' Racing folk will be wearing out their replay buttons on this one for years to come.

Monday nights at Windsor

If ever I feel my zest for racing flagging, a day at Windsor soon sorts things out, especially on Monday evenings in the summer. Londoners can catch the train down to Windsor and Eton Riverside, amble along the towpath with the castle looming above and board a French Brothers boat down the Thames to the course. On race nights there is a service every fifteen minutes. A drink from the onboard bar, swans and geese floating alongside and the *Racing Post* on your lap make for the perfect contemplative journey. True, the landing stage says 'Deep Water' as you arrive, but bet wisely on Richard Hannon's horses and you can stay out of that. 'If you become a millionaire tonight,' said the captain last time I was on board, 'then remember who brought you' – but no one has handed him enough to retire on yet.

Inside the track, jockeys thread their way from weighing room to parade ring between families picnicking on lush green grass. Jazz bands stroll between the champagne and Pimms bars and, rarity of rarities on most racecourses, you can even find somewhere to sit down, a true mercy for those of us with occasionally dodgy backs. Most of the girls dress up, although without an Ascot fascinator in sight, and most of the men don't bother with a tie.

The fast food outlets are the freshest you will find and they even show some style. One time I was there in a football-focussed week in 2010 the wine bar was advertising its Gavi di Gavi as having 'a finish better than Balotelli's'. The lively Windsor management, treading a fine line between enticing newcomers and not upsetting the traditionalists, are great believers in theme nights. You might find yourself there on a South African night or a cider night or a sausage night. 'Ladies Nights are so popular we'd have one every night if we could,' sales director Matthew Foxton-Duffy told me.

That night in 2010 was a good one for Italy with jockey Andrea Atzeni knocking off a double on Mezzotint for his compatriot Marco Botti and Vasily for fellow Newmarket trainer Robert Eddery. Mezzotint was owned by former QPR Football Club chairman Gianni Paladini, who positively bounced around the winners' enclosure, declaring emotionally, 'Last week we got bumped and beaten a neck. This is one of the best feelings in my life. I just can't describe it. Everyone needs something like this in life.'

He bought Mezzotint after his, shall we call it, 'colourful' time at QPR – enlivened by stories of a gun levelled at his head by thugs who wanted the former players' agent to quit – and at Windsor he showed what racehorse ownership can do for you instead by insisting, 'I'm so excited. I got promoted to the highest level with QPR but this feels better.' You could see his point. At least Mezzotint wouldn't be demanding impossible wages, getting in punch-ups on the pitch or spending his downtime in nightclubs with brain-dead blondes.

Some owners seem to avoid Windsor: you rarely see any of Hamdan Al Maktoum's horses running round its curious saucepan-shaped track. But others have told me they love it. Said one chief executive, 'It's close to the City, it's easy to get to and it's always a party atmosphere. It's a place where deals get done.' Trainer Richard Phillips put his finger on Windsor's secret: 'Show me one other course where the jockeys are so relaxed they come out and sit on the weighing room steps.' In fact, relaxed Windsor is a good place for spotting emerging jockey talent: it will often be the lesser meeting of the day with racing staged also on a more fashionable track. Top jockeys will have travelled elsewhere and that provides opportunities for young riders on the way up or stable number twos.

The day of Mr Paladini's success was typical. Those who scored included the then little-known Atzeni, Pat Dobbs, George Baker and the since prematurely retired Ian Mongan, whose admirers included Sir Henry Cecil.

Of course the top jockeys don't always stay away. Dean McKeown told me once of a time when as an apprentice he rode a horse called Miss Merlin, a 33-1 shot, at Windsor. The stable had its money on and there was every confidence. He was drawn in the number one slot and admits he drifted slightly across the course but he won easily: 'I never saw another horse,' he said.

Unfortunately for him the rider of the second horse was one Lester Piggott. McKeown and his trainer were amazed to hear that Lester had objected to their horse and it turned out he had done so on the bizarre grounds that the apprentice-ridden horse, by drifting left, had 'frightened my horse out of racing'. McKeown was called in by the stewards and told that his horse had been disqualified and the race awarded to Piggott.

As the two riders went back into the weighing room, the racing idol turned to the apprentice and said, 'You learned something today son. Bullshit beats brains.'

Windsor seems to be something of a gambler's course. Following the money there often pays, but following Richard Hannon's horses does so even more. Some punters call the Thameside track 'Hannonland'. 'We always try to bring a nice two-year-old here,' said assistant trainer Richard Hannon junior. 'Our horses seem to run well here. At the yearling sales a lot of owners want something they can run at Windsor on a Monday night.'

On the evening in 2010 described earlier, the only person grumbling was Barry Dennis, Britain's best-known bookmaker. 'Ten years ago,' he told me, 'I would take £60,000 in bets on a Monday night. In recent years it's been down to £20,000. Tonight I've hardly taken £10,000.' But then it was the night before the Budget. We all had to keep something in our pockets.

It was perhaps a wonder that I ever became so fond of Windsor. Once in my time as a political correspondent I was invited by the MP Spencer Le Marchant, a generous-hearted and utterly convivial man who was then a Conservative whip, to join him and a couple of others playing hookey from the House of Commons to go and watch his horse run at Windsor. He hired a limo – a Rolls, I seem to remember – in which we went down to the course drinking unfortunately warm champagne from plastic cups. He was so convinced that his horse would win that he promised to buy us all dinner afterwards on the proceeds at the famous Michelin-starred Waterside Inn at Bray. Unfortunately the horse ran a stinker, Spencer rowed publicly with the blameless jockey Willie Carson and instead of the fabulous dinner promised, the evening finished with us eating takeaway pizza from a car boot in the car park of a Holiday Inn. It was an early lesson about politicians' promises.

Ascot and the King George VI and Queen Elizabeth Stakes

I love Ascot. True, the modern stands can make you feel at times that you have wandered into an airport concourse by mistake. True, it is irritating through Royal Ascot week to find the place cluttered with people who are there to be seen rather than to watch the racing. Even back in 1912 *The Times* recorded, 'Ascot is notoriously the best place in England to see beautiful women in elegant clothes and also less beautiful women in very odd clothes.' Back in those times, apparently a famous actress's garish outfit in the parade ring startled a two-year-old, who reared up. The actress in turn leapt in panic and gashed a general with her parasol, after which she declared, 'It's scandalous that they allow horses in here.'

What you always get at Ascot though is top-class horses competing for proper prize money, and in recent years we have been blessed with a management team determined to turn Ascot into a true centre of international racing, attracting top-class runners from France, Germany, Australia, Hong Kong and even the conservative and rarely adventurous stables in the USA. Such is the competitiveness of Royal Ascot that the only certainty of the week is that the Queen's will be first of the four carriages across the line in the procession.

Champions Day with its Qatari sponsors is emerging as a proper finale to the season, but my favourite Ascot raceday remains the King George VI and Queen Elizabeth Stakes, instituted in 1951 and since then the crucial test over the Derby distance for three-year-olds and their elders to take each other on. What many see as the greatest race of all time, the epic contest between Grundy and Bustino, took place at Ascot in the 'King George' and there have been several renewals since which have left true racing aficionados emptying the hyperbole bottle and reaching for the smelling salts. I always get to the parade ring early for the King George to get a good look at the contestants.

In 1999 for example there was Daylami. I don't much like swagger in the human race but I adore it in horses. Watching the parade for the 1999 King George VI and Queen Elizabeth Stakes you could not have had a better display. Eight intelligent heads topped eight perfectly prepared bodies. The gleaming flanks of the Hong Kong bay

Indigenous might have been freshly lacquered. Oath may have been smaller than some but he carried himself with a bearing as if to say 'Don't mess with me folks, I won the Derby'. Fruits of Love and Silver Patriarch arched their necks with fluid athleticism, obviously confident of their right to be in the all-star line-up as they in turn studied the packed crowds under the Ascot limes.

But it was to be Daylami's day and with my money already committed to Fruits of Love I felt the first prickings of doubt as I watched the Godolphin grey saunter round with the self-regard of a world heavyweight boxing champion. A silk dressing gown across the shoulders would have been entirely appropriate for his burly frame. In the race Daylami just murdered them. Staying power and the readiness to battle are important qualities in a racehorse but there is nothing so exhilarating as sheer speed. As they entered the last quarter-mile Daylami, who takes about a furlong to wind up to top gear, simply shot away from his rivals. Frankie Dettori told us afterwards:

> Coming into the straight I gave him a crack and the turn of foot was so instantaneous that it gave me goose pimples. When I went by Gary Stevens [on Nedawi] he shouted 'Go get 'em Frankie' and the voice was getting fainter and fainter. I was able to spend the last hundred yards watching on the big screen how far I was in front.

So cocky was the horse himself that he gave an exuberant buck and kick on the way to the winners' enclosure. Well, why not: by then he had proved it all. The five-year-old had won nine of his eighteen races in four countries over distances from a mile to a mile and a half, earning well over £1 million. Owner Sheikh Mohammed and trainer

Saeed bin Suroor had ignored the doubters who urged them to keep the horse to the ten furlongs of the Eclipse. No, they said, he already had that T-shirt; they would confirm him as an all-round champion by moving up another two furlongs. Fortune had duly favoured the brave.

The King George in 2000 was special in a different way: it was the one chance for British racegoers to see the great Montjeu racing on our turf. As ever it was a joy for us gawpers and baskers in reflected glory to watch the principals before the race – not the gangling adolescents we often see on the racecourse but hard-tuned professionals accustomed to success. There was the Aga Khan's Coronation Cup winner Daliapour gazing intently at the crowds. The Japanese hope Air Shakur looked magnificent, his dark bay coat glistening like a guardsman's boots and pink bandages on his legs. Almost last in was Henry Cecil's Shiva – hard to say in her case whether she or the trainer was best turned-out, although Shiva wasn't shod by Gucci.

At last in came Michael Tabor's Montjeu, a brilliant horse who knew he was brilliant and didn't always see why he should do things that ordinary horses do. He had been reluctant to enter the paddock but his regular work rider slipped into the saddle for a few strides and coaxed him along. 'With a horse this good we don't hassle him,' said French-based trainer John Hammond. 'We just work round his little foibles.' And there he was, the winner of nine races, tall and imperious.

As Michael Kinane was swung up into the saddle Montjeu tossed his head in acknowledgment as if to say 'We both know what we're here for, now let's get on with it'. The race itself was more like a procession. The Aga Khan's pair blazed the trail into the straight and the crowd began to cheer as the 3-1 on favourite ranged alongside. But they never had to shout to encourage the burst of acceleration that was Montjeu's trademark. He simply cruised past the leaders on the bridle. Mick Kinane barely had to move. We could scarcely believe it: he was winning one of the top events in the racing calendar as if it were an exercise canter. It was like Linford Christie motoring past a gaggle of puffing parents on school sports day. Until Frankel came along I never saw a top race won so easily. Kinane said he had never been at more than three-quarters speed: 'The horse was enjoying himself; we haven't got to the bottom of him yet.' It was awesome – and some.

The sadness was in the sequel when Sheikh Mohammed challenged Michael Tabor to run Montjeu against his own pride and joy Dubai Millenium over a mile and a quarter for a $6 million sidestake. It brought echoes of the great sporting challenges of the past, but no sooner had the media begun to salivate than poor Dubai Millenium broke his leg on the Newmarket gallops and his racing days were over. What a race that would have been.

A King George that truly was a horserace was the contest between Galileo and Fantastic Light in 2001. In the parade ring beforehand, the tough St Leger winner Millenary and the French Derby winner Anabaa Blue had loped around contentedly, oozing equine status. John Dunlop's other runner Golden Snake, his wins in Germany and Italy having been followed by an unsuccessful bid for the Japan Cup, probably thought he'd had a rather shorter trip than usual to the races but still eyed up the crowd as cockily as a likely lad with a lager in his hand.

Fantastic Light, the crooked white blaze on his face curving up above his eye, tossed his head with the arrogance of a horse with ten victories behind him on three continents. Among the last to enter was Galileo, his head held low amid his four-handed security escort. But he surely knew he had won two Derbies already in Britain and in Ireland.

The race itself was everything we had dared to dream. The pacemakers set a hectic tempo. Two furlongs out, the crowd roared as Galileo cruised to the front, the bushy-eyebrowed Mick Kinane crouched low in his dark jacket. At this point in his Derbies Galileo had simply surged clear. This time Fantastic Light too came clear of the pack and set out after the younger horse under Frankie Dettori's driving. He came up to him and even perhaps headed Galileo for a stride or two. For the first time Coolmore's darling was in a real race, forced to show character as well as class. But Kinane gave Galileo a couple of cracks, he dug deep in response to the challenge and went away from Fantastic Light, who was anchored by a 12lb weight concession, to win by a couple of lengths.

From that point on we saw the sportsmanship of two great teams united in the pursuit of thoroughbred perfection. Joint owner Michael Tabor said of Galileo, whom he shared with Sue Magnier, 'It's a pedigree to die for. He has the conformation and now he's proved himself on the track. This horse has everything.' Said Fantastic Light's owner Sheikh Mohammed, 'I respect the courage of the other team in coming here. They were the ones with something to lose, but they were not afraid to find out just how good he is, and the winner is racing.'

The 2002 King George was another fine struggle and it was memorable not just for the all-out efforts of the two horses who were separated only by a head at the finish, Golan and Nayef, but for the showcase of riding and training skills it provided. Golan, ridden by Kieren Fallon, was last away and had to be scrubbed along by his rider to stay in the race early on, which was no part of the plan. Fallon kept his cool and crept slowly through the field, hugging the inside rail. As Golan's trainer Michael Stoute had told him, 'You don't win races by coming round the outside'. Meanwhile the long-striding Nayef, trained by Marcus Tregoning and ridden by Richard Hills, was making the best of his way home. In the final furlong Kieren pounced and drove past the leader, only for Nayef to fight back gamely and start closing the gap again. Richard Hills had kept just a little in the tank for such an eventuality. It took all Fallon's considerable strength to keep his mount's head in front at the line but he did so to win in the colours of Lord Weinstock, who had died that Tuesday. As the jockey commented on dismounting, 'The horse really stuck his neck out, which he has never done before. Maybe he had help from somewhere.'

Both horses had given their all under two intelligent rides, but the real achievement was that of Golan's trainer. The previous year he had sent out Golan to win the 2,000 Guineas without a prep race. He was not the first or the last to do that for a race so early in the year when none of his rivals was likely to have had more than a single run. But here again the King George was Golan's seasonal debut, the horse having suffered a setback before the Eclipse. To have a horse cherry-ripe in those circumstances to win one of Europe's premier middle-distance races in high summer against others who have been honed to race-hardness through the season really was a supreme test of skill.

Foreplay, I noted after Doyen's victory in 2004, can be even more fun than the real thing. For contests like the King George VI and Queen Elizabeth Stakes, where older horses take on the current Classic generation, the parade-ring preliminaries are an essential part of the public's enjoyment. These top horses – hard-toned athletes with a few miles on the clock – know why they are there. They are mostly mature individuals who know how to cope with the pre-race adrenalin surge. The globe-trotting Sulamani, calm and impassive, cast an intelligent eye on the crowd. Phoenix Reach, his forelegs bandaged, gleamed with health, the sun glinting off the brushwork on his quarters. Hard Buck from America looked lean and muscular. The old warrior Warrsan stopped inquiringly for a moment before leaving the parade ring: a tug on the reins persuaded him 'Yes, there is serious business ahead'. The French filly Vallee Enchantee picked up her feet fastidiously as if you could not trust those perfidious English not to have left something nasty on the path. But one horse stood out in the preliminaries. As his rider Frankie Dettori later said, Doyen swaggered into the ring looking as if he owned the place. The big Sadler's Wells colt was up on his toes, his neck proudly arched, ready to eyeball anybody who wanted to look at him. It was pure assertion. 'At home,' said Frankie, 'he just slobs around. But here he has so much presence.'

Through working abroad I had missed Doyen's course-record victory at Ascot in the Hardwicke Stakes, and being mindful that no horse without a Group One victory to his name had won a King George I had come prepared to back the battle-hardened Warrsan or Kenny McPeek's American raider Hard Buck against the favourite. (McPeek not only has a degree in business studies; on top of that he had learned Portuguese so that he could go and buy good value horses like Hard Buck in Brazil. Not many in Newmarket or Middleham, I suspect, have contemplated that kind of homework).

But having seen Doyen lording it over his rivals in the parade ring I was an instant convert: I went straight off to back him instead. Handsome is as handsome does and fortunately for me Doyen ran up to his looks. He cruised into the straight behind the leaders, was asked to pick up a furlong and a half out and smoothly went three lengths clear of Hard Buck, who held on well for second. That detail was precious to me: I don't have too many exactas paying 62-1.

I was that day at a sponsored function and our hostess had put me on public trial as a tipster against the list of selections provided by her daily cleaner, apparently a near-infallible source of endless winners. The daily and I each produced two winners that day, but the each-way odds on the 33-1 Hard Buck, I argued, put me ahead in terms of profit. 'Typical journalist,' was my wife's retort. The daily, she pointed out, clearly had alternative career prospects as a tipster: she would not recommend me as a cleaner to anybody.

* * *

I cannot leave the subject of Ascot without reflecting too on the jockey who made the course his own with a formidable feat

Frankie Dettori not only puts the *joie* into *joie de vivre* on the racecourse, he helps us take a little out of the bookmakers' satchels. I won't forget one tortured soul, I think it was Gary Wiltshire, halfway through Dettori's feat of riding all seven winners at Ascot in September 1996 shouting 'Nine to four's Dettori's horse and nine to four me for the Labour Exchange'.

Maddeningly, my duties as a political correspondent meant that I had to leave Ascot that day before the feat was completed. It was a bit like being dragged out of Headingley with Ian Botham on 60 racing towards a century or being hauled out of your seat at Le Caprice before the entrée had arrived. The applauding thousands who were able to stay on and witness the final flying dismount from Fujiyama Crest had an 'I was there' story to tell for the rest of their lives. Even now, I suspect, the sheer quality of Frankie's legendary achievement that day has not been fully digested. Alec Russell's remarkable record of riding six winners in a day had stood since 1957. But his six were rattled up on a standard day's racing at Bogside. Bog standard? Dettori's seven were accumulated at the Ascot Festival of Racing across as competitive a card as we had seen all season. The cumulative odds were 25,091-1, even after the frantic hedging on his later mounts had brought their prices down to totally unrealistic levels. Anybody who had linked the seven at morning ante-post prices would have enjoyed a return of 235,834-1.

Wall Street, his first winner, was 2-1 favourite but no easy ride. Many had questioned whether Wall Street was really bred to last a mile and a half, so to lead all the way and beat a horse as good as Salmon Ladder in the final challenge by half a length required a truly sensitive judgment of pace.

In the second race Frankie was lucky. Walter Swinburn's mount Lucayan Prince had to be covered up and produced only in the dying strides. Swinburn was sitting on a whole lot of horse but he encountered traffic problems as he came to challenge. Two strides beyond the line he was in front, but at the post it was Dettori on Diffident who had prevailed and while Diffident did come from the then all-conquering Godolphin operation, he was scarcely one of their stars, having run a stinker to finish last at Newmarket on his previous appearance. His 12-1 price was if anything rather cramped odds but Dettori's driving crouch, clamped to the horse's neck as if man and horse were one being, somehow got him to the line on time.

Third was the big race, Mark of Esteem's success in the Queen Elizabeth II Stakes. There was no doubt there that Frankie Dettori was on the right horse for this one. Mark of Esteem had looked superb in the paddock and his acceleration when he came to take on that lovely filly Bosra Sham, the pair of them clear of most of the best milers in Europe, was awe-inspiring. Said the jockey of his final furlong burst, 'The delivery was like a fuel injection – it just knocked me out of my seat.' Dettori had obeyed Sheikh Mohammed's 'wait and wait' instructions to the letter, something which takes a really cool head in that class of race. Frankie had earlier agreed with Ascot officials not to indulge that day in any of his 'flying dismounts'. After that he could not resist and his leap from the saddle brought an appreciative roar from the crowd.

By the time of the fourth race, the hotly competitive Tote Festival Handicap, punters had realised that Frankie was on a roll. In came the price for his mount Decorated Hero from 12-1 to 7-1, a totally unfair price for a horse carrying the top weight of 9st 13lb (including a 5lb penalty) in such a seven-furlong cavalry charge. Dettori manoeuvred his mount across from the dreaded far side draw and went clear at the furlong pole for his most comfortable victory of the day. 'Don't touch me – I'm on fire,' he told a fan who reached out to him and clearly he had got that message through to Decorated Hero. The grinning jockey walked his mount into the winner's enclosure holding up four fingers. Bookies were beginning to sense the chill and the BBC decided to extend its coverage beyond the four races planned.

Confidence is the key. You need confidence in timing a challenge, confidence in how much you can ask of a mount, confidence in going for a fast-diminishing gap. Even the irresistibly bubbly Dettori has had to work for that confidence at times. I remember him declaring of a comeback ride after injury how he had doubted himself just for a moment and wondered if the old reflexes would be there. That day at Ascot we needed to remember that earlier that season Frankie had shattered his elbow. Many had scarcely expected him to be back in the saddle by then, let alone riding like the angel in God's chariot.

Inevitably Fatefully in the fifth came in from 11-2 in the morning books to 7-4 favourite. Weaving through the pack and again taking it up at the furlong pole, Dettori occasioned a stewards' inquiry by accidentally interfering with Questionia. This time he had a real race of it as his friend Ray Cochrane, later to pull Frankie out of a blazing plane and then to retire and become his agent, drove after him on the 25-1 outsider Abeyr. They closed on him but Frankie had kept just a little in the tank and on a rapidly tiring horse he just held off the effort of Abeyr by half a length. There was a frisson of alarm from punters when the stewards' inquiry was announced but the stewards, wise fellows, saw no reason to deprive Frankie of the race.

In the sixth, trainer Ian Balding had told him to drop in behind on co-favourite Lochangel and bide his time. Instead Frankie took the filly into the lead and stayed there all the way, the sort of move that is praised as genius when you win and castigated as cockiness when you lose. Co-favourite Corsini, with Pat Eddery aboard, battled all the way to the line but Dettori was not to be denied. This time even the officials applauded him in.

It was in the last race on Fujiyama Crest over two miles that the confidence factor was really confirmed.

There was no reason for Frankie's mount to be in with

a chance at all. The horse had not won that season. It had not run since finishing tailed-off second last in June, and again it was humping top weight of 9st 10lb, 16lb more than it had carried when winning the same race two years before. Some bookmakers reckoned this was their chance to take some mugs' money and mitigate their earlier losses but they miscalculated. Again Dettori made all the pace and came home the winner.

Some sportswriters have wondered if on that extraordinary day some of the other jockeys let Frankie have it easy in the last. But racing is not a team sport and I need no more proof of the genuine nature of his victory than the name of the jockey riding Northern Fleet, who at the post was just a neck away from ruining Frankie's day. It was one Pat Eddery. They don't come any more competitive than the several-times champion jockey once nicknamed 'Polyfilla' by Joe Mercer because he would fill any gap the others left him.

If Fujiyama Crest's connections really had been planning something for this race, one can only feel sorry for them landing it at a starting price of 2-1 when 20-1 would have been more realistic.

Dettori's feat was all the more enjoyable for its sheer bravura and the rapport he established with the crowd. He had displayed every facet of race-riding: instinctive judgement of pace, strength in the finish, swiftness in decision and above all that precious capacity to instil in his mounts his own will to win. Bookmakers may have been contemplating throwing themselves into the Thames, the egos of a few other little men might have been irreparably dented but the seven-timer was an extraordinary achievement and it was so good for racing. Every sport needs its superstars to pull in the punters and Frankie was established in that role for evermore.

Doncaster and the St Leger

I think it was Jack Berry who first told the story of former athlete and racehorse owner Chris Brasher arriving one day at a northern racetrack to see one of his horses run. He had left his credentials at home and he arrived at the wrong entrance on the far side of the track. No, said the steely-eyed gateman, he would not take him on trust and let him in to walk across and collect his credentials. If he wanted a free badge he would have to walk round the outside of the course, past the stands, through the main car park and then there was a little green door where he might find the manager …

'How far?' asked the perspiring owner, whose horse was due to run in the first, and was told it was around three-quarters of a mile. 'Oh come on, just let me in,' he implored the jobsworth. 'Here's the card in the paper. That's my horse Run Like The Clappers and I'm Mr C. Brasher.'

'Ah,' said the gateman, recognition dawning, 'is that Chris Brasher the four-minute miler?' 'Yes, yes,' said the relieved owner, hope in his eyes at last. 'Well in that case it won't take thee very long then, will it?' said the gateman.

Sadly, bound close to Westminster by my day-job duties, I haven't done as much racing in the North of England as I would like to have done but I love Haydock and Chester and the glorious Knavesmire at York where the gatemen and other staff have always been delightful. My favourite northern track though is Doncaster. In September 2002 I wrote:

> I love Doncaster on St Leger day. There are plenty
> of good racecourses in Britain and making them
> work isn't exactly rocket science. You need good

viewing facilities, clear signposting, decent catering, clean loos, an informative public address system and friendly staff. Doncaster has those with some added ingredients. It is not just the pleasant walk under the trees to the welcomingly open saddling boxes or even the vast red-carpeted betting hall which throbs like a 1960s rock and roll ballroom. It is the sheer buzz of a crowd determined to respond to the invitation to enjoy itself. The back pocket wads are thicker at Doncaster, the beer goes down faster and the frills, feathers and diamante whatnots are gloriously over the top. A pundit once advised inexperienced lady punters to stand by the parade ring and 'back anything which winks at you' – unless it's Kieren Fallon because that probably means he's looking straight down your cleavage.

Given what is generously displayed at Doncaster it is a wonder the mounted jockeys don't fall out of the saddle.

The stands have been rebuilt since then but the sentiments remain the same. Five years earlier still I had written resisting calls for the St Leger to be shortened or opened to older horses, insisting that what I liked best was the courage shown by most St Leger winners.

In 1997 it was John Dunlop's long-backed grey Silver Patriarch who won. I had backed him for the Leger after the Lingfield Derby trial, which he finished like a horse who could have gone round again and enjoyed it. Silver Patriarch had then finished a close second in the Derby to Benny The Dip and was a touch burly when he returned in the Great Voltigeur at York and again went down narrowly to Stowaway.

A big horse who always took time to wind up, Silver Patriarch looked for a moment at Doncaster as if he was having trouble going the pace. Pat Eddery's arms were pumping from a long way out but when he took him to the front, facing into a near-gale-force wind, his mount responded like a champion, first seeing off the French challenger Vertical Speed then going away. He showed himself to be a real toughie: the more his rider asked of him the more he gave, and the knowledgeable Doncaster crowd cheered in horse and rider. At the age of 45, it was Pat Eddery's 4,000th winner in Britain. I swear that I saw a tear in the eye of the normally imperturbable rider, but he would probably insist it was just the wind.

Pat was a true champion. So too is trainer Sir Michael Stoute. But even the best have their days of anguish amid the triumphs and I won't forget one of those days for Sir Michael at Doncaster in the year 2000. I feel sorry for myself when a 10-1 shot I have backed gets mugged on the line, probably sorrier than anybody in history except Eeyore, according to Mrs Oakley, but that day my piffling little losses were put into perspective. Sir Michael even then needed only a St Leger to complete his full hand of British Classic successes. When John Reid took his Air Marshall into the lead in the last furlong of the Leger at Doncaster that year it looked as though this was to be the triumphal moment. Sadly for both trainer and jockey, it was not. John Dunlop's Millenary, a true racecourse fighter, would not be denied. After a race that had been run at a hectic gallop in the fastest time since 1935, he came again, passed Air Marshall before the line and won by three-quarters of a length under Richard Quinn.

Sir Michael, as he always does, took that in good part with a rueful smile and a slight sucking-in and puffing out of the cheeks. He then joined the journalists clustered around a TV set in the press room to watch the Irish Champion Stakes at Leopardstown in which his Greek Dance was taking on Coolmore's Giant's Causeway and

Godolphin's Best of The Bests for the £486,000 prize. It promised to be one of the races of the season and it delivered.

On Best of The Bests Frankie Dettori shadowed Giant's Causeway and took him on two furlongs out. The pair burst clear of the field. But one jockey had other ideas. Because Giant's Causeway – who had won five Group One contests in four months – was such a fighter, always ready to take on any horse which sought to pass him, the only way to beat him was to swoop late and, if possible, not too closely alongside him so he did not have time to collect himself and fight back. So in Leopardstown, just at the moment Giant's Causeway had clearly mastered Best of The Bests, Johnny Murtagh brought Greek Dance flying in pursuit. He was travelling seemingly twice as fast as the two horses ahead of him. If his final lunge came off it would be the shock – and the ride – of the year; but it failed by a fraction of a second.

Whether Giant's Causeway had just had time to sense what was arriving and respond, whether Johnny Murtagh had been a millisecond late in launching his challenge, we will never know, but he just failed to make it. Beside me, Greek Dance's trainer let out one huge, strangled shout from deep within his frame. It was part exultation at a plan that had come so tantalisingly close to perfect execution, part agony at failing so narrowly to bring off an amazing coup. After the close defeat in the St Leger just before, it was wounded stag-at-bay stuff, a cry all the way up from the vital organs expressing the generic frustration of trainers down the years at what might have been. Someone once defined racehorse training as 'months of agony, moments of bliss'. Sometimes that maxim is reversed. Never again, I decided after witnessing such pain, would I whinge about my fiver lost in a photo finish.

The Leger so often seems to bring a story with it. In 1996 for example it gave John Gosden, the Newmarket trainer with the Roman senator's profile, whose post-race explanations are a masterclass in the art of horse preparation, an overdue first British Classic. In a memorable scrap on Town Moor that year Frankie Dettori on Shantou triumphed over Pat Eddery on Dushyantor by a neck after the Derby second and third had tussled all the way down the straight.

John Gosden had learned and originally plied his trade in the USA. One of his mentors there, D. Wayne Lucas, declared wickedly, 'I taught him all he knows, but not all I know' and by 1996 Gosden must have been wondering if there was some magic ingredient missing. He had trained horses to finish second, third and fourth in the Derby but although he had an Irish Leger success he was still to win a British Classic. On Shantou Frankie delivered for him and he was on the way to that deserved champion trainer's crown in 2012.

In 2002 when Bollin Eric triumphed it was a first Classic success for Tim Easterby and a first British Classic for Kevin Darley, a naturalised Yorkshireman, not to mention success for a breeder, Sir Neil Westbrook, who had had horses with the family for 40 years. Not that the Easterbys were going over the top. Was Tim off to celebrate that night? 'Let's get home first.'

Bollin Eric's form figures before the race read 32233. I shared a taxi from the station with one of the country's foremost students of form and he had agreed that while Bollin Eric was a horse it was good to have on your side in a scrap, he could be discarded from calculations because 'he just doesn't seem to win'. What we didn't know was that jockey Kieren Fallon, forced to miss the ride with a suspension, had assured Sir Neil after the Great Voltigeur that Bollin Eric would stay the extra two furlongs and should beat Bandari and Highest next time out. Sure enough, the big Shaamit colt accelerated past Bandari two furlongs out and never looked like being caught by Sir Michael Stoute's candidate Highest. Not surprisingly, when I asked Tim Easterby if he saw any reason to change the St Leger, he replied with the single word 'Never'. Even more encouragingly, I received the same response that day from John Sanderson, Doncaster's chief executive.

It took many years and the arrival of Mickael Barzalona before the break finally came but I always felt that things were never quite the same again between Frankie Dettori and his long-time boss Sheikh Mohammed after Frankie took the ride on Scorpion for Coolmore in the 2005 St Leger. That year I remember it was pelting with rain, but the elements can never dampen the ardour of the Donny crowds. I wrote then:

Doncaster is the world capital of hair gel, a cornu-copia of spray-tanned decolletage, the last redoubt of the 'party frock'. Trousers are poured, not pulled on. The rule seems to be 'the colder the weather, the shorter the hemline' and everybody enjoys themselves. One lady in pink pulled me under her umbrella in the Tote queue after my second drench-ing, confiding that she had won £235 on the previous race. So where was the party, I asked, only to receive a look of scorn. 'It's all free drinks where we are'. Of course.

Mind you, Women's Lib still has some way to go in Doncaster. I saw one Charlotte Church lookalike ordered to join a four-deep crowd at the bar to fetch five pints while her other half worked on the next bet with his cro-nies. Another version in frills was being steered through the throng by a very firmly clutched left buttock. I don't think I would try either with Mrs Oakley.

Out on the course the pressure was all on Frankie Dettori. He knew questions were being asked about him taking the ride for Coolmore, the great rivals to his retaining Godolphin team. The conditions were dire, with the official going changed to 'heavy' after the second race. Scorpion himself was keyed-up: even with three handlers he could scarcely be restrained in the paddock. Having been second in the Irish Derby and having won the Grand Prix de Paris, Scorpion was odds-on. If Frankie were to slip up or ride an injudicious race for Godolphin's rivals we could all imagine the hullabaloo, and yet still he had enough confidence in the clock in his head to make every yard of the running. Setting a steady pace and then grinding through the gears on the descent from Rose Hill he repelled in turn the challenges of Kong, then Tawqeet and finally The Geezer. It was perfection. The only slip-up came, literally, from the horse. Inside the final furlong, as Frankie sensed the arrival of The Geezer in his slipstream and gave his horse a crack, Scorpion stumbled and veered almost into the running rail before thundering on. 'When I asked him for a final effort he went to quicken again and just lost his footing – he was trying so much to please me,' said Frankie. He insisted that had anybody else come at him, his horse would have been able to pull out a bit more. 'He dug deep like a true champion.'

He conceded that it felt a little weird to be winning a Classic for Godolphin's rivals – 'I've got mixed emotions as I usually win these races for Sheikh Mohammed' – but what struck me before he donned the traditional silk cap given to the winning rider was the intensity of Frankie's focus, the steely determination. It was Frankie himself who volunteered that this was his tenth Classic winner and his third St Leger victory. After a year in which his champion jockey's title had gone by default thanks to the disappointing form of the Godolphin horses, a suspension through Royal Ascot and a broken collarbone halfway through the season, he looked and sounded lean and hungry.

For me the St Leger of 2008 was a glorious spectacle, with Frankie Dettori once again the star. It wasn't just the sight of Dettori launching himself at Sir Michael Stoute like an exuberant child vaulting into a parent's arms for a hug, nor even the view of the mildly embarrassed trainer, a bonhomous but stiff-backed bear of a man, wiping off the smacker of a kiss that Frankie gave him later. Those represented extra relish. No, it was simply the triumph of Conduit, trained by M. Stoute and ridden by F. Dettori in the last and longest of the English Classics, the one mile six furlong St Leger.

For some years then the St Leger had been the Cinderella Classic. Modern breeding is excessively focussed on speed at the expense of stamina and, some of us suspect, at the expense therefore of the durability of the modern racehorse. The French, as already noted, have succumbed to fashion by trimming the distance of their 'Derby' to a mile and a quarter. The US Breeders' Cup authorities were in 2008 absurdly entitling the mile-and-a-half Derby distance race on their programme the 'Breeders' Cup Marathon'. Largely because of that mindset, some St Leger fields in previous years had been small and of rather limited quality. The ten-furlong Irish Champion Stakes, often run the same weekend, had begun to attract more publicity and more top-drawer horses. English or Irish Derby winners were becoming more likely to turn out at Leopardstown than on Doncaster's Town Moor. But its 232nd running with a field of fourteen runners gave glorious witness that the oldest English Classic could still be both a thrilling spectacle and a contest worth winning.

For a start it included Look Here, the filly who had won that year's Oaks, and Frozen Fire, who had won the Irish Derby for Aidan O'Brien. There cannot be much wrong with a race for which the all-conquering O'Brien sends over a team of five from Ireland and in which Sir Michael Stoute, England's champion, fields three. What was truly heartening for Doncaster regulars was to see one of those three succeed. Sir Michael had at that stage won five 2,000 Guineas, four Derbies and a brace each of Oaks and 1,000 Guineas, but despite his 24 runners in the St Leger, including Shergar, he was yet to win it – although he had five times provided the runner-up.

Ironically when he did finally tick that box on his illustrious CV it was not in association with his stable jockey Ryan Moore: of the Stoute trio Moore had chosen Dr Fremantle. But since Godolphin had no runner, Frankie Dettori was approached to ride Conduit in a race he had already won for Godolphin, for O'Brien, for John Gosden and for Jeremy Noseda.

Dettori's post-race antics as he works the victory 'high' out of his system – the hands raised to Heaven or whatever he sees up there, the flying dismounts, the crowd-conducting, the kisses sprayed around connections – are of inestimable value to a sport short on characters with his ebullience and popular appeal. What tends to be forgotten is his sheer tactical brilliance and instinctive horsemanship. Amid all that crowd-pleasing, there are often valuable words to be heard in Frankie's post-race analysis. 'They went off very fast,' he said on this occasion, 'and I knew I was on a stayer.' While Hindu Kush, Warringah and Maidstone Mixture pulled the field along at a stiff pace, Frankie was content to wait near the back in the pale blue silks of the Ballymacoll Stud. Two furlongs out, feeling plenty of horse under him, he knew it was time to press the button. He cruised to the front and dared the others to come and peg him back. Only the two fillies in the race, Look Here and Ireland's Unsung Heroine, proved capable of setting out after him, but Conduit, despite one jink to the right, ran on readily to win by a comfortable three lengths. At last Sir Michael had shaken off the hoodoo, even if it was at the price of a public smacker from Frankie.

Sandown's Coral-Eclipse

Sandown, for me, has got the lot. Class without formality. Continuity without stuffiness. A few big, historic races mixed with tantalising big field handicaps. On site there is easy access to the parade ring, a natural arena spreading down the hill to the railway fences along the bottom straight, a testing final hill and a knowledgeable crowd. Sandown, once a monastery whose inhabitants were wiped out by the plague, also stages one of my favourite races: the Eclipse Stakes is the first occasion in each year's racing programme when the three-year-old Classic generation (done no favours by the weight for age scale) takes on the older horses over a challenging mile and a quarter.

The original Eclipse, foaled during the 1764 solar eclipse which gave him his name, was a phenomenon unbeaten in eighteen races in his century. As one contemporary wrote, he was 'never beaten, never had a whip flourished over him or felt the tickling of a spur or was ever for a moment distressed ... outfooting, outstriding and outlasting every horse which started against him.'

The race that bears his name has seen some wonderful performances too. In 1971 Mill Reef was sublime: he made the talented French colt Caro look one-paced in winning by an easy four lengths. That was before Mill Reef went back to a mile and a half in the King George and beat the others so easily that his jockey Geoff Lewis declared, 'It was daylight that was second. If I'd given him a slap the judge would have left his box before the others got home.'

The superstar Pebbles was the first filly or mare ever to win the Eclipse Stakes in 1985. Nashwan (1989) and Sea The Stars (2009) are among very select company in having achieved the Derby–Eclipse double. And there have been some major shocks too, notably the defeats of Park Top in 1969 and Bosra Sham in 1997, not to mention Ard Patrick beating the great Sceptre back in 1903.

Among trainers one of the shrewdest race-readers is Mark Johnston and I was fascinated one year recently when he told us of the Surrey course, 'Sandown is a perfectly straightforward track but it's amazing how many people try to complicate it.' Jockeys, he said, are too inclined to sit in behind the leaders thinking they have got a double handful – and then they find they haven't. 'First up the hill takes some getting past. Horses sitting behind going well haven't the momentum into the hill and won't quicken up so are relying on others stopping. It takes an awfully good horse to get past.'

Sandown was for much of my racing life my local track, and the best Eclipse I ever saw was in the millennium year of 2000: the battle of the pensioners.

With Mick Kinane suffering from a bad back, Aidan O'Brien had turned to George Duffield, at 53 then the oldest man in the weighing room, to partner Giant's Causeway. Sir Michael Stoute, forced to find a substitute for the injured Kieren Fallon on Kalanisi, went for 48-year-old Pat Eddery. Neither could have made a better choice.

The hefty Giant's Causeway was a horse who needed cranking up and O'Brien told Duffield, 'Whatever you ask him for, he'll give you. Go when you straighten up and let them come for you.' George obeyed the instructions to the letter, going past the Derby second Sakhee soon after the last turn and setting sail for home. But entering the last furlong Eddery drove Kalanisi, in the Aga Khan's famous green and red silks, up to the leader. It looked like another triumph for the Aga. The last sight in the world any jockey then wanted to see was Pat, determination in full motion, coming upsides. But the old grey fox had seen it all before, including that scenario, and he was conceding nothing. Fifty yards out, Pat had Kalanisi's muzzle in front but Duffield and Giant's Causeway outgritted them. Just before the line the Irish horse got his head back in front for an epic victory.

As the crowd applauded both of them back, Duffield was sportingly pointing at his mount, as if to indicate that victory was all down to the horse. It was his triumph too but the courage shown by Giant's Causeway did seem to me to cast doubt on the argument that the horse is not by nature an inbuilt competitor with a will to win. On that display I found it impossible to believe that Duffield's driving of Giant's Causeway would have received the response it did unless there was an inbuilt desire to win in the animal too.

Cynics might take a different view, as I noted at the time, because there was an unfortunate postscript to the Eclipse. Duffield had hit Giant's Causeway more than fifteen times with the whip in the straight; Eddery had given his mount a similar number of reminders. Both jockeys were referred to the Jockey Club for 'excessive use' and were stood down for a number of days, once again fuelling the whip controversy.

The Eclipse in 2010 was truly an emotional occasion. When Henry Cecil won with Twice Over it marked the return to the top table of one of Britain's best-loved trainers.

For *Spectator* readers I described what nearly became a personal disaster:

> Feeling for my wallet en route to Waterloo for the train to Sandown my heart sank as my hand went into an empty pocket, and then I remembered. Mrs Oakley, by then uncontactable at the Royal Academy summer exhibition, had borrowed it to extract some cash the night before.
>
> Shorn of cash and credit cards for rail ticket or racecard I slunk home, reconciled to TV racing. But then I wondered: didn't Mrs O have somewhere a secret cash-stash for window cleaners, charity collectors and emergency taxis? Ten minutes' search proved successful (and no, friendly burglar, it was not in the cocoa tin marked 'Rice'). Thirty seconds later, with folding stuff in my top pocket, I was back en route for Sandown, convinced it was my day.
>
> I had several objectives, mostly financial. I was planning support for William Haggas's Triple Aspect, a horse who goes down to the post like a goat and comes back like a cheetah. Sir Mark Prescott, who does not tilt at windmills, had entered a promising filly in the Coral Distaff, a Listed race. And Andrew Balding, who does not often use the former champion, had booked Kieren Fallon, still for me the strongest rider on the circuit, to ride his Kakatosi. The other objective, all being well, was to join the crowds cheering home another Coral-Eclipse winner for trainer Henry Cecil in the Eclipse, 32 years after his last one, Gunner B. Triple Aspect prevailed by half a length. Sir Mark Prescott's Virginia Hall made

all and won by a comfortable three lengths at 11-2 and Fallon showed all his strength to bring home Kakatosi by a head. But the serious business of the day was in the big race itself. At only 13-8 I hadn't backed Henry Cecil's Twice Over but his was the success I cheered the loudest, not least because it was so bravely done.

His experienced trainer and young jockey Tom Queally had determined beforehand not to let the race degenerate into a sprint so, after sharing the pacemaking duties with the mare Dar Re Mi, who gets at least two furlongs more, Queally drove clear at the three-furlong marker and stretched out, defying his pursuers to catch him. His judgement was spot on and they did not get to him. But both Sri Putra and Viscount Nelson were closing at the finish as the tired Twice Over, his stride visibly shortening, just made it to the winning post in time, having lost one of his stick-on shoes in the struggle. Owner Prince Khalid Abdullah was visibly chuffed. Even more so was young Tom, who declared, 'I'm delighted for Henry, the prince and everyone in the yard, but more so for the horse. He has a wonderful character. I've ridden him work from day one. I knew he had ability and I was just mad about him. I got a real kick out of this.'

Twice Over himself, picking up Cecil's characteristic diffidence, paused before entering the winner's enclosure, as if embarrassed by all the fuss. His trainer, head tilted, softly spoken, immediately praised his jockey and stable staff. But when a voice in the crowd called for 'Three cheers for Henry' and got them with real enthusiasm, their subject simply pointed to his throat to say how he felt. He may be a toff in the non-toff age but his vulnerability makes Cecil the people's toff. He's been through so many travails – broken marriages, the loss of a twin brother, the withdrawal of top owners' horses, his own stomach cancer. But he's trained more Classic winners than any British trainer alive and he's back at the top where he belongs.

For some of us, Twice Over's victory also helped to make up both for Bosra Sham's controversial defeat in 1997 and for Henry Cecil's public denunciation of his own jockey Kieren Fallon on that occasion. Like many, I had been a passionate devotee of the lovely Bosra Sham since I first saw her run as a two-year-old. I had backed her the previous autumn for the 1,000 Guineas, which she won with a bruised foot after nearly being pulled out of the race. And like many I was shocked by her fate in the race in 1997.

In 1997 there were as many people round the saddling enclosure before Sandown's Coral-Eclipse as you would find normally around the parade ring proper. Like me, most of them had come to pay homage to the Queen. Not the mere mortal with a handy tied cottage at the end of the Mall but Wafic Said's chestnut filly Bosra Sham, who rules the hearts of so many racegoers. As delicately as a picture restorer working on a smoke-damaged Rembrandt, her trainer Henry Cecil washed out her mouth with a pink cloth and scratched her between the ears. The lady herself, before she resumed her imperious, head-erect stroll around the circle of her admirers, kicked out fastidiously with her white ankle socks as a fly or two had the temerity to buzz around her quarters. Her magnificent backside was turned towards us, ridged with muscle and gleaming like the patina on a cherished violin.

Heedless of the fact that only two fillies had won the Eclipse in its previous 99 years we piled the money on to the odds-on favourite. Had not Bosra Sham convincingly defeated Halling, winner of the last two Eclipses, in last year's Champion Stakes? Had not John Gosden, trainer of Derby winner Benny The Dip, declared 'She is an Amazon of a filly with a weight allowance. I don't think she is beatable'? The others, including the Breeders' Cup winner Pilsudski, looked to be running only for the place money.

But although Benny The Dip made the running as expected, he did so only at a moderate pace. Pilsudski bided his time and then got first run at him while Bosra Sham's rider Kieren Fallon managed to find himself in a traffic jam in a five-horse race. As the helicopter pictures demonstrated, he went for a gap on the inside, which was, quite legitimately, closed down. He had to snatch up and switch to the outside and in what then became a helter-skelter sprint for the line it was too late for the big filly, who needs time to wind up to her top speed, to make up the ground on Pilsudski and Benny The Dip. I wrote then:

A man talking through his pocket must always be treated with caution and although I do not normally back 4-7 shots I had done so heavily this time. But I am not one of the 'Get Fallon' brigade who reckon Bosra Sham's jockey never had the class to be Henry Cecil's first jockey. I urged readers to back him to become champion jockey this season (he currently leads the table). I have praised him before as one of the strongest riders I know in a finish. But has he yet developed the tactical racing brain he needs to complement his other skills? One racing sage I met after the Eclipse was willing to lay odds against Fallon still being Cecil's first jockey next season and the rider himself was pretty defensive in his early comments on Saturday, saying 'it would be typical of people to blame me'.

Well, yes Kieren. Her trainer was content he had Bosra Sham ready to run the race of her life. The jockey agrees he was on the best horse in the race while complaining there was no real gallop. But if the pace of the race was not suiting Bosra Sham, who likes to be covered up in a truly run contest, then it was up to her jockey to do something about it. We cannot be sure that Bosra Sham would have beaten Pilsudski in a better-run race: what we do know is that she was not given the chance of doing so. After the traffic problems he has managed to encounter this season on Reams of Verse and Sleepytime, too, it is not surprising that questions are being asked about Kieren Fallon because even when he wins he is giving Cecil's horses a harder race than they should have.

Since I wrote those words Henry Cecil has himself made plain his displeasure at Fallon's riding of Bosra Sham and it seems unlikely that Wafic Said will persevere with the Warren Place jockey on his horses even if the trainer continues to give him the benefit of the doubt. All that said, we should not detract from the triumph enjoyed by Pilsudski's connections. When you have just picked up a £115,000 prize it is perhaps easier to be honest. But all praise to Michael Stoute for blaming himself for Pilsudski's defeat in his previous race at Ascot, saying that he had obviously not got this big, gross horse to his peak by then. All credit too to big race specialist Mick Kinane for his enterprising tactics in striking when he did. And let us not forget what a cracker of a race it was too from Benny The Dip.

On Benny The Dip Willie Ryan once again rode a copybook race as he had done in the Derby. He had plotted the tactics with John Gosden, who thought that if he went too fast then 'Benny' would merely be setting it up for the older horses. The irony is that Ryan, attached to Henry Cecil's stable, is not rated highly enough at Warren Place to ride the stable's top prospects except in their work.

I stuck with Fallon in a column I wrote the next week. Complaints, I noted, do not always bring the anticipated result. When a couple of golfers missed their putts on the eighteenth green on a famous northern golf course they turned the air blue with expletives, upsetting two members' wives taking a gin and tonic on the overlooking terrace. The ladies complained to the committee, who deliberated and then issued a firm ruling: in future, ladies were to be banned from the clubhouse terrace.

Those who had been hoping that the Bosra Sham affair would bring about the downfall of Kieren Fallon as Henry Cecil's retained jockey must be feeling a little like those lady complainants. After a turbulent ten days, Fallon is now more firmly established at Warren Place than he was before his error in the Eclipse. What is more, Fallon has turned the affair to his benefit. This, remember, is a jockey whose colleagues have borne the bruises to testify to his short fuse, whose disciplinary record once ran a close second to that of Billy the Kid. Instead of cracking under the pressure, Fallon has been a model of restraint, despite his jocking off the Wafic Said horses. He has faced the heat in the hottest of kitchens with the composure of an elder statesman. His answer to the critics was to go out and ride fourteen winners in the next week, six of them at the hotly contested Newmarket July meeting.

After the public criticism from Henry Cecil, that was no mean feat. An owner was telling me at Lingfield on Saturday not to back one of his horses because the jockey was going through a crisis of confidence, the stable's main owner having refused to put him up on his horses – and that was without a whisper of publicity.

Writing immediately after the Eclipse was run, I never imagined that the Fallon/Bosra Sham affair would become the epic it did. I remain critical of his ride in the Eclipse although I begin to have my doubts how much the stable had worked through the tactical options for the race before it was run. But I had no wish to become part of a pack hounding the jockey and I remain confident that when advising readers of this column last August to back Fallon (then available at 4-1) for the jockeys' championship I was offering sound advice. He is currently at 5-4 and in terms of the return to a level stake on his mounts he is well clear of the field.

Fallon has shown a champion's confidence and has come out of it rather better than the brilliant trainer for whom he rides. One senior figure in racing who counts himself a friend of Cecil's was appalled by his public criticism of his own jockey before he announced he was keeping him on for next season. 'If you are going to get rid of somebody, you do it. Otherwise you shut up.' Getting ratty with the media, as Cecil chose to do instead, is never an answer. We are not always convenient to have around but as Enoch Powell once said, 'Politicians who complain about the media are like ship's captains who complain about the sea.' At Henry Cecil's level that goes for trainers too.

And Fallon did finish that season as champion jockey.

Newmarket

The first training centre to seduce me was Lambourn, partly because it was close enough to Oxford in my student days for me once or twice to savour the sight of racing strings jig-jogging along the skyline and, let's be honest, to enjoy a pint or two in its pubs, hoping to spot one of my racing heroes. But I was blown away by my first experience of Newmarket Heath.

The anticipation builds as you drive along from Six Mile Bottom, slaloming through the traffic-calming islands (Oh no, officer, only at 39mph), and then pass alongside the huge wedge-cut hedges bordering the training grounds. Coming in from the other end of town you might glimpse a mare or two in the paddocks of some of the 60 studs where the stars of the future are bred.

As you move along the high street past the Jockey Club's elegantly imposing home, the number of short-legged men in breeches collecting their *Racing Post* from Tindall's quickens the appetite. The town where the tradition has always been that one-time racing premises should be kept that way rather than salami-sliced into yet another characterless borough dominated by redeveloped supermarkets, car parks and petrol stations is threaded through with sandy walkways allowing the racing strings to pass in comparative safety from stableyard to Warren Hill or to the Al Bahathri gallops and back again. And though the heath itself was once described as 'miles and miles of bugger all', it never looks that way when the training battalions sweep out from Henry Cecil's Warren Place, from John Gosden's Clarehaven or from Sir Michael Stoute's Freemason Lodge to show their paces in front of knotted groups of owners, racing managers and bloodstock agents – not to mention the work-watchers with whom I spent a fascinating morning in August 1997.

In pink Ralph Lauren shirt, monogrammed blue suede riding boots with tassels and blue velvet riding hat, Henry Cecil, astride his wife Natalie's skewbald hack Poteen, was effectively holding court on Newmarket's Limekilns to a covey of owners and stud managers, a visiting tour party and assorted correspondents. The trainer of nineteen Classic winners so far, tall, elegant and authoritative, Cecil is the nearest equivalent to a King of Newmarket since Charles II frequented the gallops with his hawking friends. It is, he told me, the oldest piece of cultivated grassland in the world, unploughed since Carolingian days. Newmarket's precious turf with its peat dressings and well-knotted roots is also one of the largest mown grass areas in the world. (It is even claimed that Boadicea used to practise her chariot manoeuvres on the turf where the occupants of 70-plus stables are now put through their paces.)

I was with two men of remarkable skill, work-watchers and Newmarket correspondents David Milnes and Tony Elves. On duty respectively for the *Racing Post* and the *Sporting Life*, they can recognise on sight virtually all the inmates of Newmarket's racing stables. Both have an encyclopaedic memory for horseflesh and an easy relationship with the rest of Newmarket's professionals born of long experience.

Down below us on the Long Gallop, first to show were some well-regarded two-year-olds: Star Trech, a half-sister to Lady Carla, with Kieren Fallon up, and Jibe, a full sister to Yashmak. Both were moving nicely, as was the Rainbow Quest filly Tuning. A little later came the stars. Along the Round Gallop, now appearing, now disappearing behind the undulations as sheep grazed beyond came the Oaks winner Reams of Verse, last year's Derby second Dushyantor, Besiege and the beautiful, buxom Bosra Sham, the low morning sun streaming through her mane like an orange halo as she motored clear of her galloping companions. Both Bosra Sham and Reams of Verse went into the notebooks as 'impressive'.

Once there used to be twelve work-watchers at Newmarket for the *Sporting Life* alone. Now David, a quiet, intense former electrician from Selby, and Tony, a more extrovert Sunderlander, are virtually the last of the breed. It may sound like fun earning your living watching the Cecil stars in the early August sunlight: it is less so when you are out in the biting wind at dawn in early February, your fingers too numb to grip the pencil as you watch three lots from each of the leading stables, trying to memorise the characteristics – a white sock here, a blaze there, a style of head carriage which will help you tell apart the 2,000 and more horses being trained at Headquarters.

It is certainly not a restful pursuit. Earlier we had bumped across the grass in Tony's battered red Escort, having dashed through the town and past the racecourse to the watered gallop (which costs trainers £10 per horse per day, slips posted in a box under the watchful eye of the Jockey Club's heathmen) to see Luca Cumani's and Michael Bell's strings at work. Tom and David even helped the trainers to identify their galloping charges. Before that, on the Polytrack beside the road to Six Mile Bottom we had watched some of David Loder's multi-horsepower stable, then dashed through town again to the Al-Bahathri track to see more of his plus David Morley's horses. A quick word with owner Trevor Harris here, with jockeys Willie Ryan and Ray Cochrane there, then bustling back through the high street again as the four-legged reasons for Newmarket's very existence proudly stalked the sandy horsewalks, their riders, some nursing hangovers, discussing last night's football or that morning's page three girl in the *Sun*.

David and Tony watch for many things – for a horse rated 70 which works upsides with one rated 95, for a horse clearly getting back its sparkle after a spell off the racecourse, for a top jockey brought in to get a feel of a likely prospect while the regular work-rider, temporarily grounded, taps his whip against his riding boots in frustration. 'Just like with a human athlete,' says Tony, 'you can sense when they are doing the work with something in hand. It's the ones who don't do anything at home but only on the racecourse which fox us. But then they usually fox the trainers too.'

Relations with most trainers, I can testify, are good and they won't watch work on behalf of bookmakers, only for their papers. 'It certainly wouldn't do you any favours if you were known to be a bookmakers' nark. They mostly get their information from staff in the yards,' says Tony.

So with their privileged information, do they personally make their betting pay? 'You wouldn't rely on betting for your income,' says Tony. 'There's a difference between making it pay and making your living from it,' adds David. Realists both. But Tony did go the first six weeks of the season without a loser. I think I could stand a few cold Februarys for that …

Unlike Lambourn or Middleham, Newmarket has its own racecourse too – in fact a pair of them, the Rowley Mile and the July course. The former, the scene of so many thrilling contests down the years, sets you instantly re-hearing the thunder of hoofbeats past. The more accessible little July course, with its hanging baskets and sausage stalls, trainers in blazers and chinos and the horses in the winners' enclosure close enough to snatch an ice cream, reminds us all of simple summer joys. It is one of those familiar pleasures, like slipping into a comfortable old pair of suede shoes, eating baked beans on toast after a week of lunching politicians at fashionable restaurants or getting halfway through a Dick Francis and realising that you have read it before but luckily can't remember the ending anyway. The staff smile with you, nobody looks askance at those who choose not to wear a tie and the fillies in silky pastels are as beguilingly under-covered as those in a risqué Edwardian pencil sketch. Flowers abound beside the parade ring and unsaddling enclosure, and I have never agreed with my late mother, who used to complain of others' gardens, 'Marigolds, dear ... so common.'

The July course has been 'modernised', on the whole without losing its character. But not all the changes are welcome. I can no longer find the board where a man used to chalk up the results from other courses and I was disturbed to find that the old Tote Credit Club building where riff-raff like me consorted had become 'The Pink Bar'. Indeed, so uncompromisingly pink has it been painted that I wondered about the precise qualifications for entry. I won't be risking it without a few of my more flamboyant friends.

It was Charles II who staged the first racing under prescribed rules at Newmarket – still, with the Guineas, the home of the first two Classics of the English summer – and he won one of those races himself. The Rowley Mile is named after the favourite hunter he used to exercise there. In those days of course there was no imposing Millennium Grandstand: Charles and his chums had to watch the races from the Bushes, one and a half furlongs out. But truly the horse has always been king here: close your eyes and you can see again battles like the one which enthralled racegoers at the 1971 2,000 Guineas, the only time the two heroes Brigadier Gerard, trained by Dick Hern, and Mill Reef, Ian Balding's superstar, ever met.

Mill Reef and My Swallow dominated the betting, the latter having beaten the former a head in the Prix Robert Papin. Again the two took each other on down the centre of the course but a furlong out Joe Mercer on Brigadier Gerard, who hadn't raced since the Dewhurst the previous season, gave his mount a slap and it was all over. He scorched past the pair with a breathtaking burst and was three lengths clear of Mill Reef at the line. Mill Reef was never beaten again, Brigadier Gerard just once in his remaining thirteen races.

This was the course on which Tudor Minstrel left his field for dead in 1947 with his blinding speed and on which Frankel repeated the feat when Tom Queally unleashed his turbo-charger in 2011. Up the same run from the Bushes Petite Etoile and Bosra Sham, two fillies adopted by the whole racing public, won their 1,000 Guineas and Oh So Sharp took the first of her three Classics. Nashwan, Nijinsky, Dancing Brave and Sir Ivor demonstrated their brilliance in the male equivalent.

If I could take only one rerun with me to my desert island, however, it would have to be Persian Punch's victory in the 2003 Jockey Club Cup. David Elsworth's hefty warrior was passed two furlongs out by three horses, caught a whip-stroke from another jockey across his nose, and yet then, in a gut-busting effort up the final rise, reeled in all three of them to beat Millenary by a short head on the line. It was what horseracing is all about.

Brighton

Brighton for me is one of the jolliest, most informal of race-courses. Most of my years as a political editor, party conferences were held in the seaside town and often the political circus would happily coincide with a race fixture. This race-day in 1998 was typical of the seaside course's fare:

Brighton on a Friday isn't exactly Goodwood or Ascot. Where they are worn, the suits are shinier and sharper, the ties a good deal gaudier. Your binoculars pick up the runners at the seven-furlong pole over the top of a block of council flats in mid-course. But there is a lot to be said too for a track where families can get out a picnic blanket within yards of the parade ring, where pushchairs are welcome and the staff actually ask if you are having a good time. It is too the sort of course where many of the winners seem to be ridden by weatherbeaten work-riders or fresh-faced apprentices while the star jockeys are away at more fashionable tracks. It also gives those with yards full of lower-rated handicappers the chance to snap up a race or two.

Five minutes before the first, having backed Sean Woods's My Learned Friend I encountered Epsom trainer Roger Ingram, who fancied his five-year-old gelding Random Kindness. I managed a wan smile as Random Kindness led all the way under a canny ride from Tony McGlone, holding off My Learned Friend as Roger, his daughter Rhian in his arms, whooped home his horse with cries of 'Come on Randy'. An appropriate slogan, I guess, for the spiritual home of the dirty weekend.

Noting that Lambourn handler Brian Meehan had won the second race the previous year I had intended to back his La Tavernetta. But I fell into conversation with ex-trainer Gerry Blum, who had travelled to the course with another handler who fancied his runner. Since Gerry and his sister seemed to be the lucky sort (they had won thirteen races in three seasons with two-year-olds trained by Jack Berry) I switched my bet. Only to see the animal fade out of contention as La Tavernetta broke clear of the field with Rod Simpson's newcomer Sampower Star and won by a short head.

The ever-colourful Simpson was stretching even Brighton's informality as the first trainer I have ever seen in the parade ring actually wearing trainers, combined with a colourful sweater and shorts of a bagginess I had only ever glimpsed previously when encountering a khaki-clad Denis Healey on holiday in the Cote Vermeille. When asked if he had mistaken the way to the safari camp, Simpson tartly replied that there were plenty of camels around the parade ring. Whatever he looks like, he can certainly train racehorses.

A touch of class was visible in the next. Walter Swinburn rode the Aga Khan's Aliabad, but they were beaten by Henry Cecil's Grimshaw, owned by Prince Fahd Salman and ridden again by the under-rated Cecil work-rider Tony McGlone. When someone asked the dismounting McGlone when he had last ridden a double, he grinned and said, 'Surely it wasn't that long ago?' How sad that the Aga, Prince Fahd and Henry Cecil all gave the occasion a miss. If they come to Brighton's next meeting I will buy them all ice creams.

In the next race I could not decide between the merits of my chum Simon Dow's Perfect Poppy and Annabel King's May Queen Megan, so I backed the pair, only for both to fall in the last furlong as Tony Clark's mount Natalie's Pet interfered with them. Yes, you are right, it was a Flat race. There are not many people who can back two in a race on the level and have two fallers.

Richard Hannon doesn't mind where he goes for winners, and he doesn't often leave the seaside track empty-handed, so I backed his nine-year-old sprinter I Cried For You in the next and restored the bank balance somewhat when Richard Hughes drove him home. The trainer was just telling me that this was I Cried For You's first success when up popped ex-car salesman, ex-seaside crooner and ex-local trainer Charlie Moore, a man who once nobbled a fellow singer who was getting better applause by pulling out his microphone cord. 'Who owns that one then Richard?' he cried, 'Johnny Ray?' At Brighton you can rely on enough pensioners being around to score with a joke like that. And there was even a happy ending in the last.

Stratford-upon-Avon trainer Annabel King was so upset by May Queen Megan's fall (both horses were unscathed, although jockey Matt Henry was taken to hospital with a suspected fractured cheekbone) that she could not bear to saddle her last race runner, especially as her previous Flat runner at Nottingham had also extraordinarily been a faller. But the well-named Step on Degas, a bay mare by Superpower out of Vivid Impression, prevailed in a photo finish at 20-1. When the result was announced she came bounding out of the weighing room dragging on a borrowed cigarette and in such voluble form that she was probably still talking hours later. The team said they weren't going to let her saddle up a horse again. Who says racing people aren't superstitious? But what is for sure is that you can have just as much fun racing with the minnows as among the big fish.

Jockeyship

Former champion jockey Bob Davies once met a trainer for the first time in the parade ring and asked him, about the horse he was about to ride for him, 'How does he jump?' He received the rather disconcerting reply, 'That's for you to find out.' One of the most fascinating elements in racing to me is the chemistry which bonds horse and rider. It is a subject I have often tried to explore when profiling jockeys for my *Spectator* column or when sharing a platform with the likes of Richard Dunwoody, Ruby Walsh or Mick Fitzgerald for book launches. I have devoured jockey biographies over the decades in search of clues.

Horses are individuals: some like to be up there with the pace at the front, others like the hurly-burly of pushing their way through a crowd. Some shrink from contact or stop the second they have their heads in front: jockeys therefore get horses to run for them in different ways. Race-riding cannot be a one-size-fits-all business. Sometimes they need strength, more often they need intuition. But above all they need the ability to transmit to their mounts the will to win. Kieren Fallon, riding as well in his 40s as he has ever done, whistles at his mounts to make them go. The late Greville Starkey used to try and disconcert his opponents in a tight finish with his brilliant imitation of a barking dog. The Duchess of Bedford showed me a photo of him doing just that in the Japan Cup that Jupiter Island won for her and Clive Brittain in the hands of Pat Eddery.

One thing often forgotten is that jockeys often have no more than the time between climbing aboard a horse in the parade ring and the gates opening at the start of a race to get to know their mounts. In the autobiography he put together with the perceptive Jonathan Powell, Frankie Dettori reflected on the need to use that five minutes on the way to the start to become a horse's friend:

> You climb into the saddle and feel how it walks, how it places its feet and how it looks at you and you must understand. When I sit on a horse I can tell its character within five seconds, its nature, its temperament and best distance, even whether it has got a kick or is one-paced. That is something I was born with.

When a jockey like Frankie rides a horse into the starting stalls the animal does not know if he is going to be running half a mile or two miles. He doesn't know where the winning post is:

> So it is down to me to make sure we become friends so that he will respond to whatever I ask him. You must work to build that bond. He has to have that trust in me to slow down and quicken up when I ask. Only then can you control the release of that huge potential energy during a race ...
>
> The most important thing between man and horse is trust. You find it by body language and feeling. Horses have a sixth sense about the person on top. They can even feel you blinking. If they realise you are frightened they are just as likely to drop you straight away and bury you. It's their natural instinct. They won't stand for just anybody on their backs.

An equally inspired horseman, Mick Fitzgerald, reckoned Frankie's timescale a little optimistic. He told me:

> You've got ten minutes when you walk out into the paddock, five minutes while you take it to the start,

five minutes to become acquainted with a horse before you ride it in a race. You'll know very soon whether a horse is amenable to you, whether you can ask that horse to do something or whether you can tell it to do something – because some horses need telling and some need asking.

It is, he says, a matter of finding out which is which: 'Some horses just make a mess no matter what you do!'

At Newbury one day Richard Hughes discussed his fondness for riding hold-up races, when he swoops from the back to grab first place on the line. One reason he does so, he replied, is that nine out of ten horses will only battle with the pain barrier for a hundred yards, so one burst is enough to ask.

Little bits stick with you from different conversations. I spoke to Flat jockey Brian Rouse when he retired and went to Hong Kong about what was the crucial quality required: common sense above all, he replied. 'Riding horses is like driving a car with no brakes. If you make a mistake you can't rectify it in one stride.' And no one conveyed the excitement of riding a top-class horse better than the talented amateur Sam Waley-Cohen, who has partnered Long Run throughout his career. The adventure-seeking Sam is a helicopter pilot, a bungee jumper and a white-water rafter but at the Cheltenham Literary Festival he described his favourite mount like this:

He's highly strung and can be a real challenge. In the stables he's like a little lamb, quiet as you like. But lead him out into the parade ring and it's as if he's pulled on a suit of armour to go out to war – 'Come out and have a look at me.' Then, bang, it can be like you're trying to sit on a box of fireworks. But when he gets into a rhythm with that ground-devouring stride he's so smooth and relentless. Of all the adrenalin rushes I've had nothing comes even close to riding Long Run.

One of several downsides of the controversies over use of the whip in recent years is that it has given the public the idea that getting horses to win races is all about physical strength and even brutality. Listen to Ruby Walsh however and he will tell you that 99 races out of 100 are won by a jockey's intelligence rather than his physical strength. He also points out that jockey fitness is different to fitness in other sports and that they use their muscles in a different way. Football and rugby players stretch to be explosive. Jockeys don't get strained hamstrings or quads because 'For us it's all about muscle compaction. When you are riding a horse the key is not to move. Everything is compressed. You're trying to achieve a stillness on a horse's back so that you can manipulate him the way you want.' To avoid giving mixed signals from the saddle requires a totally different kind of fitness.

What was also intriguing to learn is that Ruby lost 3lb when he first started riding regularly in England, simply from the race-riding, because riders in England start motoring at a much earlier stage of the race and races are truer run. 'There wasn't a snowball's chance in hell of you winning a race in Ireland if you set sail with five to jump. Not a hope. If you were foolish enough to try it you'd have three lads sitting up behind you on the bridle with smiles on their faces.'

Talk to the old pros and they will agree that the standard of riding over fences is higher today, more professional than it has ever been. The two men instanced as examples every time are AP McCoy and Ruby Walsh. But their styles are in total contrast. Says Mick Fitzgerald:

You couldn't have more different styles. Ruby is very quiet. AP is a lot more aggressive, you see a lot more movement with AP, but both are just as effective. There is more than one way to skin a cat. Ruby is brilliant at what he does. He rides a very different race to AP. He's a lot quieter, he allows the horse much more time to get into it. He does little things that you can't actually see. If you watch Ruby you'll see him make little moves, he'll sit down a little bit lower on a horse, he'll ask a horse to quicken a little but at a particular time because he wants to get into a position he wants the horse in. AP is a bit more aggressive in attitude.

The results tell you how effective they are. I've ridden too against Richard Dunwoody. I found Woody to be the best that I've ever seen. He was brilliant at what he did. He was good in a finish, strong, he was brilliant at presenting a horse at an obstacle. AP has taken that and he's found a little bit more aggression; he's a real winner, AP. Anybody who backs him, you know you're going to get a run for your money. Somebody said to me if I was skint, down to my last tenner and I wanted a jockey to ride a horse for me there wouldn't be any question, it would have to be AP every time.

Perhaps the last word should go to Martin Pipe, who has had Peter Scudamore, Richard Dunwoody and Tony McCoy ride for him. When I asked him to compare them, this was his response:

All were very good jockeys. But they all school differently, all have a different motivation. Some jockeys just like to go and pop them over the fences, some like to go a good pace over the fences. Some jockeys ride better in better races than in sellers. I like to treat every race the same. Whether it's a seller or the Champion Hurdle the objective is to try and win. It's just as important to win the seller. Not all jockeys have got that feeling in every race: 'today's the day we've got to win'. AP does like to win *everything*. He's got the determination no matter what kind of race it is. Dunwoody was a very good jockey, very stylish, perhaps he improved in big races. Scu was a natural, very good: again, a great front-running jockey. He went out, knew the pace, knew the horses would jump and got them jumping and going. Scu was very good at getting a result. AP is a genius, nothing but the best.

In the end then it comes down to will, perhaps even more than technique, and that takes us back to the chemistry.

A few jockeys have managed to combine riding on the Flat and over jumps, and a number of the National Hunt jockeys were forced into the winter game by struggles with their weight. Two top jockeys moved the other way: both Graham Lee and Jim Crowley have become top riders on the Flat after giving up jumping. Jim Crowley came from a point-to-pointing family – 'I had a pony under my arse even before I could walk' – and I talked to him at Sandown one day about the different skills required. 'You race so much tighter on the Flat,' he said:

> You have to tidy yourself up. You have to keep your horse balanced and get him in the best possible position. In jumping there's more time to recover if you miss the break and are not quite where you want to be. It's not so good on the Flat if you're seventh or eighth and wanted to be second or third ... you've got to be on the ball.

But what about the weight – moving down from a natural

9st 5lb when he was riding over jumps to a regular 8st 7lb? 'Oh I just eat more healthily,' he replied airily. 'In the summer heat with up to ten rides a day it's not a problem.' A pity that the rest of us don't have that slimming option.

Are jockeys masochists?

Wincing through the bludgeonings and knifings suffered by the heroes of Dick Francis's racing novels it struck me one day that his leading characters rarely survive a book with their bodies intact. Just as James Bond will never get through a film without being dangled from a window, thrown into a shark-filled pool or strapped to a table with his manly assets threatened by an advancing laser beam, so each Francis hero gets a going-over by thugs in a race-course car park, a deserted stable yard or a horsebox parked in a lay-by.

The Queen Mother's former jockey clearly became inured to pain during his years in the saddle and I some-times wonder if all National Hunt jockeys aren't born masochists.

I once had permission to spend a winter day in the jockeys' changing room at Newbury. As muscular, pain-fully thin young men joshed and rushed about in the ladies' tights they use to keep warm under their breeches, some still pink from the sauna, you could see livid scars on their backs and strange protuberances on the shoulder-blades and collarbones exposed by their wasting. There were the puckered scars of surgery and vivid lines down one rider's back as if he had been run over by a harrow. As Mark Perrett, who rode on the Flat as well, emerged from the shower as spare as a coat hanger, he would have been an ideal model for a medical class: there wasn't a bone in his body you couldn't see.

Mick Fitzgerald had one eye all but closed and the other bruised, and was dabbing at a nose still bleeding from a resetting operation the day before, but he was smiling: he had just learned he was to ride Remittance Man at the following week's Cheltenham Festival.

John Kavanagh, then Nicky Henderson's dependable number two, who was recovering from a broken leg, limped down the passage to be pummelled by the Jockey Club's 'flying physio' Rabbit Slattery on her treatment table. Had an old man left the betting shop walking like he did you'd have laid odds on him not making it to the pub next door; John Kavanagh came out and coaxed and drove half a ton of horse athletically over fences for three miles and then rode a stirring finish.

Jockeys loped in with their barrel-bags amid the gentle scuffing of brush on boot, the slap of saddle soap on well-worn leather as the valets – the talismans and father confessors of the weighing room – prepared their kit. One of them, Tom Buckingham, told me that Hywel Davies never went back to Doncaster after a horrific fall in which his horse cartwheeled on him and he literally 'died' for two minutes on the way to hospital.

One well-known figure was sleeping, his head on a heap of towels in the corner as he fought to mitigate the flu which had dogged him for two days and which had not been confessed to his retaining yard. When I commented on the number of smokers, another valet noted, 'Well it's a novice chase next isn't it?' As others wandered about in various states of undress, an occasional lady rider would slip in, eyes fixedly to the front, to collect her parcel of colours from the valets.

Simon McNeill, nowadays a starter, took a spectacular tumble three out to sympathetic groans from the jockeys not riding, as they watched on TV. When he came in,

Rabbit led him straight to her table. 'It's the next day they notice it,' she said. He himself was in no hurry to see the doctor, fearing the dreaded red ink entry on his jockey's passport that would mean he was stood down for two days. He had fancied rides at Stratford the next day and was annoyed that an ambulance man had alarmed people by suggesting he'd taken a blow that had left him unable to speak: 'The only reason I couldn't speak was because I was bloody well winded!' He added, 'When I was younger I used to bounce up immediately to convince others I was OK. Now I lie there until I'm sure I'm OK.'

It really is mind over matter and the market economy. Always fearful that too many days out of the saddle will see others becoming fixtures on their rides, and that owners and trainers will acquire new loyalties, they shrug off in a matter of days the injuries that would keep the rest of us off the tennis court for three months.

It is instinctive. At Cheltenham in 2011 Dickie Johnson was thrown through the running rail among photographers as his horse fell at the last. Groggy and with blood all over the place, his first words as trainer Philip Hobbs reached him were, 'Don't you start giving away my rides.'

At Ascot in November 2012 we crowded to greet the rider of J.P. McManus's winner My Tent Or Yours. No racegoer would normally fail to recognise eighteen times champion jockey Tony McCoy. But on this occasion they could have been excused for doing so. AP was 30 shades of grey, his normal pallor heightened by the bandaging all across his nose and upper lip. Twenty-four hours earlier at Wetherby a horse had lashed out with its legs and caught him full in the face. As trainer Nicky Henderson said, 'A few inches closer and AP would no longer have been on this planet.' Hearing of the accident, Nicky had started making plans to put AP's friend and rival Barry Geraghty on his Ascot runner instead, especially when McCoy's agent Dave Roberts told him nobody could possibly be riding the next day after the injuries he had suffered. But McCoy, the original iron man, is different. A plastic surgeon in York had applied twenty stitches inside and outside his mouth and nose, his dentist had fixed him up with a couple of temporary teeth and he reported for duty the next day, telling us through swollen lips that his injuries were 'superficial'. Just to make sure it did not hinder his chances of riding the next day, McCoy had had the medical work done on him without anaesthetic, though there was a flicker of memory across his face as he recalled, 'They were a little time doing it.' Even Nicky Henderson, who has seen plenty of brave and determined jockeys in his time, had been shocked when he saw the man about to ride his horse. He told Jonjo O'Neill, McCoy's most regular employer, 'I wanted a jockey, not the Phantom of the Opera.'

McCoy had already ridden a hundred winners that season before the success of My Tent Or Yours and was 25 winners clear of his nearest pursuer in the championship, Richard Johnson. He could easily have afforded to give himself a few days off to recover, but that would not be the real McCoy.

McCoy's great friend and fierce rival Ruby Walsh is the same. In March 2011 the most colourful sight at Sandown on the Saturday before the Cheltenham Festival was not the jockeys' silks but the vivid bruising around Ruby's eye as he returned on his first winner since breaking his leg in November. The blues, reds and yellows visible on his stitched-up face were the result of a fall on King Of The Refs at Naas three days before. Had he feared the worst as his mount had gone down? Oh no, said Ruby matter-of-factly, in a jump jockey's life there is all the difference in the world between 'ordinary nuisance pain' and 'oh my God I've broken it' pain.

I remember too Graham Lee in his days as a jump jockey after he had won the Betfred Gold Cup at Sandown on Hot Weld in 2007. Few had expected him to ride that day, after a crunching fall in Ireland on the Tuesday. Hadn't he been worried too, after the field had galloped on without him and Aces High? 'Well you know how you react to a broken bone and I didn't react that way ... when you know it isn't a broken bone you just bash on.' It was the sheer matter-of-factness of the comment that struck me.

In his autobiography Mick Fitzgerald talks harrowingly of 'the pungent smell of bone on bone', the shattered ankle and two broken necks, the second of which ended his riding career. The first time he did it he lived with the pain for eleven days before going to see a specialist. 'How did you get here?' he was asked. 'I drove.' 'You won't be driving back – you've broken your neck.' Admittedly the stoic Mrs Oakley walked around for twenty years with a broken neck before it was revealed by a skiing accident. It does happen. But fortunately she doesn't ride over fences.

The jump jockeys were just as hard in the old days. Once when Jack Berry broke a leg in his riding days he got a horrified St John Ambulanceman to drag him off the course. He didn't want to be taken to the local hospital but one nearer his family, so he kept himself going with nothing but a few cigarettes until the end of the day's racing. When his friends finally got him to hospital the surgeon found the leg was broken in six places. Before long Jack was out riding exercise, complete with his plaster-of-Paris pot. And on the day he returned to the saddle he broke his wrist.

It was Australian Les Carlyon, one of the finest racing writers there has been, who told me the ultimate story about suffering jockeys, in the shape of the Adelaide-based Les Boots. So regularly did Les Boots finish up in hospital after a ride that his wife used to pack his pyjamas in his racing kitbag. His record on the Flat was depressing: he never rode a winner, in fact Boots never even collected any place money either. Over jumps it was worse. He was fine riding work but on the racetrack his record was 39 starts for 42 falls. Yes, those figures are the right way round. Les Boots never completed and in one race he fell, remounted and fell again. The extra fall was the one he took from tumbling off the stretcher on the way to the medical room.

When he retired from the saddle I asked Mark Perrett about the difference in the weighing room atmosphere between Flat and jumping jockeys. He replied, 'They're a great bunch, the jocks, all game for a laugh. But the jump jockeys are much more so. It's the money. On the Flat there's so much more at stake. It's big business. Jumping jockeys are more down to earth.'

Ah yes, it's only their lives they are risking over jumps ...

Don't marry a jockey

Back in the mists of time I proposed to Mrs Oakley in the rather naff Caribbean bar of a fashionable London venue patronised by a set we couldn't afford to join. I prefaced my question with a long preview about the perils of marrying a journalist. Fortunately she did not take me seriously. Since then she has stuck with me through a train-wreck life of cancelled dinner parties, curtailed holidays and mortally offended ex-friends with more predictable occupations. I have come to realise since that she could have done worse: she could have married a jockey.

Every time I pick up a rider's biography there is harrowing confirmation. You wouldn't find a more affable, intelligent and considerate guy than former jockey Mick Fitzgerald. Not out of the saddle. But in his autobiography *Better Than Sex* (the title deriving from his famous comment to Desmond Lynam about what it was like riding Rough Quest to win the Grand National) he was entirely candid about his priorities. The book was a red flag warning to any lady not to become involved with a rider over obstacles. The day he rode a treble at the Cheltenham Festival Mick's wife wasn't there and he reflected: 'She just wasn't a factor. She was largely irrelevant. I was going to Cheltenham with four good rides on Gold Cup day and that was massive. What my wife did that day was simply not even a green dot on my radar' – even if he did later feel guilty and leave the celebration party early.

The warriors who day after day throw half a ton of horse at obstacles at speed know in their rational moments that they face the possibility of paralysis or even death. To push that thought to the furthermost recesses of their mind they have to convince themselves that they are immortal and invincible. The best way of obliterating a worry that might otherwise intrude or hinder performance is to persuade themselves that nothing in life even climbs on the other end of the scales when balanced against their need to win.

Having spent a little time on the book promotion circuit with Richard Dunwoody I can confirm how charming and rational he is out of the saddle, even if he can rarely bear to go racing since injury forced a premature retirement. But in Richard's unsparing biography *Obsessed* he revealed how his all-encompassing desire to win destroyed all perspective in his life when he was riding. Mistakes in the saddle turned into an extreme form of self-loathing that made him a danger to himself and those around him. After a fall at Newbury when he was tussling for the title with Adrian Maguire he had a row with his wife 'who didn't have a mean bone in her body' in which 'all the malice and the anger came from me'. He played the video of the fall more than a hundred times: 'There was no excuse that was acceptable, no way that I could allow myself even one mistake.' He raged about the house, battering himself against door-frames and walls in self-reproach. Later that month he saw a photo of himself coming in on a winner, sporting a lurid black eye. That injury was not down to a previous fall: it was self-inflicted in another rage after he had been unseated at a fence in front of Huntingdon's stands. A sports psychiatrist once told Dunwoody that he was addicted to speed and danger.

In Tony McCoy's autobiography, the bravest jockey we have seen is chillingly honest about how he became a control freak and engineered endless fights with his wife-to-be Chanelle, driving her frequently to tears or walkouts. He was not, he admits, fit for a relationship:

> All I wanted to do was to ride winners, to ride big winners, ride more winners than anybody, be champion every year and I felt that in order to do that I had to remain focussed, I had to devote everything I had to horses and riding and racing. In my head I wasn't talented enough to be better than everyone else, so I had to work harder than everybody else. There really wasn't room for anything else, there certainly wasn't room for a partner.

He once told a friend: 'It's all right for you, you don't have to live with me.'

Like Dunwoody, McCoy would wear out the rewind button on his video control, constantly replaying the races in which he had not ridden the winner. He convinced himself that he had to do that to see what he could learn. Never mind that the horse might not have been up to it: it had to have been his fault as the rider. He had to go back and back to analyse what his mistake might have been. In what was to me the most revealing comment, McCoy says, 'I did decide that I would ride particular horses a little differently but I think I was punishing myself by watching the tapes as much as I was. I think I felt that if I watched the race again and again I would have served the appropriate penance for getting beaten and then I could move on.'

It was Dessie Hughes, Richard Hughes's trainer father, who pointed out to me as we talked about Cheltenham Festivals past what a significant change the video recording has wrought in riders' lives. To me, some riders' obsessive use of them has become akin to the self-flagellation of medieval monks obsessed with their supposed sins. Yes, the videos have improved overall standards in race riding but how good are they, you sometimes wonder, for the state of mind of the perfectionists at the top of the jockeys' tables? Former jump jockey Warren Marston, somebody who always gave a horse a decent ride without ever expecting to reach the highest echelons of his profession, put it into perspective for me one day when he said:

> Lads come into the weighing room, a horse has fallen with them and you'd think their world has ended. I say, 'Watch the football tonight. Someone will miss a penalty but they'll be on the field the next day ...' You've split-seconds to make a decision and sometimes horses do go on the floor because of a rider. Too many people think every jockey can ride every race and never make a mistake. But you mustn't be frightened of making a mistake.

The will to win and the ability to transmit that to a horse is admirable, crucial perhaps. But some just can't help themselves from taking it to a dangerous degree. When Tony McCoy broke his back in January 2008, most people would have chosen three months in plaster followed by a slow recovery. He opted for the fast track, the insertion of metal plates in his vertebrae, in the hope of getting back in action by the Cheltenham Festival in March. As AP looked for ways of speeding the healing process following his operation, former trainer Charlie Brooks recommended cryotherapy, the use of a cold chamber subjecting the body to extremes of temperature. Taking the treatment, Tony McCoy inquired what was the lowest temperature anybody had endured and was told that the footballer Shefki Kuqi had managed to get down to a temperature of minus 145 degrees. McCoy of course had to beat that: despite the fact that he already had burn marks all over his body, including his testicles, he managed a three-minute session at minus 150 and he was, of course, back riding seven days before the Cheltenham Festival. After such a massive operation the consequences of a fall could be serious, but the thought of not riding at Cheltenham never occurred to him – and that despite his reflection: 'I don't think I've ever ridden at a Cheltenham Festival and not got buried – you have to take risks at Cheltenham.'

It is no wonder that riders become obsessives. British jockeys both on the Flat and over jumps face two added strains compared to other sportsmen. Cricketers, cyclists and footballers don't have to torture their bodies to get down to riding weights which are totally unnatural for their frames, nor do they have to travel the length and breadth of the land daily to around 50 racecourses, often after having risen at an unearthly hour to ride work for a trainer who needs them to familiarise themselves with particular horses. Both those added strains – and perhaps the regularity of champagne-fuelled celebrations where tongue-tied country boys can find themselves mingling with the rich and famous – increase the possibility of alcohol or drug dependence. And in what sport would you find large numbers of its participants as smokers: jockeys smoke as an alternative to food, as an appetite suppressant.

Again, many riders' life stories reveal the strains. Blessed with the softest of hands in the saddle, jump jockey Timmy Murphy is a shy man to whom social exchange does not come easily. Off the course he used to fuel himself with booze to counteract that, and the alcoholism to which he finally admitted reached its most disastrous point when he got drunk on a flight back from Japan early in 2002. Amid other offensive behaviour, little of which he could recollect, he molested a female flight attendant and earned himself several months in Wormwood Scrubs wondering if he had a future. Fortunately the racing community, without condoning the offences, kept things in perspective. While he was away serving his sentence, fellow jockey Andrew Thornton refused to allow anyone else to hang their silks on Murphy's peg. Alcoholics Anonymous, leading owner David Johnson and the trainers who continued to use Timmy Murphy when he came out have enabled the talented rider to rebuild his career. Good for them and good for him.

A comeback I thrilled to particularly was that of Irish jockey Bobby Beasley. A series of bad falls, difficulty controlling his weight and the drink forced his early retirement. He ballooned to fifteen stone. But AA and his friends helped Beasley restore his mental and physical fitness and as he started scratching for rides, Pat Taaffe was looking for an experienced jockey to handle the talented tearaway Captain Christy. In 1974, with a couple of wins in novice chases and a couple of falls behind them, Beasley and Captain Christy took on stars like Pendil and The Dikler in the Cheltenham Gold Cup.

A canny instinct had Beasley move out from behind the leader High Ken just before that horse fell three out, bringing down the luckless Pendil. Captain Christy jumped the second last well but then hit the final fence with his chest. Crucially, Beasley gave him a few strides to settle before setting off up the hill after The Dikler, who always stayed on well. They caught him and went away on that merciless run-in to win by five lengths. Although many in the crowd had lost their money on Pendil and The Dikler, Beasley and Captain Christy were given a hero's welcome. The grateful Beasley reflected, 'As the crowd gave me three cheers I was thinking less of the actual victory than my gratitude to Alcoholics Anonymous and the others who had helped me to knock the booze and use racing as a means of rehabilitation.' When he retired again from the saddle Beasley showed how far his recovery had come by running a pub. Friends say he was in the habit of coming down in the morning, eyeing the optics behind the bar and saying, 'You little bastards thought you were going to get me, but you didn't.'

It isn't only jump jockeys who face injuries that can sometimes trigger other problems. In April 2008, for example, I talked to Flat race jockey Robert Winston who at only 28 had already been through as many ups and downs as a fever victim's temperature chart. The jockey, who started his racing life riding ponies bareback around burnt-out cars on the council estates of Finglas near Dublin, had three years before been leading the jockeys' championship in August. With 98 winners already in the bag he seemed likely to become champion. Then he suffered a fall at Ayr in which he smashed both his upper and lower jaws. His title hopes ended that afternoon and months of enforced idleness saw him spiral into alcoholism. He was, in his own words, in a big black hole drinking himself to death.

What made the Ayr accident especially hard to take was that it was the second time Winston had broken his jaw. His reins had broken and he had gone 'out the back' in an accident at Haydock: it was during the three months lost then that his alcohol problems had begun. He had worked his way out of that but by the time of the Ayr accident things were going awry in his personal life – 'Everything seemed to catch up with me' – and he had made a mistake in a race by dropping his hands too soon. Those of us who don't have to steer horses at speed and do their thinking for them forget what a precious commodity confidence is. It only takes a couple of worries to start nibbling away at it.

In February 2007 Robert Winston's problems were compounded when he was banned for a year for passing information, although it was a lesser sentence than those meted out to others because there was no suggestion that he had ridden any horse to lose. Robert Winston too has battled back and has ridden for plenty of top trainers since his enforced absence, but his story is symptomatic of the pressures and potential pitfalls faced by today's jockeys.

The most spectacular example of redemption we have seen recently is of course that of 2012 champion jockey Richard Hughes. The 5ft 9in jockey has always had to watch his weight. Asked one day at Newbury what he had on his breakfast toast, he replied, 'Salt and pepper.' Having read the biography he put together with the *Racing Post*'s Lee Mottershead, most people would wonder how his wife Lizzie ever came to marry him, even more why she stayed with the character he admits to having been until he kicked the booze.

Hughes charted in relentless detail how riders like him and the equally talented Johnny Murtagh have first taken to alcohol for its dehydrating effect and then become dependent both on the booze and on diuretics (or 'piss pills' as they call them in the weighing room) in their efforts to mount the scales at a riding weight. In Richard's case the crisis came when after a bottle and a half of champagne, followed by fourteen piss pills (most jockeys would stop at three), he passed out in an Ascot car park toilet shortly before one of the biggest races of the year, the King George VI Stakes.

Riding, he said, was easy. Controlling his weight was the hard bit. He drank champagne as if it were fruit juice, using its dehydrating effect to keep his weight down and to help suppress his appetite. He wrote:

The more you drink, the more dehydrated you become. Not only does it dehydrate, it slows the rate of rehydration while also increasing the need to pee. Given that up to 60 per cent of a person's weight is water, getting rid of that water will inevitably trigger weight loss. For a jockey that is bingo.

Among the downsides of this lifestyle was the fact that 'Piss pills make you feel nauseous, woozy and weary. They could leave you with severe cramp. They could suck out every last jot of energy from your body. But they also made you lighter, albeit not for long.' Come the morning and a drink of water, and the weight was back on again.

The other problem was that Richard Hughes's excesses designed to keep down his weight turned him into an alcoholic. 'I thought alcoholics drank from bottles concealed in brown paper bags,' he recounted. 'It turned out that they came in all shapes and sizes. One of them was a 5ft 9ins Irishman.' Every aspiring young jockey should read Richard Hughes's book, not just for his race-riding advice but much more for the lifestyle advice he has to impart.

The jockey's life is one of quite unnatural strains. More medical and dietary help is available these days and the Jockeys' Association does much to warn riders of the potential perils. But it was intriguing to hear the highly successful trainer Mark Johnston in 2006 state his belief, 'I've always believed that if I wanted to give up training horses and instead train jockeys I could create a champion jockey ... I think there's a desperate lack of lifestyle coaching and management where jockeys are concerned.'

But there is pressure and pressure. Keith Miller, the Australian fast bowler had flown Mosquitoes over Germany in the Second World War, an experience, he said, that gave him perspective. He said, 'When athletes these days talk of pressure they only reveal what they don't know of life. They've never had a Messerschmitt up their arse. That's pressure.'

Dean Gallagher

Keeping your weight down to improbable levels and forcing your body back into physical action too soon after injury imposes formidable strains on jockeys. But their lifestyles sometimes bring challenges of a different kind too and I encountered jockey Dean Gallagher several times as he met some of those.

Life is really about how we recover from our mistakes. The best example I ever heard was provided by the tenor

Lauritz Melchior. Singing in Lohengrin he was supposed to conclude an aria by jumping on a giant swan and gliding off the stage. Unfortunately he was too late and the swan had gone, whereupon he turned to the audience and inquired, 'Anybody know the time of the next swan?'

Dean too didn't do too badly recovering from mistakes, some made by others, others which he made himself, and I remember the special quality of the cheers when he rode Teaatral into the Sandown winners' enclosure after winning the valuable Tote Hurdle in February 1999. The racing world was enfolding one of its own to its collective bosom and showing once again that it cared for the gutsy 29-year-old with the cherubic grin.

'For more than a year now,' I wrote, 'Dean Gallagher has lived with a nightmare':

In January 1998 police officers came knocking at his door before dawn. Along with two other jockeys he was arrested in connection with an investigation into alleged doping and race-fixing. Since then the other two have been released from the investigation but though no charges have been brought against Dean or anyone else, he has to report to the police yet again on March 10.

Race riders are under relentless scrutiny for every minute they are on the course and living under the kind of scrutiny he has supported for a year would have broken a lesser man. Instead, in this test both of Dean Gallagher and the racing fraternity, both have emerged with real credit.

It would not have been the same in politics. When the rumours start to circulate, the lunch dates there dry up rapidly. Those due to appear on platforms with you suddenly discover important appointments elsewhere. Former friends pass by on the other side of the street. But when I spoke to Dean an hour before his Sandown triumph it was a different tale he had to tell. Racing actually does live up to the belief that a man is innocent until proven guilty.

Not one of the trainers he had ridden for before his arrest has failed to continue supporting him. 'Had I not had that kind of support I don't know that I would have been able to handle it.' Day in, day out it has been difficult, he admits. At first he lived with the fear of being abused as he rode a mount around the paddock. But never once has he had a bad response.

'When I rode my first winner after all this happened I was heading back into the paddock wondering what kind of reception I would get – boos or jeers or what. Instead it was like coming in after winning a race at the Cheltenham Festival – enormous cheers and congratulations and calls of "Keep it up" and "We're behind you". It sent shivers down my back. It makes you feel good and want to keep battling on.'

The choice was simple, said Dean. 'You can either go down or try to keep going and I have always had a never-say-die attitude. Nobody has ever given me anything for nothing. I've always grafted since I was an apprentice. I've known nothing but hard work and this has given me the inspiration to keep going ... In a weird, silly way I love it. People who didn't know me before are saying "Let's have a look at him and see how he rides". I'm riding the winners and I've gained respect from quite a lot of other trainers.'

There wasn't that much to prove anyway. Having been a pony racing champion in Ireland, Dean Gallagher, dreaming of a career as a Flat jockey, began as an apprentice with Jim Bolger. Increasing weight forced him into a career change and he worked for six months with Dessie Hughes to see if he would like the jumping world. He has been in love with it ever since. In England he began with Rod Simpson and then worked for Jenny Pitman before Charlie Brooks took him on as second rider to Graham Bradley at Uplands. He rode Hennessy Gold Cup winner Couldn't Be Better for Brooks and partnered quality horses like Royal Athlete, on whom he won the Long Walk Hurdle, for Jenny Pitman. A winning Gold Cup ride remains his ambition: 'That race is the pinnacle. From the word go it is so fast. I've ridden in top-class hurdle races but in that race you just can't afford to miss a beat, you can't miss a stride. When you come back afterwards you are drained. That is the race I dream about' ...

Understandably Dean would not, could not talk about the police investigations. But full face on I found a man who was confident of being cleared and in the meantime the likeable Gallagher has showed his mettle by riding more than 30 winners this season, putting him on schedule to beat his previous season's best of 43. He has shown character, but so has the racing world. It may not be a world in which nobody has ever bent a rule. It is not peopled entirely by those who would take first place in the queue for spotless surplices at the Pearly Gates. But racing's principled treatment of Dean Gallagher makes even a part-timer proud to be part of it.

That, it turned out, was only episode one of Dean's one-man soap opera. He continued to hold his head up. He rode 51 winners that season amid the pointing fingers and the whispers. A couple of months later he was indeed told that, like the other riders concerned, he had no case to answer on the race-fixing charges. But it had not all been as easy as Dean had made it look and he paid a price.

To meet his legal fees he had to sell the first house he had ever bought: closing the front door for the last time, he said, was a scene forever etched on his memory. To help fuel his bravado through the bad times he also turned to drink and then to use of a little white powder.

That was not just a mistake, it was a disaster. A jockey on drugs is a danger to others as well as himself and a six-month ban followed his first positive test. Again Dean Gallagher worked his way back. Again some good people refused to cast him into the wilderness and when he came back he rewarded owner Paul Green and trainer James Fanshawe by winning the 2002 Champion Hurdle on the quirky Hors La Loi II. I caught up with Paul just after the race and his first thought was for his jockey: 'Today is Dean's day. He's fought and he's never given in. The guy was on the rocks and he's back again. He's a superb jockey.' But then the Bad Fairy struck once more. In France Dean Gallagher once more tested positive for cocaine and this time, at the age of 33, he was banned from riding for eighteen months. Most of us thought we had seen the last of the compact, muscular bundle that is Gallagher in the saddle, a horseman who blends with his mount, creeping quietly through a field of jumpers to strike after the last fence. The professional obituaries were written. Dean's self-worth fell to pieces and he felt like crawling under a stone.

But trainer Richard Hannon offered him stable work and PR opportunities with owners. Richard Dunwoody counselled him not to write off his racing life, warning him 'You're a long time retired'. The eighteen months passed and then back came the Good Fairy. As Dean's ban expired, François Doumen's jockey son Thierry suffered a shoulder injury which ended his career, and his father hired Dean to ride his jumpers. More opportunities followed with François Cottin and Gallagher's career was extended, largely in France, until he retired at 40 in 2009.

Of course he was an idiot to have drifted into the use of cocaine in the first place. Burning your boats not just once but twice isn't exactly a career enhancement. But you can see the strains he faced and in the end it was a remarkable story of one man's rediscovery of self-worth and of the racing community's ability to rescue one of its own.

Kieren Fallon

Teachers tell you that it is the ones in the class with a little bit of naughtiness who are the most interesting. In racing, the characters who tangle regularly with the authorities, the ones who sail a little close to the wind from time to time and finish up on the front pages as well as the sports pages often have a particular appeal. Over jumps Graham Bradley intrigued me. I enjoyed his cheerful company when writing my book on Lambourn and I was saddened that one of the most talented horsemen we ever saw in the saddle also got himself banned for years for associating with the wrong people. Racing folk remain equally divided, it seems, about the character of former champion Flat jockey Kieren Fallon. It is harder for part-time racing writers to get to know jockeys than it is with the more regularly available trainers. I have only ever had brief conversations with Kieren but I have followed him closely, equally fascinated by his talent and by the turbulence of his career.

Fallon has figured in court cases, he has been banned for drug-taking, he has had to spend time in clinics to cope with a drinking problem, he has won and lost jobs as stable jockey to three super-power trainers and he has mixed with some of the wrong people. But he also possesses a supreme talent and he has somehow never lost his public appeal.

When it emerged the day after he had shown ice-cold nerve to win the Prix de l'Arc de Triomphe on Dylan Thomas that he was facing a second lengthy ban for cocaine use, many predicted that Fallon's career was over. But it was not. The week before he returned to the saddle the *Racing Post* ran a week-long series on Fallon and the day he came back the gate at Lingfield doubled. Now in 2013 he is being classed as a 'veteran' rider but he is still first choice for Luca Cumani and he has been drawing rave reviews for some of his performances.

When Henry Cecil chose his new stable jockey in 1996 I told *Spectator* readers:

> The racing world has affected to be much surprised that Henry Cecil, England's most successful trainer, should have chosen Kieren Fallon, the hot-headed bad-boy, as his stable jockey for next season. It has created the sort of consternation that Tony Blair might by appointing Dennis Skinner as Chancellor of the Exchequer or the Queen by opting for Max Clifford as the Press Secretary at Buckingham Palace.
>
> The stepson of Sir Cecil Boyd-Rochfort, training in Noel Murless's old yard, Cecil in some ways personifies the racing Establishment. But what those now fluttering their fans forget is that it takes real determination as well as ability to collect as many trainer's titles and as many top races as he has done. This is a man dedicated to winning and all the more so since his falling-out with the Maktoums made him determined this season to show he was as good as ever without their horsepower.
>
> I wrote earlier this year that if I had to choose a

jockey to ride the horse carrying my last fiver it would be Kieren Fallon and Cecil has clearly recognised a fellow spirit in the will-to-win department. Together they could produce a formidable racing chemistry. Henry Cecil has been training English Classic winners since Bolkonski took the 2,000 Guineas in 1975, at a time when the accomplished Luca Cumani was Cecil's assistant. Those who have preceded Fallon as stable jockey include Lester Piggott, who was forced to part ways with the stable when the volcanic Daniel Wildenstein ruled in one of his periodic eruptions that Lester would never ride a horse of his again. There was the silky smooth Joe Mercer, the brilliant young American Steve Cauthen and at one stage that underrated horseman Greville Starkey.

To those who wonder how Cecil will cope with the wilder side of his new acquisition, one experience with Starkey surely offers a clue. The trainer, jockey and owner Lord Dunraven once went to the Mirabelle to celebrate after winning a big race at Deauville with the filly Katie Cecil. Starkey, who had been wasting hard to take the mount, was somewhat affected by the fine wine and began to perform his celebrated imitation of a barking dog. Noting that the other diners appeared a touch put out by this, Cecil handled it with aplomb. As the bill was requested he looped his napkin around Starkey's neck and led him, on all fours and still barking, to the door ...

But to return to racing: what raises eyebrows over the Fallon appointment is that he has been notorious for the shortness of his fuse and the regularity of his clashes with racing's ruling authorities. The most notorious was the six-month ban he received for pulling fellow jockey Stuart Webster from his saddle after a finish at Beverley in 1994. Their weighing-room exchanges afterwards, it seems, were not confined to the verbal. After another fracas when Fallon went for a gap that wasn't there at Haydock, his eight-day ban cost him the chance of his first century of winners. Even this season there was trouble when Fallon failed to turn up for a Jockey Club inquiry after riding when his medical book pronounced him to be 'unwell'. But the jockey himself, who sensibly spent his six-month suspension honing his skills by work-riding in California, reckons that at 31 he has settled down.

It is worth remembering that Joe Mercer, Steve Cauthen and Lester Piggott all won the jockeys' championship while riding for Cecil and I believe that Ladbroke's opening offer of 4-1 against Fallon winning it next season is a price worth taking.

Fallon parted from Henry Cecil amid lurid tabloid headlines about the trainer's wife, and the Cecils later divorced. Kieren Fallon then rode for another Newmarket giant, Sir Michael Stoute. Again there were run-ins, over timekeeping and reliability. But there were also some sublime moments of success before Fallon was attracted back to his native Ireland to ride for Aidan O'Brien and the Coolmore team. Among the great moments from the Stoute days was Fallon's victory on Kris Kin in the 2003 Derby. I wrote then:

Fame of a sort is so easily acquired today. Minor celebs can fashion a career from little more than getting out of taxis in short skirts. A couple of gossip-column mentions can briefly make a chef fashionable enough to charge three times what his food is worth. So let us celebrate real quality when we see it, as those of us lucky enough to be at Epsom on Derby Day did in the richest race ever run in Europe.

The magic of racing is that the truth is often so

much more exciting than the fiction. This year's Derby was won by a horse Kris Kin who is described by his highly experienced trainer Sir Michael Stoute as one of the laziest he has ever trained, running for only the fourth time in his career. The horse is owned by Arab businessman Saeed Suhail, who had been happy for the trainer to scratch it from the race last autumn and then buy his way back in five days before the race by paying a £90,000 supplement. And it was ridden by a jockey, Kieren Fallon, who was not long ago dropped off his horses by that same owner, a jockey who nearly lost the use of his arm in a horrific accident three years ago and who spent 30 days of the past winter in a clinic sorting out an alcohol problem, but who after spending six years grafting for his first 40 winners has become a towering presence in his sport, a sure bet for the jockeys' championship as long as he wants to keep chasing it. Fallon has worked for his fame and deserves every minute of it.

Kieren's ride on Kris Kin was a truly great riding performance. The horse was over-excited at the start, sweating copiously, but somehow Kieren kept him calm, knowing that he would be asking questions of him early in the race.

All through the Derby Day card the importance of being up with the pace in races on the switchback course was amply demonstrated and Fallon forced his mount to compete from the start, chasing the leading group up the hill. When the scrimmaging started at the top as the field tightened towards the inside rail it became pretty rough. But Fallon is not a man to give quarter and his mount, as he put it afterwards, was 'man enough to take them' when he got a couple of bumps. The Derby course really is a test of character as well as ability.

Round Tattenham Corner Kris Kin was in with a chance but no more. To many of us in the stands it looked at the two-furlong pole as though Fallon had been pushing for a while, but he says he could feel that when he dug deep his mount was going to answer. It was then that the genius of a great jockey's split-second racing decisions showed. He sensed the leaders had gone for home early and rather than going hell for leather after them he waited, determined not to ask the final question too soon. I wrote:

> It was the kind of decision that could only be made by a jockey full of confidence, a jockey riding the way Fallon is doing this season, as if he has been clapped on the shoulder by the Almighty and told that it is his destiny to win. A couple of hundred yards out Fallon galvanised his mount, every muscle in that formidably strong 5ft 4in body of his brought into play to will his mount forward. A horse turned within a few minutes from boy to man answered, stretched and grabbed the ground. They won going away by a length. Saeed Suhail's £90,000 gamble became an £852,000 prize.

For the bookies it was a disaster. When Kieren announced he would be riding Kris Kin the odds tumbled from 25-1 to 14-1. On the day of the race, a massive racecourse gamble clipped that price down to 6-1. As William Hill's representative stated: 'Turnover is through the roof thanks to the open nature of this year's race, but the roof has caved in.' In the old days, the kind of people who bet only twice a year, on the Grand National and the Derby, used to ask what Lester Piggott was riding and plump for his mount. A fair few nowadays probably go for Frankie

Dettori, who is yet to win the race. But now there is a real Fallon Factor.

(Frankie, incidentally, was not letting the fact that he had now ridden eleven Derby losers get to him. I encountered him as he rode down the chute to the course on Muhareb, his mount in the next race. He was singing.)

The most notorious episode in Kieren Fallon's career was his arrest as part of an alleged race-fixing inquiry, a case that when it made it to court was thrown out by the judge. So how was the racing world, ever ready to insist that smoke rarely filters upwards without some combustion beneath, going to behave on his return? We soon knew.

In September 2009 I wrote about his comeback, listing his past misdemeanours and bans, the drink and drug problems, the departures from big stables and the hideous injury which threatened to cost him the use of one arm and left him with a scar from elbow to shoulder.

Should we cheer him or shun him? There was nothing special about the race on Wolverhampton's all-weather track last Friday night, a twelve-furlong handicap won by Paul Howling's Our Kes, nothing special except the fact that the jockey on board had ridden his last winner in Britain back in July 2006, at which point his licence was suspended because police believed he was involved in a race-fixing conspiracy …

If racing had a naughty step it would by now have moulded to fit the Fallon backside. The jockey who so often finds himself in the headlines for the wrong reasons jumps with unerring aim from the frying pan into the fire. A man who can enter a room of 40 people and, by his own admission, somehow end up talking to the dodgiest character there, he could almost list hara-kiri as a hobby.

When the last drug offence was revealed one headline summed up the rest: 'Fallon: no way back'. Some of the best judges in the sport wrote his racing obituary: 'He will be yesterday's man by the time his suspension expires in the late summer of 2009'. Yet now Fallon is racing again. The *Racing Post* devoted a week of special features to his return. The Lingfield gate nearly doubled on the day he started riding again. And the racing authorities, who could have gone on pursuing him over matters revealed in the failed court case, have instead agreed to his resuming riding, albeit subject to random drug tests and with his acceptance that he has in the past been 'reckless' in his attitude to passing inside information.

They are right to do so, partly because a man who has served his time must be allowed the chance of redemption but also because his is a sublime talent. In an insightful biography of Fallon Andrew Longmore revealed the insecurities which have dogged the plasterer's son from rural Ireland who left school barely able to read and write. But despite those insecurities and a slow start in racing Fallon has ridden fifteen British Classic winners and won the jockey's championship six times. His life out of the saddle has sometimes been a disorganised shambles but when riding he is utterly controlled. He may have had trouble coping with his own demons but he has many times shown a sympathetic genius at sorting out the minds of difficult horses.

Fallon is the strongest, most focussed jockey I have ever seen. Ice-cool rides like that on Kris Kin in the Derby and Hurricane Run in the Prix de l'Arc de Triomphe will live in my mind forever. He owes racing, but he deserves one more chance. Let us pray the demons don't get at him again.

Trainers

Paul Nicholls' chief patron Paul Barber once offered the intriguing thought that it is the lesser jockeys who tend to make the best trainers: 'Jockeys who haven't been successful have the time to see what is going on, to think, to watch, to pick up an awful lot so that when they go into training they have it half thought out.'

It is not, obviously, a hard and fast rule. Fred Winter was both champion jockey and champion trainer in his time. David Nicholson was one of the top riders and he took the trainers' championship too. Jonjo O'Neill not only rode Dawn Run to success in both the Gold Cup and the Champion Hurdle, the only horse ever to achieve that double, he has also trained 22 Festival winners himself. He remains the only man to have both ridden and trained 100 winners in a season. But to take just a few random examples, those two supremely talented Flat jockeys Pat Eddery and Walter Swinburn have never won so many, nor such high quality races as trainers as they did when they were in the saddle. Neither Tom Dascombe, who rode just 96 winners in his ten years as a jump jockey, nor Clive Cox were names to conjure with in their riding days but they were soon on a rapid upward trajectory as trainers. The same applies now to David O'Meara.

Having over the years visited yards up and down the country, I have a huge admiration for those who achieve success as racehorse trainers. Good jockeys are usually born with an instinctive flair, which the best ones then develop with application and experience. But many who have made the switch to training, as Mouse Morris and Jamie Osborne have done, concede that a jockey's life is very much simpler. As a jockey you ride your race, chuck the reins at a stable lad, utter a few banalities to the connections and off you go. As Mouse says, 'When I became a trainer I had to stay around afterwards and explain what had gone wrong.' Soon after Jamie switched roles, he told me that his head lad Ron Thomas was head of personnel and his secretary Jenny was head of the office:

> I'm head of marketing, I'm head of communications and I'm head of the work programme. In a normal business this size you would have finance and marketing directors. In racing that's me – and I'm not trained for any of them.

Young trainers I met in their early days like Jamie and Harry Dunlop confessed to over-eagerness as they learned on the job. Harry Dunlop told me, 'I galloped the tripes out of one or two of them before they ever saw a racecourse: now most of mine improve for their first run.' He added, 'Winning first time out can be the kiss of death anyway. You've then got to go on to higher company before they've got the experience to cope with it.'

Even experienced handlers worry about whether they are doing it right. I remember Mick Channon on the gallops when he was preparing Flashy Wings for the 1,000 Guineas in a spring so cold, he complained, that they'd found two dead polar bears in a thicket. 'The last two gallops aren't for the horse at all,' he said, 'they are for you. You wouldn't want to be going to a Classic with a horse that wasn't fit, looking a prat.'

Often on the racecourse I am with a pack of media folk in the winners' enclosure talking to owners, trainers and jockeys after a race victory. Most of my fellow scribes have to concern themselves with future plans for the successful animal: I love to hear too about the preparation for the victory and the tactical choices, the wider reflections from a trainer's race-reading. Some trainers are good at articulating what they do; many are not. Among my favourites are Mark Johnston and John Gosden.

I remember John telling us one day that Ascot, with its short finishing straight, makes a jockey look a genius or an idiot, rarely anything in between: 'At Ascot when you get shuffled back to last you have one choice: stay on the rail and pray for a gap, because if you attempt to come around the field you will always be the unlucky third.' At Goodwood when his natural front-runner Mutahir won, he explained how he always worked him from behind at home: 'If you work a front-runner in front they never really learn how to relax and use their stride properly.'

Horses are not the robust creatures they look to be from a Saturday afternoon armchair in front of the TV. They are frighteningly delicate animals bred over 300 years to install the maximum engine in the most streamlined frame – a recipe for constant injury and breakdown. It is an achievement to get most of them to the racecourse, let alone win a race with one. Even when you do have quality horses a mystery virus can blow in and lay low your yard for a season or more. Then there are the staff to manage, often including a fair proportion of restless itinerants. One Newmarket chaplain claimed to have encountered a lad who had been in every stable except the original one in Bethlehem.

On top of that trainers must bear in mind the competition for the leisure pound: they have to be astute marketing directors and public relations paragons, patrolling the racecourse bars and the right dinner tables in the hope of increasing their orders for the sales. Sometimes that gets taken to extremes. One comely female trainer was said to have kept one elderly patron for years by supplying services of a strictly after-dinner nature. I am sure that it works the other way too: I once heard a lady at Kempton confide to her companion as the elegant François Doumen went to saddle a horse that she wouldn't mind at all if he'd been coming to saddle her too. It brought to mind the tale of the Lambourn dinner party at which the conversation had turned to the rights and wrongs of pre-marital sex. 'I didn't sleep with my wife before we were married,' said one upright owner to his trainer, 'did you?' 'I am not sure,' came the unthinking reply, 'remind me of her maiden name.'

One thing has always struck me as unfair. Given the days, weeks and months that a trainer has to devote to his charges compared with the jockey's few minutes in the saddle, it does not seem right that they are rewarded with virtually the same percentage of the winnings – especially when the quality of a well-prepared horse has given the jockey virtually an armchair ride. It was a different matter in the days when most horses were ridden by retained stable jockeys who had been true working partners, helping to develop the horses step by step. Nowadays the dominance of the jockeys' agent providing the top ten riders with a much bigger proportion of the best rides leaves little room for that kind of mutual loyalty, although some trainers still see it differently. When I visited her yard, Emma Lavelle told me, 'There's nothing more irritating for an owner than having a jockey get off a horse and say "If only I'd known him a bit better ...".'

There is of course no rigid set of rules for training: different approaches work. Emma, for example, is against what she calls the 'picnic in the woods' approach, insisting, 'Horses like routine. Magical mystery tours just wind them up.' But Henrietta Knight used to send her string off through the woods in twos and threes to make their lives more interesting and you can hardly question her results.

Lambourn

The first racing book I wrote was a portrait of Lambourn, *Valley of the Racehorse*, published in 2000. Poring over every available racing biography and memoir over the years I had long been thrilled by the over-the-wall rivalry of Fulke Walwyn and Fred Winter, which had given Lambourn its profile. Jenny Pitman's breakthrough achievements had added a new lustre while on the Flat Peter Walwyn had won the Derby with Grundy and Barry Hills had taken every other English Classic as he built a racing dynasty. Just up the road from Barry his chum Nicky Henderson had won three consecutive Champion Hurdles with See You Then and pretty well every other race worth winning at the Cheltenham Festival. In 1995 Kim Bailey had brought off the Gold Cup and Champion Hurdle double.

I spent a year in and out of Lambourn talking to owners, jockeys, trainers and stable lads, with many a convivial evening in the Malt Shovel pub or the Hare and Hounds run by Henry Cecil's twin brother David, a figure every bit as elegant and stylish as the great Newmarket trainer.

I tried to depict a year in the collective life of the Lambourn community and 1999/2000 turned out to be an eventful one indeed with huge Cheltenham success, another Classic for Barry Hills, the unwarranted involvement of Lambourn figures in corruption trials and the passing of the training baton from Jenny Pitman to son Mark. But what was just as fascinating to me as getting into the top stables and seeing how they were run was hearing about racing as it used to be from some great veterans.

Three of them, all now sadly passed on, I remember with special affection and respect.

Doug Marks had been in Lambourn since 1962 and was certainly the only trainer there to have ridden two Classic winners, which he did as an apprentice in 1940. Dick Francis could not have made up his career.

Doug's father, a First World War veteran, had written to the Prince of Wales for help and his son was taken on as an apprentice by royal trainer William Jarvis. 'I was four stone and that was mostly head. Father took me to the stables saying I loved horses but actually I'd never seen one. I was so useless I was on the stable pony for eighteen months.' When the Prince of Wales visited and inquired after young Marks the trainer said he was thinking of giving him a ride soon. 'I rode a winner at Newcastle and nobody said "well done" because the money wasn't down.'

The young apprentice fell in love with a yearling and the trainer gave way to his entreaties to be allowed to look after her. Known in the yard as 'Judy', she was named Godiva and she was a handful. She kept dumping other riders so he was allowed to ride her in a Classic trial, which they won at 16-1. He had a fiver on himself.

Next time out with someone else riding Godiva refused to start 'and literally pissed all over the starter'. Then jockey Jackie Crouch was killed in a plane crash and Marks was put back on, duly beating a filly ridden by Gordon Richards, who had won the Queen Mary by ten lengths. After a third in the Middle Park when she had been off work with a blood blister he agonised all winter if he might get the ride in her three-year-old year. 'When jockeys came to the stable and looked at her I felt as a man does when someone else eyes your woman.' Eventually Jarvis told him he would ride her in the 1,000 Guineas, saying, 'For God's sake don't do anything stupid because if you do it won't reflect on you because you're only a little boy.' Doug Marks won the race by five lengths, after impudently shouting 'Come on Gordon' as he passed the champion jockey.

When Godiva then ran in the Oaks Trial at Lingfield he was told the other jockeys were conspiring to force him to make the pace. He did so, but only at half speed and Godiva had enough left to win all the same. Then came the Oaks itself and again he had heard they would try to force him to make all and expose Godiva's stamina. He was ordered into line at the tapes but dropped her in behind anyway as they broke and was well last at the first turn. It didn't worry him: 'When you're in a Rolls-Royce you don't worry about cyclists on the road ahead.'

Trainer Jarvis was on top of the stands and when he heard his favourite was last he started down the steps to avoid humiliation by getting lost amid the throng. He was three steps from the bottom when the crowd started to cheer on Godiva as her young rider threaded her through the field to win.

The next phase in Doug Marks's wartime life was a grim one. He told me:

> I went into the Air Force. I wouldn't have been a pilot, I would have been an air gunner and the odds are you would have been talking to my ghost but I got TB in the bone and I was in hospital for three years. You were totally immobilised in an iron and leather frame with your legs in plaster boots. We lost about a third of those being treated. They left you in five years and you either died or got better. When I came out I couldn't walk.

It may have saved his life but nobody wanted a jockey who had been three years in hospital and he finished up driving dumper trucks. Eventually he got back to stable work and survived by punting. One day after much pestering he was allowed to ride a dodgy customer for Jack Holt's father and they finished fourth, full of running. 'Unsaddling the horse the Guv'nor hissed "Be quiet". The horse then won eight of his next nine races, the first time at 100-6.'

Later Jack Holt senior was 'warned off', quite wrongly Doug insisted, and he went training himself, at one stage having thirteen consecutive winners at Newton Abbot.

When Doug trained near Ascot, Jack Holt was his head lad, Reg Akehurst his conditional jockey and David Elsworth too was on the team. Doug won the Chester Cup with Golden Fire, bought for only 400 guineas, and then they backed him at 28-1 for the Cesarewitch. His orders to David 'Flapper' Yates were 'Don't win too far' but Bill Williamson crossed Golden Fire and they finished second. Marks borrowed a tenner to lodge an objection and they were awarded the race.

As those who worked for him soon came to know, Marks was a great practical joker. He once tricked his highly undependable paperboy: for weeks the trainer regularly fed one of his horses from a bowl placed in the paddock on an open newspaper. One day, when the paperboy was late again, he told him, 'You're really upsetting my horse. He gets in a right state if he doesn't get his *Sporting Life* on time.' As the paperboy argued that this was nonsense, Marks spread the paper down on the floor. Immediately the horse trotted over to sniff the paper, looking for his bowl of oats but appearing to be scanning the headlines. After that the papers arrived on time.

When he came to Lambourn Doug Marks, affectionately known around the village as 'Sir Douglas', first bought the Uplands Stable later made famous by Fred

Winter, paying £17,000. He trained for many showbiz personalities including Danny La Rue, Frankie Vaughan and Jimmy Tarbuck. He gave Tarbuck a winner with his first runner Tattie Head at 8-1, with Tarbuck and his solicitor each putting on £600. The comedian sent Marks a case of vintage champagne and a note saying, 'I hope we can do this on a regular basis.' Said Doug, 'I think he expected it to run once a week like a greyhound.' Tarbuck once said that he had to have horses in training with Doug Marks to stop the trainer taking over his job as a comedian.

* * *

One thing that was striking in visiting Lambourn thirteen years ago was to see the number who still called out from the passing strings to a small figure with a well-weathered, outdoorsman's face, a man as adept on the dance floor in his 70s as he was in the saddle in his 30s – the one-time champion National Hunt jockey Jack Dowdeswell, who took the title with 58 winners in 1947. Modesty personified, Jack Dowdeswell never made much of his achievement, insisting, 'I am and always was just a stable lad who happened to ride a few winners.' But others recognised it: when I visited Jack and his wife Betty at the time of their diamond wedding anniversary, the card which took pride of place amid many others was one from the Queen.

Hearing Jack Dowdeswell tell the story of his racing life was a reminder not just of the sheer grit required of those who ride over jumps for a living but of the carelessness, even callousness the racing community showed in the past about the meagre rewards for the stable staff who keep the whole show on the road. Some regret the passing of the old-style apprenticeships and the craft-learning that could go with them. But they were also a licence for exploitation.

Jack Dowdeswell had been on horseback since he was four. A tough father who worked with a hunt and then ran a riding school as well as fronting the Craven Arms at Enborne had put him on anything and everything around the pony classes and show-jumping circuits. As Jack put it, 'A lot of parents bought ponies for their Little Lord Fauntleroys and then found they couldn't handle them so I got all the hot ones to ride.'

He arrived in the village at the age of fourteen in 1931, apprenticed to Ted Gwillt at Saxon House in Upper Lambourn on just two shillings a week. 'Why my father ever dreamed of doing it I cannot imagine. It was slave labour fourteen hours a day and I was never taught a thing. I couldn't have gone to a worse stable. He never gave apprentices a chance, he never 'made' a jockey.'

The youngster would get up at 5.30 and go round with the head lad helping with the feeding. Then there would be a cup of tea, mucking out and working around the yard until lunchtime. 'I was the only apprentice so there was the afternoon work when the others went off.' Even in his 70s he could remember his list of tasks in order: Hay. Oats. Carrots. Wood. Chaff. Copper. Mash. And in his spare time he was expected to do the weeding. There was another cup of tea before two hours on evening stable duties, which finished around 7.00pm.

> After that I had to walk down to Lambourn and fetch the Guv'nor's evening paper. There was a station here then. I think I earned my two shillings a week. All I did was ride the yearlings, break them in and ride them away. I learned to ride yearlings well but in five years I probably only did ten gallops. All I ever did was canter.

Stable routine, he said, was much the same as today: first
lot around 7.30am, then second lot and then the 'roughs
and scruffs'. But he did ride three winners from the half-
dozen rides he was given in the first few years by Gwillt and
Marcus Marsh. When Epsom trainer Walter Nightingall
inquired of Jack's father what had happened to the pony-
club star, Dowdeswell senior wrote to Gwillt asking if Jack's
indentures could be transferred to Nightingall. There was
no reply. Eventually the apprentice plucked up his courage and asked for a response. He received just two words
in reply: 'Definitely not.'

At the end of his five years the trainer said to young
Dowdeswell, 'I suppose you'll be staying on then now
you'll be getting £2 5s 0d a week as a lad.' 'Definitely not,'
replied the ex-apprentice, with emphasis, and he left that
night.

He went to Captain Bay Powell at Aldbourne and by
the next day was riding schooling. He began getting more
race rides and rode six winners from just a handful of
opportunities. Shortly after that there was what he called
'a terrible argument'. The trainer asked him to go a good
gallop on a horse that was being schooled over fences,
directly into the wind. He thought this crazy and came
at a steady pace instead. After the bawling out he went
back to the yard for breakfast and was summoned to the
trainer's house.

'I thought it was curtains,' he says. 'Instead he invited
me to come shooting that afternoon. When I said 'I don't
shoot' he said, 'Come and look at the Racing Calendar.'
We never had another cross word. He was the nicest and
the best trainer. I was always straight with him and told
him when I thought I'd ridden a bad race, come too early
or whatever. He would always say, 'Jack, you did your best.'

Although Captain Powell was later 'warned off' after

one of his horses was found to be doped, Jack Dowdeswell wouldn't hear a word against him: 'In those days trainers had to carry the can. He wouldn't have known how to dope a horse.' Jack reckoned he had ridden some horses that were doped and he reckoned he knew who was behind it, but he wasn't saying.

After six years away in the war with the Royal Horse Artillery, Jack Dowdeswell came back in 1946 to win at Wye on his first ride back. The next year he was champion. But it was a different life then. There were no sponsorships or endorsement fees or free cars.

> I think horses ran for me. I was always kind. I didn't like using my whip and the form book told me I was getting results as good as those who did. Though of course if a horse made a mistake I would give it a couple to wake it up. I'd love to be riding today at £85 a ride [as it then was]. When I rode it was three guineas a time and if the race was worth over £85 you got a fiver. But there were no percentages for winning riders. You hoped for a 'present', but there were more promises than presents.

Nor was there then an Injured Jockeys Fund. Back injuries finally forced Jack Dowdeswell to retire from the saddle in 1957, but not before he had broken 50 bones in all. The worst injury was when a following horse virtually ripped his arm from its socket after a fall at Taunton. His wife dashed down from the stands and he was in so much pain he bit through the glove she gave him. When he was eventually given morphine and supposedly out cold, the doctor told his anxiously inquiring fellow jockeys, 'I'm afraid he'll never ride again', at which point Jack sat up and exclaimed, 'Oh yes I bloody well will.' It took him eleven months though to prove it.

* * *

Another sorely missed Lambourn veteran, Snowy Outen, I spent time with both when writing my Lambourn book and later when putting together a biography of Barry Hills, whose head lad he was for many years, having been with Barry from his start-up in 1968. Officially Snowy (whose hair was white from childhood) 'retired' from Barry's Faringdon Place at the age of 70 in 1994. But he went straight back to the yard and continued 'doing his four' or any other tasks he was handed, saying that he would be bored silly just walking his dogs three times a day. The only concession he made was to stop riding out; instead, when the others were legged up, he went to collect the eggs from Barry's chickens. To all of Lambourn's delight, Snowy was at Newmarket leading up the horse when Haafhd, ridden by Michael Hills, was an impressive winner of the 2,000 Guineas ten years later in 2004.

Snowy had started as an apprentice alongside Doug Marks in William Jarvis's stable in Newmarket back in 1938, but this was the first time he had led up a Classic winner. It was Snowy who had legged up all five of Barry's children, two to become trainers themselves and the twins jockeys, on their first childhood mounts.

In a house filled with racing memorabilia like the signed photograph from Steve Cauthen thanking him for his friendship, Snowy showed me the fraying letter from trainer Jarvis to his mother setting out his apprentice terms: £1 0s 0d a month for the first year, rising to £11 3s 4d for the fifth year. Board and lodging were free but 'if you can afford to fit him out with breeches and leggings those are more serviceable than trousers,' wrote the trainer.

As with the other veterans there were calamities along the way. Riding the King's horse Ocean Swell in

1941 Snowy clipped heels with another horse: he had 68 stitches in his head and suffered two broken legs, a fractured skull and a broken shoulder, but he was back riding again before being called up in 1943. Having applied for the Veterinary Corps he was sent to the Mule Corps used for transporting gun parts, even though at 6st 7lb he was too light even to lift shells. There were exercises in Scotland and in Europe, then jungle training in India for an Orde Wingate operation. He volunteered in 1946 for the British occupation force in Japan after Hiroshima, where an officer keen on racing found him 40 gardeners and they laid a racecourse for monthly meetings at which Snowy rode eight winners. Two years in Hong Kong followed, during which Snowy heard the War Office was planning to put down twenty ex-service horses. He arranged for some officers to buy them and start a riding school. When he came home there were stable jobs with Ginger Dennistoun, Florence Nagle and Ian Balding before he began with Barry.

Snowy was not one to believe that everything was better in the old days: 'When I first went in and you did your two you scrubbed your horses to death. You worried them with it. It made them sour, drove them silly.' In Barry's early days in Keith Piggott's old yard, he remembered the horses did not have mangers, just buckets for their water. Snowy never drove a car, so 'My wife and I used to walk up at 9.30 to 10.00pm to ensure that each horse had a full bucket for the night and I would have a pint myself on the way home. If they kicked a bucket over in the night and made a noise it was Barry lying in bed who would hear it and have to go and fill it for them.'

Snowy would be up again in the yard around 5.00am to give the horses a feed before seeing in the lads at 6.30. Not surprisingly, he rated Barry as a master of the training art, telling me, 'He doesn't kill his horses. If work-riders go a stride faster than he wants, he'll go pop. He doesn't want them leaving their races on the gallops. He likes to bring on his horses nice and steadily. It's no good working a horse to death when it's not ready.'

It was from Snowy that I began to get a sense of the rhythms of the training year in a big Flat yard:

> In the spring you bring on the two-year-olds. They tell you themselves if they are going to be early types. As they run, you give them a rest and then you pick them up again. You look at them every night and you can see them maturing. You have your Guineas horses, Classic animals, then you think about Ascot, then Goodwood. After Goodwood [at the end of July] you are beginning to think about the new crop of yearlings.

Snowy was always fascinated by the veterinary side. 'I like to try to find a "leg" before it becomes a "leg",' he said, and he was heartened by the advances in horse care: 'Now they deal with colic by calling the vet and having an injection into the horse's neck. In the old days it was a matter of staying up all night trying to get the horse to break wind and pass a dropping. Once they laid down quiet it was OK.'

He didn't believe in the iron fist approach of his own young days but said that a head lad had to know how to lead. 'They used to rule by the rod, a toe up the backside, but no more. I would never ask a lad to do anything I wouldn't do myself. I believe in manners and in saying please and thank you. Manners help with your staff. But they'll shit all over you if you get too familiar.' Not a mistake the master of Faringdon Place, B.W. Hills, would ever have made.

Clive Brittain

I have rarely had such fun from my racing as during the eighteen months I spent putting together a biography of Clive Brittain. I wanted to write about Clive for many reasons. The first of those was his sheer list of achievements. Not only has he trained the winners of 50 Group One races, including six British Classics, he was, with the magnificent filly Pebbles, the first British trainer to win a race at the Breeders' Cup. He was the first to win the Japan Cup and the second place he achieved in the Kentucky Derby with Bold Arrangement in 1986 still remains the best placing achieved by a British-based trainer.

I wanted to write about Clive too because of the way he broke the glass ceiling. He had been a stable lad with Sir Noel Murless before he set up on his own and in those times former stable lads just didn't do that. To make it as a trainer you needed a background in the services, a nodding acquaintanceship with a reasonable proportion of the entries in Who's Who, an old school tie and a decent legacy. Clive had none of those.

The other reason for telling his story though was a simpler one: every time I saw Clive on a racecourse he was enjoying himself. As the ace American jockey Steve Cauthen told me, 'One of Clive's biggest qualities is that he made everybody around him have a good time. The owners around him were all getting fun.' Says George Duffield, 'He's what racing's all about. He enjoys racing, full stop. Day in, day out. He's so buoyant and full of the joys of spring. He just gets on with the job, no whingeing and moaning. Just goes and does it; what will be will be.'

As everybody kept telling me, Clive and his wife Maureen are simply the nicest people in racing. They live for their horses (and their Labradors Hoover and Sweep) and never say a bad word about anyone. But their achievements are extraordinary. Brought up as one of thirteen children in Calne, Wiltshire, where his father stuffed sausages in the local bacon factory, Clive taught himself to ride by jumping bareback on to Welsh mountain ponies in the field opposite. Soon he was supplementing the family income by helping local horse dealers to break and sell their ponies in Chippenham Market.

For 23 years then Clive was a stable lad to Sir Noel Murless; Maureen was stable secretary. He was never paid more than £17 a week although his canny backing of the Murless horses produced an added annual income of £5,000. He was never even head lad but he was of especial value to the yard where horses like Petite Etoile, St Paddy and Crepello were trained: Clive was the man who could and would ride anything, the natural horseman who sorted out the problem animals. As fellow trainer John Gosden puts it, 'He was as a young man, and probably still is now, the bravest rider there has been. There was nothing he wouldn't get on.' And yet in all his time with Murless Clive was never addressed by his first name, or even by his surname, only by where he came from. It was 'Calne, do this, Calne do that'. No insult was meant, it was just how things were in a more forelock-tugging age.

As Murless approached retirement Clive set up on his own. Within a few years he was the first trainer in Newmarket to have more than 100 horses. A restless innovator, Clive was the first to build an equine swimming pool, the first, says Steve Cauthen, to use horse walkers to warm up his charges before exercise. Especially, he was the first to travel his horses worldwide. It was six years before any other British trainer replicated his Breeders' Cup victory. Clive was hoovering up Group races in Germany and Italy before others had even found the racecourses on a map. As Cauthen told me:

> When I first got to Britain in the late seventies and early eighties, guys like Henry Cecil and even Michael Stoute were taking the attitude 'We would rather stay at home, why bother with abroad?' But Clive saw the opportunity. He started winning these things and it forced other people to follow him because their owners were saying, 'How about it? If he can do it, why can't we?'

Clive is famous for getting his horses out on the heath in the dark while others are still fumbling for their bedside alarms. It is not an affectation. He had to be up before dawn to move the ponies he looked after in his teens, sneaking them back from an owner's grazing before anybody was up to see them. He found too, when handling the awkward cusses in Noel Murless's string, that he achieved the best results by taking them out early alone.

As for becoming Newmarket's dawn-breaker, Clive's long-time pal Willie Carson told me:

> It came about in the days when there were so many trainers in Newmarket and Newmarket Heath was only allowing so many gallops to be opened in order to save the ground. Clive planned to get the best ground by getting there first. Henry Cecil and Michael Stoute might have 50 horses in one lot. If you followed them it was like going up a ploughed field – you had to keep in-between the bushes – so Clive's early start was a clever plan to get the best ground and stop the chance of getting his horses injured. He was looking after his horses.

Clive is famous for his celebration dances in the winner's enclosure, a reaction as eagerly sought by the TV cameramen as Frankie Dettori's flying dismounts. And he is famous too in some eyes for aiming his horses at what others see as over-ambitious targets. Let the purists scoff. Clive's record is studded with successes like Rajeem's 66-1 victory in the Falmouth Stakes, Braughing's 50-1 success in the Cambridgeshire or Terimon's second place in the Derby at 500-1. As he puts it with a quiet smile, 'I've been criticised for tilting at Group One windmills with horses some people reckoned shouldn't be running at that level, but I've managed to knock down quite a few of those windmills.' His is not, of course a policy that is always favoured by jockeys. They would rather have one more on their winner total than the second or third place in a 'black type' race which pleases owner-breeders.

If there is a story which sums up Clive Brittain's attitudes and abilities it is that of the two Royal Ascot victories scored by Radetzky, in the St James's Palace Stakes and the Queen Anne at prices of 16-1 and 25-1.

Clive can't bear unfulfilled potential and Philip Robinson, his long-time stable jockey, told me how much joy Clive obtains from trying to find the key to the awkward horses: 'A lot of horses show ability but don't come up with it on the racecourse. That's one of his real pleasures in life, trying to work them out and, if you like, get one over on the horse, getting them to enjoy their racing.'

In 1976 Clive ran two horses in the St James's Palace Stakes. One was Patris, owned by his first major stable patron Captain Marcos Lemos and being ridden by stable jockey Willie Carson; the other was Radetzky, a cranky horse very much with a mind of his own, owned by banker Curtis Elliott and being ridden by Pat Eddery. Carson had angered Captain Lemos by accepting a retainer to ride the next season for Dick Hern and both owners had wanted Eddery to be on their horse. Both owners too liked their due amount of attention and Clive and Maureen had to mount a diplomatic offensive in the parade ring moving between two mutually suspicious clusters.

Turning for home in the race, Radetzky was in front and Willie Carson set out after him, colliding with the French favourite Earth Spirit on the way. Patris and Radetzky flashed past the post together. There was a long pause for the photo and then a dead heat was declared between the two Brittain-trained horses. Both groups were up in the air cheering and went off for a champagne celebration together. But meanwhile a stewards' inquiry was called.

Captain Lemos had seen Willie bump the French horse and feared Patris was going to be disqualified. He was right. In the end the stewards demoted Patris to third place and Radetzky was left as the sole winner, but Lemos took the decision with good grace and ironically he and Curtis Elliott from then on became good friends.

A dead heat between a trainer's two runners in a Group One at Royal Ascot was remarkable enough. But the sequel was even more so. Two years later Radetzky had been retired to stud but was not attracting too many mares. A few weeks before Royal Ascot in 1978 Curtis Elliott asked Clive to take him back into training. Clive agreed to give it a try and found himself with the big, almost black Radetzky corned up to the eyeballs and behaving like a king.

Fearful that the horse might injure a stable lad, Clive rode him himself, and found he was in a battle of wills with a stallion used to being the boss. He reared, he spooked, he planted. He refused to go in any direction he was asked so in the end Clive backed him all the way to the training grounds, about a mile and a quarter. The horse never got a slap. Clive sensed that every time he attempted to take control the horse tensed up. Eventually they got to the closed Round Gallop. Clive backed him into a hedge and they were off and galloping: the breakthrough had been made. So it went on for session after session, including a gallop at Yarmouth racecourse with the then 9st 10lb Clive in a 10lb saddle riding Radetzky in most of his work.

Says Clive, 'He absolutely cruised past his lead horse and I knew he was as good as before, if not better. *L'amour* had obviously done him the world of good.' Word soon spread at Carlburg House and the staff were on him to a man at all sorts of fancy prices when Radetzky went down to the start for the Queen Anne Stakes at 25-1.

The horse had given trouble going to the start in the past but that day he went down like a lamb for Edward Hide and came back like a lion, making every yard of the running and leaving the rest strung out like the washing as he coasted home four lengths clear. It was a famous victory – and whatever Radetzky had won, Clive had lost 10lbs in the process.

Barry Hills

Of the many racing figures in Lambourn, one who fascinated me from the start was Barry Hills, so much so that ten years after writing my portrait of the village, I persuaded him to let me write his biography. It was not just that Barry had the biggest, most successful team in Lambourn but the sheer dogged character of the man who created a £3 million state-of-the-art training establishment and a racing dynasty, with sons John and Charlie following him as trainers, Richard and Michael among the country's top jockeys and George successful in bloodstock and horse insurance in America.

Few in racing can resist the story of a betting coup that comes off and Barry's breakthrough was founded on one of the classic coups. When he was travelling head lad to John Oxley in the 1960s, Barry used to get together with the head lads to Harry Wragg, Cecil Boyd-Rochfort and Jack Watts and settle on a few 'good things' on which they would invest a few hundred – at a time when he was earning just £25 a week.

Barry's personal pot was augmented among other good 'touches' by successful bets on Sky Diver in the Stewards' Cup at 50-1, on Jack Watts's Ovaltine winning the Ebor at 100-8 and on Harry Wragg's Lacquer taking the Cambridgeshire at 20-1. 'We didn't bet big but we had some yankees and cross doubles. We more or less cleaned up in our own small way,' is how he puts it. But the horse who was to transform his fortunes, literally, was Frankincense, trained by John Oxley and owned by Lady Halifax.

Ex-trainer Syd Mercer, who had proved a shrewd punter with the horses he handled himself, including the famous stayer Trelawny, sent Copper's Evidence, a horse who had won five races in a year, to Oxley to be trained for the 1968 Lincoln Handicap. Although Copper's Evidence was a decent horse, watching the two on the gallops Barry became convinced that Frankincense was far superior.

> One day he gave Copper's Evidence two stone and beat him out of sight. I remember ringing Syd Mercer and telling him about it. But Syd wouldn't have any of it. His words were 'Lad, the Lincoln Handicap trophy is on my sideboard.

At that point Barry went out and started backing Frankincense for the Lincoln:

> We backed him from 66-1 to 5-1 favourite, though he drifted back on the day [to 100-8]. He was a certainty. He worked on Side Hill at Newmarket one day and beat the others out of sight. You didn't need to see any more. We toured round bookmakers' shops putting small bets on everywhere.

Ironically Barry and his punting friends continued to get a decent price because Syd Mercer kept backing Copper's Evidence. They were aided too by the fact that Frankincense had been allotted 9st 5lb by the handicapper and no horse had ever won the Lincoln with more than 9st 1lb.

Come the day of the Lincoln at Doncaster and the Irish-trained Bluerullah, ridden by Lester Piggott, was made favourite. Also fancied for the race was Tom Jones's Waterloo Place. Stable jockey Greville Starkey, who was to become godfather to Barry's twins, had taken some persuading to ride Frankincense rather than Copper's Evidence. With Frankincense's big weight, the plan was for him to swoop late but Starkey found his mount going so well that he sent him on down the centre of the course a furlong out and then held off the late challenge of Waterloo Place by half a length. He said afterwards that from the break he had never doubted his horse would win. Bluerullah burned out early and Copper's Evidence finished fifth.

Barry and his fellow punters didn't celebrate that night. He had his travelling head lad's duties to perform. He has never been famous for displaying his emotions and when I asked him if it had felt like a life-transforming moment he replied, 'I was expecting the horse to win and he did. It was mapped out. It happened. After that it was simply a matter of looking for a stable to buy.'

There was a fun session though the Sunday afterwards when those who had shared the gamble, like Eddie Mills, one of Barry's earliest owners, counted the proceeds from the betting shops at the Mills family home. Said Dorothy Mills: 'All my life I have wanted to take a bath in fivers: now I can!'

The £60,000 which Barry won, worth more than £1.5 million in today's money, enabled him to buy the South Bank Stables in Lambourn Village from Keith Piggott, Lester's father, and set him off on a training career which brought him more than 3,000 winners, including a Prix de l'Arc de Triomphe and five British Classics. The only Classic which eluded him was the Derby, in which Hills-trained horses four times finished second.

Barry is not a loquacious man, rather one of those who prefers to let his achievements speak for him. Nicknamed 'Mr Grumpy' by the family, he is famous for his bollock-ings of jockeys and staff who fail to meet his meticulous standards. His wife Penny has a cushion in their drawing room emblazoned with the slogan 'Sometimes I wake up feeling grumpy and sometimes I let him sleep'. But there is a great deal more to Barry Hills than the occasional gruffness which he has built in as a trademark.

He is a genuinely brave man who fought cancer uncomplainingly for twenty years and in many ways he is a traditionalist, always impeccably turned out whether on the racecourse or the gallops. He would win the best-turned-out trainer award in every race if there was one.

One of my fascinations was trying to understand what made him such a great trainer. Much of it, I was to dis-cover, boils down to instinct and to the fact that he is as consistently patient with his horses as he can be impatient with human failings. Now he has handed over the reins at Faringdon Place to son Charlie, Barry's greatest pleasure is in his garden. The Chelsea Flower Show is as much a fixture in his diary as Royal Ascot, York's Ebor meeting or Doncaster's St Leger and his study holds as many books about horticulture as it does about horseracing. He says that horses are like flowers: 'They bloom when they are ready, you cannot force them.'

He does not overcook his horses at home, he says, preferring to give them 'nice, progressive work'. Overdo things on those stiff Lambourn gallops, he argues, and you will soon be in the workhouse:

> I never ask my horses too much at home. The secret is to get them to peak fitness without really testing them. If you make a horse happy it will generally do well. They must like work and if they are used to doing a good day's work then, like a human, they will be happy.

Barry is no mere traditionalist. Immense thought went into the design of his barns at Faringdon place, where he reckons he took the lessons of Manton and 'Rolls Royced' them. Light and ventilation are calculated to protect the horses from sudden changes in temperature but to ensure regular changes of air so as to avoid infections. They were built with concealed taps in every stall, rubber floors to minimise injury risk, and rails designed to prevent horses getting cast in their boxes.

Back in 1999 he told me that horses like routine:

> They are herd animals. They like company. They like rhythm and routine. The knack is getting them to a peak and keeping them there. You can't push

them. They'll tell you when they can go. They soon
get knocked off colour, especially early in the year
when the weather can change three or four times
in a day. In bad weather you've just got to let them
tick over. Freddie Maxwell used to say 'Never gallop a
horse when the wind is in the north east' and he was
absolutely right. They can't cope with stress.

Happy horses, he argues, will eat up well and can be given
more work to make them fitter, although he does not
believe in over-feeding. Routine is the key: 'They have to
have the temperament and the constitution as well. It's
like training soldiers. Only some will make it. You've got
to get them into a good routine, you've got to get their
heads right.'

John Francome says Barry is 'a proper stockman'
attuned to the rhythms of the countryside. John Hills says
his father never forces horses. 'He has the ability to spot
if they are thriving and taking what he is giving them. He
sees before most people when he needs to back off. He's
got an instinct.' What Barry's team told me was that he
had an extraordinary capacity for looking at a horse and
saying what race he would win with it in several months'
time.

That capacity, it seems, begins very early. Jack Ramsden
told me that Barry was a wonderful judge of a yearling:

I would back him in front of anyone to go and buy
one. He would have a look at a pedigree but he
wouldn't allow it to dominate his mind. The training
and everything else is done on instinct. It's an absolutely natural thing like being able to go into a sales
ring and pick a couple out and end up with the right
ones. Everything is done on instinct. You've either
got it or you haven't. He's got it in bucketfuls.

Paul Nicholls

It takes a lot to keep me away from Newmarket's Champions Day meeting but the prospect of an hour on stage at Cheltenham's Literary Festival with Ruby Walsh and Paul Nicholls talking about Paul's autobiography *Lucky Break* was lure enough in October 2009. The champion trainer's careers master might have been surprised to find the ever-reluctant schoolboy there. When Paul said he wanted to go into racing, he warned him, 'You will never make a living out of horses.' Uh-huh? At the time of the book event, Paul's horses had won some £3.5 million in each of the previous two seasons.

The 'lucky break' occurred when a horse kicked out in a Devon lane in 1989 and painfully shattered Paul's left leg. Not most people's idea of good fortune, but for him it was the turning point towards a training career. Even as he lay awaiting the ambulance he dreamed of the big meals awaiting him in hospital. He had for nine years tortured himself to keep a big policeman's body (both his father and grandfather were in the force) two stone at least below his natural weight in order to go on being a jockey.

Much of his riding life, he admits, was like being terminally ill as he starved, tossed down the 'pee pills' and sweated as he drove to the races in a tracksuit, coat, a woolly hat and bin bags with arm holes cut out, with puddles of perspiration on the floor beneath him.

The champion trainer is unduly modest about his achievements in the saddle, accepting the label of 'journeyman' and saying, 'I was exactly the kind of jockey I would not employ now'. In reality he twice won the Hennessy Gold Cup and had a Welsh National to his credit too. But the second lucky break came when big-time dairy farmer Paul Barber, whose ambition was to milk 1,000 cows and win a Cheltenham Gold Cup, chose Paul from the applicants to be the tenant of Manor Farm Stables in Ditcheat. He now milks 3,000 and Paul has given him two winners of the Gold Cup in See More Business and Denman.

Paul Barber noted that as well as his drive and ambition, Paul had from early on too that touch of arrogance you find in most of those who get to the top.

In the early days Paul used to find it hard watching others ride his horses. He bawled out those who didn't do it exactly as he wanted. Gradually he mellowed, and the long relationship with Ruby Walsh, who had no retainer with the yard, just a gentleman's agreement to a sort of open marriage as he rode also for Willie Mullins in Ireland, was a harmonious one until Ruby's decision in 2013 to focus on the Irish scene for his family's sake.

Gambler Harry Findlay, for a while part-owner with Paul Barber of Denman, named another of his horses Herecomesthetruth because he said that is what you always got from Nicholls. Certainly he is one of the most open in the sport and in his autobiography, excellently crafted by collaborator Jonathan Powell, there are some stark revelations. Nicholls had to be restrained by friends from punching his arch-rival Martin Pipe after Pipe's Cyborgo, ridden by AP McCoy, squeezed See More Business out of a Gold Cup race as he pulled him up injured. Now Paul totally dismisses any conspiracy theory and praises Pipe for leading the way in getting horses fully fit. But he and Pipe never managed to rub along.

Owners looking at the vet's bills for their horses stabled with other trainers will have noted Paul Nicholls' dismissal of trachea washes and blood counts and endless weighing. Fitness is all, he says. 'I do more with a horse in a day than others do in a week', and that can be assessed by eye. He won't delegate the training of his animals to vets.

Of course, with horses like Kauto Star, Denman and Master Minded winning prizes so consistently, Paul was regularly sent the best. But he improves those who seem restricted by breathing problems with a wind operation which vet Geoff Lane calls 'the Nicholls'. His only coy moment on stage was when I asked him who had been given the operation that summer.

Horses

In the end our sport is all about the horses and I was happy to get the chance of telling some of their stories when Icon asked me in 2012 to put together a volume on those I considered to be the hundred best. What was rather more daunting was that they asked me to rank them in order, a near-impossible task when they included both Flat racers and jumpers.

Initially it brought to mind my favourite limerick:

A crusader's wife slipped out of the garrison
And had an affair with a Saracen
She was not oversexed, or jealous or vexed
She just wanted to make a comparison.

Comparisons as they say of course are odious and I certainly set off a few pub arguments when producing as my top ten Arkle, Brigadier Gerard, Frankel, Sea The Stars, Seabird, Kauto Star, Golden Miller, Mill Reef, Sceptre and Red Rum. We went to press with Frankel yet to run over further than a mile. When he had proved even more impressive over ten furlongs I elevated him above Brigadier Gerard to second place for the later paperback version.

In making my choice I was influenced not just by victories amassed and records broken but by how much I judged particular horses had seized the public imagination. All of us, I guess, have our personal lists of horses who have come to mean something special to us, giving us a kind of emotional part-ownership when they performed. Among those for whom I developed a particular affection or admiration were Dawn Run, the incredible mare who remains the only horse ever to have won both the Champion Hurdle and the Gold Cup, Persian War, the much patched-up three-times Champion Hurdler, and Giant's Causeway, who to me was one of the greatest battlers I have seen on a racecourse. Then there was Mill Reef, one of the most graceful movers across the turf, the gorgeous Pebbles, with whom Clive Brittain became the first British trainer to win a Breeders' Cup race, and Best Mate, superbly handled by Henrietta Knight to win three Gold Cups. But here are six horses who somehow became extra special to me.

Mandarin

The first of them, Mandarin, I only ever saw run twice but he was the first horse to make me realise how important courage and tenacity are in a racehorse as well as speed. Like Persian War he was constantly in need of the vets' attentions and like Arkle he ran not just in championship races like the Gold Cup and King George VI Chase but in multi-runner handicaps too.

Owned by Madame Peggy Hennessy and trained by Fulke Walwyn, little Mandarin won the Hennessy Gold

Cup (later a fixture at Newbury) when it was held for the first time at Cheltenham in 1957. He was passed by the Gold Cup winner Linwell at the last but fought back typically up the hill to re-pass him. Four years later, Mandarin won the Hennessy again with the likes of Grand National winner Nicolaus Silver and the Irish National winner Olympia in the field, fencing fast and cleverly despite his top weight and going away on the run-in. There were regular visits to equine A & E departments to have his tendons fired and a stifle bone repaired but in between Mandarin also twice won Kempton's King George VI Chase, in 1957 and 1959, and three times had been second in the end-of-season Whitbread Gold Cup at Sandown.

Peggy Hennessy once declared that she only kept steeplechasers in training in Britain because she wanted to win the Cheltenham Gold Cup and in 1962 Mandarin gave her her heart's desire, winning the supreme championship at the age of eleven and doing it in his accustomed style, gutsily passing Ireland's hope Fortria on that daunting final rise to the winning post. That was his eighteenth victory in Britain but it was his next race which turned Mandarin and his rider Fred Winter into racing immortals.

I was not there but thanks to one of the finest pieces of sporting journalism I have ever read, the report of the race by rider/journalist John Lawrence, later Lord Oaksey, I have always almost felt I was. John Oaksey described in vivid terms how, as they approached the fourth obstacle, the bit in Mandarin's mouth broke and his jockey was left without any contact with the horse's mouth or head. Effectively he had lost brakes and steering. His only handhold was the reins held by the martingale around Mandarin's neck and the neck strap attached to his girth:

The man, with no means of steering but his weight had to rely entirely on grip and balance. The horse, used to a steady pressure on his mouth, had to jump 21 strange and formidable obstacles around a figure-of-eight course with his head completely free, a natural state admittedly but one to which Mandarin was totally unaccustomed.

Winter had to rely on rhythm to get them around four 180-degree turns, although the French jockeys sportingly helped with a little shepherding. Mere survival would have been an achievement, especially after a swerve at some bushes left them in fifth place at the final turn. Two out they were seven lengths behind the leader but with Winter using all the power in his legs to impel his mount forward, Mandarin responded gallantly and took the lead at the last. There was then a frantic tussle all the way to the line with the French hope Lumino. It went to a photo but Mandarin had it by a whisker. After their incredible achievement Winter, suffering from stomach cramps, had to be carried into the weighing room. But Mandarin had also had his problems. One of his tendons had 'gone' again three fences out. He really was the bravest of the brave and in his retirement he fully deserved the regular supply from Whitbread's of the stout he relished in his food.

Russian Rhythm

How do you choose which football club to follow? Family tradition? Locality? The colour of the kit? I am not quite sure what makes me 'adopt' certain horses and follow them devotedly through their careers. Often it is a thrilling performance, a display of courage or exceptional speed. But with Russian Rhythm, trained by Sir Michael Stoute, it was a case of love at first sight.

I first saw Russian Rhythm, a chestnut daughter of Kingmambo, in the paddock at Ascot towards the end of July 2002. She was like a statuesque woman who comes into a room dressed by the best couturier in the expectation that she will be the focus of attention – an expectation immediately confirmed. Certainly she was not petite. Her imposing physique was built on substantial lines but there was something about her challenging head, her direct and intelligent gaze as well as the obvious power source of her high-muscled rump. She had cool, she had presence and when she went out on track to contest the Princess Margaret Stakes she showed she had the ideal racing temperament too, quickening up impressively under a hands-and-heels ride from Kieren Fallon as she and Luvah Girl went five lengths clear of the field. Immediately in that week's column I urged *Spectator* readers to get on quickly at the 10-1 then available for the 1,000 Guineas of 2003.

After a courageous victory in the Lowther Stakes at York that summer her trainer said that few fillies could have done what she did. She was trapped and had to fight to get clear. Said Sir Michael Stoute, 'She showed acceleration and she showed guts.' Russian Rhythm became the 5-2 winter favourite for the big race. But in the autumn, in season, she was beaten in the Cheveley Park Stakes by the speedy Airwave, the only time she lost a race to one of her own sex, and as the new season began Sir Michael Stoute was not pleased with Russian Rhythm. She didn't sparkle in her work, she did not eat up well. (Nor did I, as I kept my ante-post vouchers out of Mrs Oakley's sight.) There was trouble with a bruised heel, there were stories that she was to be taken out of the first Classic, and with the direst of rumours circulating, her price steadily lengthened.

Come 1,000 Guineas Day I had been planning to double my bet as she went to post, but I allowed myself to be deterred by all the scare stories, kept my hand in my pocket, and watched in some chagrin as Kieren Fallon brought Russian Rhythm home the winner at 12-1, two points better than I had happily taken the previous summer!

The French favourite Six Perfections had a troubled run but Russian Rhythm did all that was asked of her. Afterwards her trainer wondered aloud if she had been kidding him a little in her work.

In her next contest, the Coronation Stakes at Ascot, Russian Rhythm again beat the talented Soviet Song and posted a record time for the race too. But the real thriller came when she stepped up two furlongs to take on older fillies and mares in the Nassau Stakes at Goodwood. Jockey Kieren Fallon was unable to get a clear run when he wanted to move up and challenge. He had the class to wait until his filly was balanced and ready: Russian Rhythm had the class and tenacity when he found her a clear run to chase and catch the leader Ana Marie in the last few strides and win by a neck.

It could not last forever and in October in the Queen Elizabeth II Stakes Russian Rhythm was beaten, by the ultimate alpha male Falbrav, for my money the best horse Luca Cumani has ever trained. When he overtook a Godolphin pacemaker and set sail for home she was the only one with speed and guts enough to go after him, but he had too much left in the tank for the younger filly. The Ascot crowd knew though that they had seen something special from both horses and applauded both first and second with real fervour after the race.

Although Russian Rhythm was beaten too in her final race of the season, the Champion Stakes, this time by Rakti, my fervour remained undiminished and I rolled up at Newbury for the Lockinge Stakes in May of the next year to continue the affair. I was not disappointed. In the paddock, cool as ever, the object of my affections lobbed around with her head lowered, her mane rippling silkily like a shampoo model and her powerful quarters a well muscled indication of the power still there to be unleashed. Once Kieren Fallon swung into the plate she perked up, ready for the business in hand, happy to take on the boys who included Refuse to Bend and Indian Haven, the winners of the previous year's English and Irish 2,000 Guineas. In the race, as soon as Kieren found a gap she quickened, rather too swiftly in fact, taking the lead two furlongs out. Luca Cumani's Salselon and David Elsworth's Norse Dancer ranged up on either side and briefly seemed to head her. But while the longer-term message for this exciting breeding project had to be 'come up and see me sometime', that was not the game plan just yet. The daughter of Kingmambo was ready for a scrap. She stuck her neck out, went on again and won by a gutsy half-length.

Back in the paddock when her lass Jane Saunders told her what a good girl she was and sloshed a water bucket over her, Russian Rhythm didn't need telling. She stuck out her tongue and preened as her trainer declared, 'She's got the right mind, she's got this wonderful physique and she loves racing. She's a competitor. She doesn't lack courage. She's a real pleasure to train.' He praised too the brave decision of Patricia and David Thompson of Cheveley Park Stud to keep her on the track one more season rather than rushing her off to stud, saying it was a decision taken without the trainer. 'Perhaps because they thought I'd be too windy.'

Sadly, soon after that race Russian Rhythm suffered an injury and never raced again.

Frankel

I saw Frankel most of the times he ran. My only regret is that I wasn't there for all of them. Everyone will carry their own memories of that extraordinary racehorse. Certainly I will never forget his explosive effort in the 2,000 Guineas or his humbling of Canford Cliffs in the Sussex Stakes at Goodwood. But it was after his run in the Lockinge in May 2012 that I found myself reflecting as much as anything on the sheer strain imposed on Henry Cecil and his team in looking after such a phenomenon. I wrote then:

> When they present themselves there are certain experiences you simply have to undergo to make life complete, like rounding Cape Horn, watching the waters cascade over the Niagara Falls or flying on Concorde. I would add to the list, in the five months or so while it is still possible, the absolute must of seeing Frankel in action on a racecourse.
>
> Owner Lady Beaverbrook once declared, 'I have all the art I need but nothing makes my heart beat like a horse.' And while in one way it is hard to think of something as muscular, mighty and masculine as a work of art, Frankel certainly is one. When jockey Tom Queally told him to go two furlongs out last Saturday, half a ton of horse quickened away from the second-best miler in Europe with an instant supercharged acceleration that was totally sublime.

The 14,000 of us who flocked to Newbury to see this racing phenomenon needed reassurance after the recent injury scare that could have ended his career. What we got as he recorded his tenth victory from ten starts was not just reassurance but a polished, controlled, yet dominant display that was truly life-enhancing. How we are going to report his future appearances I am not quite sure: cricket writers said of W.G. Grace in his time that he had exhausted the language of superlatives and Frankel has done that to racing already.

Frankel's trainer Henry Cecil is a steel-stemmed poppy who combines outward diffidence with inner certainty of purpose. Watching him struggle to contain his emotions after Frankel's success was a reminder of the huge strain that is imposed on those who handle quality in sport, particularly when they are tending talents which have become public property. As Tom Queally said of Frankel before dismounting, 'He belongs to racing.' One small misjudgement on Cecil's part and the whole magic story could be over.

I was of course at Ascot for Frankel's final appearance in the Champion Stakes that October and I found myself caught up in a small way in the extraordinary celebrations:

After Brad Wiggins's Tour de France victory, Mo Farah's Olympics successes and Andy Murray's first Grand Slam title any other result would have been unthinkable, so praise the Lord Frankel did win Ascot's Champion Stakes. On unsuitably soft ground and after gifting the others lengths at the start, the unbeaten star of world racing proved that he could fight as well as run. Now it is off to a pampered life in the breeding sheds with the hope of lots of little Frankels to come.

I have never seen a crowd like it at Ascot. The roads were choked three hours before. The velvet collars and City suits were there, so were the trilby and cords set. But so were the likely lads with gelled hair and ties at half-mast, the giggling girls in chiffons and high heels, the tatty anoraks and the chancers in pointed sharkskin shoes, all gathered to pay homage. In the parade ring before Frankel's Champion Stakes with the trees turning Olympic gold and the whiff of burger-frying floating past there were celebs like Bryan Ferry and plenty of owners and trainers who didn't have a runner. As Frankel's connections arrived, led into the paddock with his usual quiet elegance by the silver-haired Prince Khalid Abdullah, I looked back at the vast stand to see balconies packed with flags in the pink and green of his colours. Even so, the mood before the race was one as much of anxiety as of elation. 'He is going to win it, isn't he?' we were all asking each other before Frankel's fourteenth and final contest.

There was some reassurance when in the race before, the million-pound Queen Elizabeth II Stakes, Excelebration, the talented miler who has so often followed Frankel home some lengths behind in second place, triumphed in the style of the supremely talented and consistent horse he is too. As one commentator put it, 'Even today he could only beat Frankel by turning up half an hour earlier.' But there was still that edge, that niggling fear that Fate would deprive us of a happy ending.

In the event Frankel won splendidly against two toughies who had proved they could act on the rain-softened ground, Cirrus des Aigles and Nathaniel. Ironically, the horse whom they had feared might be too buzzy and hot-headed to reveal his best on the track had by now so brilliantly been taught to relax by the Henry Cecil team that he virtually fell out of the stalls like a sleepwalker leaving poor Ian Mongan on Bullet Train, his pacemaker, looking round nervously to see where he had got to. Jockey Tom Queally though gave Frankel time to collect himself. It is never so easy coming from behind on heavy ground but he came up to Cirrus des Aigles two furlongs out with the crowd roaring on their champion and went away to win by a one-and-three-quarter-lengths margin that could have been more.

Few held back their emotions after the race and as vast numbers of spectators dashed from the stands to be in position to cheer Frankel back into the winner's enclosure I found myself beside Sir Henry Cecil as the crowds closed in, obliterating the walkway down the steps to the paddock. With Cecil's voice reduced to a whisper by his cancer treatment there was only one thing for it. I pushed through the sea of bodies shouting 'Make way for the trainer' like some demented toastmaster. My apologies to those whose feet I trod on or whose ribs I elbowed in the process.

It was a supreme training performance by a master of his art and the Prince and his racing manager Teddy Grimthorpe too deserve huge praise for the calm way in which they have campaigned their superstar. Given the dire conditions that race was run in this year thank heavens they did not listen to the entreaties to run Frankel over a longer distance in the Arc. Frankel is special enough without that and he could provide a handy answer in a year when awarding the BBC Sports Personality of the Year is going to be fiendishly difficult. Why not this time give it to a horse?

Rainbow View

Your wishes don't always come true. Another filly I spotted early on and was convinced would win the Guineas was Rainbow View, but although she was an odds-on favourite for the Classic at 8-11 she failed to match Russian Rhythm's achievements. Trained during her English career by John Gosden, Rainbow View was a thrilling juvenile to watch and a real equine personality. This was how I wrote about her after a visit to her accomplished trainer's yard in April 2009:

> If she was human Rainbow View would be a stroppy teenager, chucking down her school satchel and heading straight out to the sort of club you wouldn't want your daughter in. One word from a parent and she would do the other thing. Threaten a smacked bottom and she'd be off to the child protection officer, knowing her rights. She is a head-tossing little madam who puts the x into minx, the original wild child. But she also inspires infinite patience because her strength of will is matched with exceptional physical ability. Given the right mood on the day, Rainbow View will confirm that by winning the first fillies Classic, the 1,000 Guineas, on May 3 for her trainer John Gosden and owner George Strawbridge.
>
> Visiting a trainer's yard is always fun at this optimistic end of the racing year. Serious questions are just beginning to be asked on the gallops. Any of the heads popping inquisitively over box doors can turn out to belong to something special. But visiting John Gosden's Clarehaven yard is an experience. The running commentary, delivered at shock-jock speed, is not limited to recitations of horse performance.

It throws in a condensed history of the great Pretty Polly, who was trained there in the early 1900s – 'She ate the colts from five furlongs to two and a half miles' – and a discussion of the Munnings and Constable Suffolk skies. There is no shortage of opinions either, for example on racecourse parades: 'It's nice for the public to see them cantering down but I've never been a believer in them marching to the furlong pole and coming back. You can do it in America where they train on track but they're all accompanied by ponies. They'll sleep on the pony and the jockey doesn't have to ride them. You get an American jockey here and tell him "You've got seven races and you are cantering them to the start and there's a six furlongs, a seven furlongs, a mile and a two miler", well, he's going to want an oxygen tank and a conveyor belt.'

Parades, of course, don't suit Rainbow View, who would have been flicking pellets and chewing gum through class roll-calls. 'She just doesn't do waiting around,' says her trainer. 'One day she got bored waiting for a canter and took off, five furlongs away. Down the walking grounds and in. She nearly took out Sir Mark Prescott's wall on the way. Of all the fillies I've trained she's a long way the wildest.' Now Rainbow View goes out on her own, with a lead horse. 'She doesn't do strings.'

In a corner box of the top yard, with its yellow brick and duck-egg blue box doors we are allowed finally to see the pocket rocket herself. The door is open but she isn't allowed out. Says her trainer, 'She'd have gone through us, broken a window and finished up in [wife] Rachel's office.'

Munching handfuls of grass from her stable hand's pocket, madam is comparatively cooperative. But the last time I saw such a naughtily flickering eye it belonged to a princess. The message is clear. 'I'm in charge. I do what I like, when I like.'

Her trainer confirms: 'She takes some riding. She can just throw shapes for no reason.' He goes on: 'That is part of her character that makes her so determined and so good. It's important not to think of beating the spirit out of them, the idea that when you "break" a horse you beat any evil spirit out of them. That's crazy. That was the old concept. I don't believe in that at all. Our job is to channel that determination, that nervous energy, to turn them into athletes.'

We are talking about some athlete. As a two-year-old Rainbow View ran four times and won the four races by a cumulative margin of more than sixteen lengths. The last was an impressive victory in Ascot's testing Fillies Mile, a Group One race. In that, despite sweating up in the pre-race preliminaries, she beat Fantasia by two and a half lengths. Fantasia, who has since been bought by Rainbow View's owner and who will not face her in the 1,000 Guineas, came out last week and spreadeagled a high-class field, winning by seven lengths.

Size, says John Gosden, is not an issue. 'It's not the case of a little two-year-old that hasn't trained on because of her physical limits. She's trained on in terms of ability. Mentally she's tough to deal with, but it's that nervous energy that gives her such a competitive edge.'

I was lucky enough to see all four of Rainbow View's performances at two. She won her Newmarket maiden by six lengths and then took the Group Three Sweet Solera Stakes by the same margin, being shaken up to lead one furlong out and then coasting clear. Progressing next to the Group Two May Hill Stakes at Doncaster as the

Richard Hughes, the master of the waiting race and an honest chronicler of the problems jockeys face with their weight.

Kieren Fallon: if racing had a naughty step it would have been moulded to fit his backside – but what a sublime talent.

Frankie Dettori: the man who puts the *joie* into *joie de vivre* for racegoers …

… and bookmaker Gary Wiltshire, who lost £600,000
on Frankie Dettori's seven-winner day.

All in a day's work for iron man Tony McCoy
– and all without an anaesthetic.

Nicky Henderson's horses on the gallops at Seven Barrows:
the early morning scene that never fails to thrill.

Nicky Henderson at Seven Barrows with Gold Cup winner Long Run.

Trainer Barry Hills with 2,000 Guineas winner Haafhd,
led up by Snowy Outen.

Henry Cecil – the nearest thing we have seen in modern days
to a King of Newmarket – supervising the morning routine.

Has there ever been a pairing like it?
Paul Nicholls with Kauto Star and Denman.

Poetry in motion: my favourite Russian Rhythm
winning the Lockinge Stakes with Kieren Fallon.

The gutsy little Mandarin, poised in second to overtake Fortria and win his
Cheltenham Gold Cup in 1962.

Singspiel at the Breeders' Cup:
a tragic end to an illustrious globe-trotting career.

Sha Tin, Hong Kong: high-class and highly organised racing for top prize money. But I do miss the bookies!

Sheikh Mohammed bin Rashid al Maktoum, the man who has used racing to build a future for his country.

A contrast in styles: World Cup day in Dubai.

1-3 favourite she was anchored in the rear and came up smoothly on the outside two furlongs out to assert her superiority over Snoqualmie Girl. Rainbow View's very best effort though was when she took on the highly talented Cumani filly Fantasia at Ascot in what promised to be one of the races of the season in the Meon Valley Stud Fillies Mile. She moved up to the leaders after the two-furlong pole, and although she did not take the lead until inside the final furlong, she was two and a half lengths clear at the line.

Naturally following that she was made favourite for the 1,000 Guineas but in that race she never quite let herself down on firmish ground and finished only fifth behind Ghanaati. In her three-year-old career Rainbow View ran in the best company but never quite had the luck of the draw and never quite realised her juvenile promise. She was fourth to Sariska in the Oaks but lost all chance two furlongs out when hampered as she improved to third place. She ran third to Ghanaati in the Coronation Stakes at Ascot, again having a troubled passage as she stayed on to be third. She was fourth to Goldikova in the Falmouth Stakes at Newmarket and second to Midday in the Nassau Stakes at Goodwood over ten furlongs. It was not until her sixth race of the season and her last this side of the Atlantic that she finally got her nose in front again, winning the Matron Stakes at Leopardstown from Heaven Sent.

After that Rainbow View went to Woodbine to contest the E.P. Taylor Stakes, in which she finished second, done for finishing speed despite leading in the final furlong, and she finished the season fourth of eight at Santa Anita. At four, trained in America by Jonathan E. Sheppard, Rainbow View did win once again in a Grade Three at Pimlico.

Denman

One day when I arrived at his Ditcheat base to talk to Paul Nicholls about Cheltenham, the invariably courteous trainer was caught up on the phone. I wandered out across the yard. There in one box was the unmistakeable slightly crooked white blaze of Kauto Star; next door was the heftier, slightly more stolid Denman. Was it just my imagination that Kauto Star looked like a star accustomed to attention and celebration, Denman more like a horse there to do a job?

Kauto Star made it into the top ten of my *Top 100 Racehorses* book, Denman was ranked in the 30s. Both were wonderful horses who generated huge excitement. I would happily have travelled the length of the country to watch either run. But because Kauto Star won five King Georges as well as his four Betfair Chases and two Cheltenham Gold Cups, and because he showed the speed and athleticism to win two-mile Tingle Creek Chases as well, he was always the one who received superstar treatment from the media. Fair enough in a way, but that always left me with a soft spot for the honest bruiser Denman, a massive seventeen-hands horse who required enormous amounts of work to get fit.

Denman excited the media as much as anything because for most of his career he was owned by the Odd Couple, the seemingly incongruous but effective partnership of the dairy farmer Paul Barber, the countryman personified, and the flashy professional gambler Harry Findlay, in Paul Nicholls' words 'an open mouth in search of a microphone', who called Denman 'The Tank'. But Denman's record too was an astonishing one. He won thirteen of his first fourteen races and over a million pounds in prize money. Not only did he win the Cheltenham Gold

Cup, beating Kauto Star when he did so, but he twice won the Hennessy Gold Cup under massive weights. He ran six times in all at the Cheltenham Festival and was never out of the first two.

It was to me a bit like Coe and Ovett on four legs. Both were supreme talents, but the one written about most was the smooth-talking charmer. Kauto Star was an eye-catching Mod, Denman an implacable Rocker.

To me the most memorable of the three Cheltenham Gold Cups they won between them was the 2008 contest. In that race Kauto Star was defending the crown he had won in 2007. For most people the only question was the margin by which he would beat his stable companion. Most had chosen to forget the Hennessy Gold Cup back in November 2007 when Denman, carrying 11st 12lb on stamina-sapping soft ground, had come home nine lengths clear of Dream Alliance. Leg-weary competitors with lesser burdens clambered over the last few fences that rain-sodden day like slow-motion clockwork creatures. Denman, clear of his field despite his heavy burden, soared majestically over the last two as if on springs. 'Awesome,' said jockey Sam Thomas. 'Awesome,' said trainer Paul Nicholls. Less decorously but with equal vehemence, part-owner Harry Findlay told everyone the result after the first circuit, roaring: 'The Tank's shit it.'

At Cheltenham for the Gold Cup the next March it wasn't the cakewalk for Kauto that most had expected. Instead stable number two jockey Sam Thomas, who had been bollocked by trainer Nicholls for an ill-judged ride in the race before, took Denman into the lead for the second circuit and remorselessly ground out a pace which none of the others could live with. Struggling to do so, Kauto Star under Ruby Walsh made jumping errors. Four fences out, 'The Tank' stepped up the pace even further.

That was how he won his races, using his big stride and his sheer physicality to grind the others into submission and he was the one who came up the Cheltenham hill well clear. Kauto Star closed the gap to seven lengths but there was no doubt about who was the champion that day.

What we did not realise at the time perhaps was just how much effort Denman had put into his victory. When he came back from his summer break for the new season Denman was listless and permanently hot. It turned out that he had an irregular heartbeat and had to be sent to Newmarket for treatment. He had to be nursed back to confidence and on his return looked a shadow of his former self. But ten days before the 2009 Gold Cup, Paul Nicholls saw a glimmer of the old Denman return and let him take his chance.

Kauto Star duly won on that occasion. But to general surprise, the only partly recovered Denman still came home in second place and the racing world was all agog for the re-match in 2010, hopefully with Denman fully recovered by then. He certainly seemed to be when he went back to Newbury for another Hennessy in November 2009. He had not been in a winner's enclosure since his Cheltenham Gold Cup victory but back he came to win again under 11st 12lb from a top-class field, this time ridden by Ruby Walsh, who had to hold off a strong challenge from stable companion What A Friend.

With a sea of Kauto Star scarves in the stands the next March, we were all entranced as Kauto Star and Denman renewed their Gold Cup rivalry. Again Denman, this time ridden by Tony McCoy, took it up on the second circuit and began to step up the pace. Kauto Star, alas, had crashed out with a hideous fall at only the fourth fence and for a while it looked as though Denman could match his feat of retaking a Cheltenham crown. In the final stages however the next generation asserted and Imperial Commander went by Denman to win. It was second place again.

The final Gold Cup contest between the two stable companions, both now aged eleven, took place in 2011. This time Kauto Star led from halfway, then Denman took the lead three out. In a finale no scriptwriter would have dared contrive, the two heroes took the last together, with Denman looking the stronger, but they were accompanied ominously by the younger Long Run, ridden by amateur Sam Waley-Cohen, and he it was who asserted up the hill with Denman once again second, seven lengths behind, and Kauto Star third.

Kauto Star, it must be conceded, was the greater all-rounder, but I would argue that at Cheltenham, jump racing's Mecca, Denman was at least his equal.

Singspiel

One reason that jump racing, or National Hunt Racing as we used to call it until racing's administrators were called in for lessons in political correctness, has held its appeal in recent years at times when that of Flat racing has flagged is the continuity, the fact that you see jumping horses around for many years more than most Flat racers, racing from the age of four to twelve, or more in a few cases. People get to know them as individuals and relish their quirks.

Kauto Star was still thrilling us at eleven, racing in the very top class. Sea The Stars, although he gave us a wonderful summer in 2009, winning the 2,000 Guineas, the Derby, the Coral-Eclipse, the Juddmonte International, the Irish Champion Stakes and the Prix de L'Arc de Triomphe, was off to the breeding sheds at the age of three, never tested against the next wave. It was as if Beckham and Ronaldo had been whisked off permanently to a life of celebrity TV shows before they had ever played in a World Cup, as if Ian Botham and Shane Warne had been dragged upstairs to the commentary box before ever playing an Ashes series.

I have enough years behind me to be prejudiced but I always think of Gypsy Rose Lee's response when somebody asked her if she was worried about getting older. 'Honey,' she said, 'I've still got everything I used to have, it's just that it's all a little bit lower.' One of the best ideas the planners have had in recent years, to my mind, are the veterans' races specifically for those chasers who have been around for a while and who can still thrill the crowds, even if they are slowing up a bit.

In the same way I have had a special affection on the Flat for the Cup horses, the late-maturing individuals who peak at five, six or seven and are kept in training by masters of the art like Sir Michael Stoute to tour the world picking up prizes in Hong Kong and Dubai, Singapore and Japan. The last of my 'favourite horse' choices therefore is Singspiel. It could equally well have been Warrsan or Fantastic Light, Daylami or Falbrav, Swain or Pilsudski but I have chosen Singspiel because I have never forgotten the picture taken of him on the Hollywood Park training track at the Breeders' Cup in November 1997. In the early morning fog he hobbled off with the leg injury that was to end his career. It was one of those pictures which told you more than thousands of words.

I wasn't there. The *Spectator*'s expenses sadly don't run to trips to the Breeders' Cup. Truth be told, they don't run to a charabanc trip to Fontwell Park. But you did not have to be there to understand that a single frame encapsulated a drama and a tragedy. I wrote then:

In Singspiel's career there have been the joyful, colourful, prancing moments that might have made
a Degas or a Dufy. But this was a grim and serious
tableau in the morning mist, fit only for the som-
bre tones of a Rembrandt. The worry etched on
trainer Michael Stoute's face and the eyeline of the
work riders and watchers clustered about the limp-
ing, stricken animal told their own story. The little
horse's neck, which we have been accustomed to seeing arched imperiously with a star's confidence in the
parade ring or thrust out reaching for the line in yet
another pulsating finish, was rigid with puzzlement
and pain.

Two days before what was anyway to have been
his last race, with Singspiel starting favourite for the
Breeders' Cup, it was the end of his career. Thanks to
the veterinary surgeons' skills it was not also the end
of Singspiel's life and in a few months, his fractured
off-fore cannon bone repaired, he will be fit enough
to take up the pleasures of a life at Stud.

Singspiel's career, I wrote, was a testament to Stoute's
patient ability to spot and nurture the later developers:

People tend to forget that Singspiel was not univer-
sally admired as a three-year-old. He won only once
in his six starts, a Listed race at Doncaster, although
it has been pointed out that a one-length bonus,
divided judiciously between the races, would have
won him also the Thresher Classic Trial, the Grand
Prix de Paris and York's Great Voltigeur.

His first significant success came only as a four-year-
old, at Sandown in April 1996, but then it was back to
second place again in the Coronation Cup at Epsom
and the Princess of Wales's Stakes at Royal Ascot.
Next came a win at Goodwood over 1m 2f before his

illustrious overseas career took off. Singspiel won the Canadian International at Woodbine over a mile and a half two weeks later, picking up £283,000. On the same track two weeks later he was second to his stablemate Pilsudski, winning another £258,000. Then a month after that he was off to Tokyo to pick up £1 million for winning the Japan Cup.

Versatility, toughness and consistency like that are rare but the gutsy little horse surpassed his four-year-old achievements with his campaign this year at five. Despite the tough race that he had endured under Frankie Dettori to beat the Prix de l'Arc de Triomphe winner Helissio in Japan he came out this year dropping back to ten furlongs with enthusiasm undiminished to beat the American horses Sandpit and Siphon on the dirt track in Dubai, this time picking up £1.4 million. He took the Coronation Cup with ease at Epsom and the Juddmonte International at York. His only defeat was in the 'Race of the Year' King George VI and Queen Elizabeth Stakes at Ascot when a deluge on the day turned the race into a stayers' slog won by Swain.

Once there were doubters. At one stage Singspiel had been second in seven out of his last ten contests. But there has been no tougher horse around these past two years. It takes a special kind of grit to travel the distance he did and to keep winning through as long a season as Singspiel did. He finished as an undoubted champion, a winner in Canada, Japan, England and Dubai, the record stakes-winner in European racing history with £3.6 million and the most potent argument we have yet seen for keeping good horses in training beyond their three-year-old careers. For Michael Stoute the Dubai victory, beating the American horses on their kind of track was the crowning moment. But this brave little battler has given us all magic moments. May he enjoy every minute with those mares.

Betting

When film stars James and Pamela Mason were bringing up their precocious daughter Portland she was allowed to do pretty much what she liked to encourage her to develop her own personality. She wore lipstick and couture dresses at four and was introduced to cigarettes at around the same time in the hope that it would put her off for life. Asked in later life how the policy had worked, her father replied, 'Well, she's down to two packs a day ...'

I sometimes wonder if my life would have been different had my father taken a firmer line over my liking for a flutter, developed in my teenage days. But then he did have a full-time job trying to cure my mother of her addiction to retail therapy. As a student I did once tip him three winners, all at 12-1 or better, on what for him was his dreaded annual corporate visit to Royal Ascot (he worked for the construction company George Wimpey who had built one of the old stands) and he gave me £25 on his return.

My old squash partner Jeffrey Archer once told me, with all the gravitas of a future peer of the realm, 'The world is divided, Robin, into those who know how to make money and those who don't. You, alas, are in the second category.' But there was one brief moment early in my gambling career when he might have been proved wrong.

When a church fête was held in the grounds of my school, the sideshows included one of those boards divided into chequered squares, on to which you rolled pennies down a chute. If your penny landed on a square without touching a line you received your penny back multiplied by the number on which it had landed. Somehow I managed to persuade the earnest cleric in charge to let me roll sixpences instead, arguing that he would make six times as much each time I lost. True. But sadly for the warmth and comfort of his parishioners it was much easier to land a little sixpence within the squares and by the time I moved on to the coconut shy I had cleaned him out.

My betting on horses has not always been quite so successful, although I did tip Jenny Pitman's Jibber the Kibber at 40-1 in one of my early *Spectator* columns and I gave Foreign Secretary Robin Cook Gingembre at 33-1 for the Hennessy. I never got a story in return to match the quality of that information.

To me racing and betting are inseparable companions. Betting is the salt in racing's soup. Going to the races without a flutter would take away an important part of the relish. To me in my youth there were few word pairings more exciting than 'betting coup' and I used to pore over trainers' and jockeys' biographies relishing the stories of legendary gambles.

Away at boarding school my punting was a largely imaginary hobby. I used to read all the racing pages in the school library, make my daily selections and tabulate the theoretical returns, concentrating on handicaps and horses with known form rather than little-raced two-year-olds. I then went racing in the holidays when I could, although on occasion I did have to walk the three or four miles home to East Molesey from Sandown Park after going for broke in the last.

I am not one for superstition. I once knew an MP who carried a lucky rabbit's foot on election days but my feeling was that it hadn't done much for the rabbit and I use no lucky charms.

One-armed bandits leave me cold and I don't go to casinos. Nor do I bet much on anything besides horseracing. I did however get 50-1 from Ladbrokes between the two elections of 1974 on Margaret Thatcher becoming the next leader of the Conservative party. We had a nice family holiday on that one and for some years I did well out of predicting by-election results. But I felt it wise to give up political betting after becoming Political Editor of the BBC. I didn't want the gossip columns accusing me of manipulating the odds in my reporting.

Occasionally I have been lured, to my shame, into a coincidence bet. But I don't generally go for traditions like backing the first trainer or jockey you see on entering a racecourse. Pulling up in the car park alongside racing personalities does though have me recalling a story Barry Hills told me of his early days as a trainer. Neville Callaghan was his assistant and they had a horse called Taxanitania well readied after a sighting run under Kipper Lynch and headed for Ripon. Neville was determined to have £1,000 on a horse for the first time and Barry, who had bought his stable thanks to winning £60,000 on Frankincense in the Lincoln, was going for a big punt too.

They deliberately didn't arrive too early at the course because they didn't want to have to tell any fibs when asked about the horse. But as they headed for the ring they were accosted by the owner Sam Lee, who was on a similar mission. He wasn't the kind of gent who had made his money selling embroidery kits to old ladies and he realised where they were heading. 'You take my price and I'll chop your kneecaps off,' he told them. 'After I'm done you can do what you like!'

The training duo held back until he was satisfied, but got their money on too. More importantly Willie Carson brought home Taxanitania the winner by three parts of a length. Willie remembers: 'The story went about that Taxanitania wasn't "off". It was a gull and he was 10-1 and it came off at 10-1.'

Barry of course was one of the shrewdest punting trainers we have seen. Interestingly he always liked his lads to be punters too:

> They work harder. They get more interested in what's going on, in looking for success. They need to get some money, don't they? What's the matter with tipping a winner if someone puts a tenner on for them? Plenty of people used to put me a score on, like Lord Wigg or Sir Randle Feilden. Phil Bull used to talk about betting as 'the pursuit of pleasure'. Racing should be about pleasure. It's a fascinating, intriguing business.

Not all trainers, however, make the betting pay as well as the training. Noel Meade once confessed that in his betting days he used to think there was no point unless you could buy a decent new car with your winnings. He would plan eight or ten bets a year and have two or three grand on each. Invariably, he said, some of them got beat. Then there would follow a series of smaller bets for a few hundred to recover the two or three grand. 'Often I would get the money back. But I never got that new car.' If he was reduced to chasing losses, what hope do we ordinary punters have?

The equally wise Willie Mullins once told me that he was always glad to get rid of gambling owners. 'You don't want a juvenile hurdler running a promising third, something to be pleased about, and then having an owner whingeing because he's got a bookie's ticket burning his arse pocket because he's had £10,000 on.' He made the good point too that 'Trainers who get into gambling never bring their horses to their true potential. They start deviating from the right route, aiming more at bookies' satchels, running in the wrong races. What's worse is that horses that have been stopped get confused about what they are there to do and may take two or three runs to recover.'

I am not a compulsive gambler like one journalist friend who lost both his house and his wife to his gambling habit. You would meet him after the first race with a wad of fivers in his pocket thick enough to stop a church door. After the last he would be touching you for the cost of a taxi to the station. As with anybody who gambles, I have had my good days and my bad days. It was a good day at Newmarket when I backed the 50-1 Land n' Stars and approached a Tote window that hadn't got enough cash to pay me. I asked the clerk to tell me again, a little louder, just for the pleasure of hearing it once more. It was a bad day at Newbury when in front of two regular *Spectator* readers the bookie from whom I collected on a 5-1 second favourite chortled, 'A winner for you Robin. It must be months since your last one.'

Being for a few years a BBC News face on television had its pros and cons. There was a drunk in Kennington, where I lived for years, who used to accost me in the betting shop and try to touch me unsuccessfully for a fiver. Luckily he used to call me 'Mr Brunson', having confused me with my rival on ITN, Michael Brunson. I fear Michael developed quite a reputation as a meanie round the Kennington pubs.

For most of my life my racing activities have had to be woven around my working life reporting politics. Some MPs and peers were aware of my dual role but I was careful not to pass on too many tips. I needed to get around and keep up my political contacts: I couldn't afford to become like the Damon Runyon character the Seldom

Seen Kid, obliged to make himself scarce on account of the amount of duff information he had passed on.

I still reckon from my political reporting days, however, that Alastair Campbell, Tony Blair's long-time Press Secretary, owes me nearly £800. One Friday in September 2003 I was at Sandown on a day off. Cutting it a little fine, I was just writing out my placepot before the first race when CNN's newsdesk called. They had a tip-off that Campbell was about to resign and wanted me back in action fast. I tucked away the ticket and headed off to Downing Street, only to discover later that my seven selected horses would have won me £789.30.

Robin Cook was one who enjoyed horse talk, one-time Conservative leader Michael Howard another. Robin argued that every politician should spend some time as a tipster to teach him humility, although I am not sure that his own fulfilling of that function for *The Herald* in Glasgow quite completed that process in his case.

Delwyn Williams, a Welsh Conservative MP whom I encountered on the track on occasion, discovered that Michael Cocks, Labour's Chief Whip in his time, was partial to a little racing information. Supplying it, he found, used to make it much easier for him to obtain a 'pair' on the Labour side when he wanted to miss a vote.

One day Delwyn was in one of the eighteen bars within the Palace of Westminster with a young lady who was the regular squeeze of a minister in the Thatcher government. Taken aback when, as he was plying the young lady with champagne, the minister suddenly appeared and asked, 'What's going on here?', Delwyn scrabbled for an alibi and declared that they were celebrating in advance the victory of a horse for which he had been given a tip. Desperately he fished out from his memory the name of the only horse he could remember reading about that morning and urged the minister to back it too. Passing a betting shop later, he thought he had better supplement his claim with a little documentary evidence. He went in and had £20 on it, and was amazed to discover the next morning that it had won at 16-1. 'Did you get on?' he smugly asked the minister the next day – I think it was the 16-1 shot rather than the minister's amorous intentions that he had in mind.

Another one-time Parliamentarian, Sir Clement Freud, wasn't the politest of men. I sat next to him once at a racing lunch where his rudery reduced to tears a woman whose only offence was to have asked him politely if he would autograph the menu for her aged father.

Freud had fun though naming his horses, like the Thatcher-teasing WeareaGrandmother. Then there was Dig Up St Edmunds, an attempt, he insisted, to cheer up the people who lived in Bury St Edmunds. My favourite was Overseas Buyer, named when Chancellor James Callaghan in Harold Wilson's government decreed that the only business expenses allowed were for entertaining purchasers from abroad. Freud set Overseas Buyer's feed costs against his tax bill. Freud argued that all racing journalists who didn't bet should be ignored: 'The most readable writers are those activated to work by bookmakers bills.'

Freud's wry humour was sometimes cruel, as when he was asked his opinion of New Zealand and replied that he didn't really have one 'Because most of the time I was there it appeared to be closed', but on racecourse cuisine he was irresistible, once describing what appeared on his plate as 'the piece of cod which passeth all understanding'.

When it comes to betting, my biggest sin is probably investing too much faith in information from those who I reckon are closer to the racing core than I am. I probably give far too much credence to snippets of information simply because they come from a ferrety-faced lad in a no-hoper yard or from the guy who delivers papers to a well-known breeder.

Professional gambler Patrick Veitch has the lifestyle to support his claims of having made £10 million punting and I reckon the best bit of advice in his *Enemy Number One* manual on how to beat the bookies is the very simple maxim, 'Any gambler worthy of the name should retain the discipline to keep records of every bet, otherwise it is human nature to remember the winners and conveniently forget the losers.'

In betting though, as in life, it is not always the advice you get but how you use it that matters. I have in mind the two hunters in the American woods. One fell to the ground, his eyes rolling in his head. His companion called the emergency services by cellphone: 'I think my friend is dead. What do I do?' The operator cautiously urged him, 'Now, sir, let's stay calm. Let's first of all make sure your friend is dead.' The line went quiet. Then there was the sound of a shot before the caller came back on the line: 'OK. Now what?'

One bit of betting advice I would pass on is that there is often value to be had with foreign imports or horses from abroad racing in Britain. We are a nationalistic, not to say occasionally xenophobic, people and sometimes bookmakers and punters don't do their homework on the horses that come from elsewhere to run here. The prime example was the Australian sprinter Choisir running at Royal Ascot in 2003 before we had become accustomed to horses sweeping in from southern parts and picking off our top sprints. The well-muscled Choisir, a horse built on the lines of a Brahma bull, had been horse of the year in Australia but in the King's Stand Stakes on the first day he was allowed to start at 25-1 (paying 37-1 on the Tote). Having won that race, he was still allowed to start at 13-2 for the Grand Jubilee Stakes later in the week, before winning that too. (It was of course a nightmare for those of us with Australian cameramen friends. Modesty in victory is not quite the Aussies' thing. They go more for the full ten-gallon, gold-plated, streamers-and-bunting, top-volume gloat. Thank God the England rugby team beat the Wallabies the same day or Earls Court would probably have been burned down.)

In the same way in June 2009 I did quite nicely when the bookmakers were struck by some sort of collective blindness over a horse called Ialysos, running at Haydock in a five-furlong sprint. Ialysos's seven previous racecourse outings had been in Greece, a country admittedly as much famed for producing top racehorses as Namibia is for turning out ice-sculptors. But there were two things to note. One was that Ialysos had won all seven of his races in Greece, the other was that he was trained in Britain by Luca Cumani and if there is anybody with a track record for doing well with imports it is Luca. Remember Falbrav and Starcraft, La Vie de Colori and Cima de Triomphe? And yet in spite of that, Ialysos was allowed to start at 14-1 and some of us did rather better than that. The bookmakers' intelligence system rarely fails – I sometimes think MI5 should be on the rails recruiting at some of our bigger meetings – but on that occasion they certainly let one under the net.

At Oxford I had a brief flirtation with system betting, having inveigled a few friends into joining a syndicate. The midday edition of the evening paper listed the selections of all the major newspaper tipsters. I kept careful records and every time a tipster reached his previous longest losing run for the season we began doubling up on his naps from that point. The theory was that we were tapping into expert knowledge at the point when the tipster was desperately anxious to provide a winner. We were running at quite a healthy profit when unfortunately I contracted glandular fever (I couldn't think why I felt sick after every rugby game, and doubled my training, getting even sicker) and was taken into the Slade isolation hospital. A fellow student failed to maintain the records and the scheme slipped into disarray. It was fun though while it lasted and my system even won the commendation later of Sir Gus O'Donnell, the one-time Treasury Secretary and former Press Secretary to John Major, who had his own ideas about roulette table possibilities.

I didn't have anything so grand as a telephone account in those days and my punting was mostly done in an irresistibly seedy betting shop near Carfax Tower. You pushed your way through one of those long shredded plastic curtains into a smoky den with lino tiles on the floor and counters beneath the pinned up pages from the *Sporting Life* barely wide enough to write out your bets. That you did with stubby little two-inch pencils handed out by the betting shop staff with the grudging air of folk who had the costs stopped from their wages.

Behind the barred counter was the lovely Lil, a statuesque lady who wore vivid lipsticks and buttoned jumpers strained so tightly over nature's provisions that you feared as you approached with a betting slip that a pink or blue projectile might suddenly detach itself and blind you with the ricochet. We wrangled often over the place odds from the 100-6, 11-4 and 13-8 shots in my yankees and trebles but Lil never gave an inch.

In the holidays I used to work on building sites and a little racing knowledge was my passport to acceptance by fellow labourers, chippies and brickies in tea breaks when we wrote out our bets for a runner to take to the bookie. All of us, that is, except mournful Joe, a Pole who constructed the hardboard columns for the concrete we poured from barrows. Why did he always look so sad, we asked Joe one day. 'Ah you see,' he said, 'back home in Poland I was a coffin-maker. Very good business. The trouble with Britain is that not enough people die ...' It takes all sorts.

In early days I sometimes used to travel to courses on raceday specials or take trains to particular meetings that were almost taken over by racing folk. Occasionally I would share a particularly smoky carriage with bookies and tic-tac men. I was invited once to join one of their card schools, but I remembered the travelling vicar invited to play by W.C. Fields, who inquired, 'Is this a game of chance?' and received the reply 'Not while I'm dealing, it ain't', and decided against. I preferred to keep my stake money intact until I got to the races. But later we did fall into conversation about betting coups and they told me what has since remained my favourite near-miss story.

At the start of one season a new, smart figure was to be observed strolling the scene at every race meeting that mattered. He arrived alone. He was invariably smartly dressed, with a distinctive flower in his buttonhole. He would walk the ranks of bookies checking the prices. Answering to the name of John, he would pass the time of day with all the rails bookmakers and knowledgeably discuss the day's prospects. But he would never, ever have a bet. Eventually it became quite a game to try to tempt him. 'Come on Johnny,' some would shout, 'a special price for you.' He would smile quietly and say, 'Not today'. Most of the season went by and then suddenly at Glorious Goodwood, on the final day, Johnny's answer changed. To the first inquirer he said he would have a thousand on the third favourite, on the nose. To the second he had another thousand. On credit please. No need for the formality of an account, was there … It turned out afterwards that he'd been round most of the ring. After a gulp or two, credit was extended, with a few little jokes along the lines of 'Well we'll always know where to find you', meaning that such a predictable figure could be relied upon to be doing the same thing tomorrow.

Johnny's selection, starting favourite with the weight of his money, was beaten half a length. And he didn't turn up the next day to pay. Or the day after that. Or ever again. Nobody knew where he lived or even his second name. He was never seen on the racecourse again, but one leading bookie returned from a holiday in Thailand tortured by something familiar about the face of the well-dressed barman who had served him pink gins in the hotel's cocktail bar.

Looking back over my *Spectator* columns over nearly twenty years I am slightly embarrassed to see how much space I have devoted to relating the circumstances of a gamble that came unstuck, or occasionally bragging about one that came off, because the one boring thing about writing on horseracing is that people will come up and tell you, 'My granny had an infallible system. She always backed a horse if there was green in the jockey's colours and a three somewhere in the number. Worked every time …' In listening to other people's gambling stories I am always mindful of a lady doctor friend of ours who told us over dinner one night how she compiled notes on her patients. When they told her how much they smoked, she doubled it. When they told her how much they drank, she trebled it. And when anybody over 50 told her how often they had sex, she divided it by four.

Do I make money from betting, friends ask, thanks to

the contacts I enjoy with owners, trainers and jockeys? The answer is that overall, year on year, I lose, but I don't lose much and I get an enormous amount of fun out of the process of losing that bit. I find betting is a bit like playing golf: in golf every round you play, however grotesque your final total, there is that one shot – or even two or three – which enables you to convince yourself, 'If only I could give it the time, I could get quite good at this game ...' So it is with betting. Every now and then I bring off a punt that has me saying, 'If only I could spare a little more time for the form books, I could really make a go of this.'

There is of course always a new way of looking at familiar objects, especially if you are an academic. In 1998 a Dr Mark Neal of Reading University spent three years visiting betting shops for a research project and concluded that they did a good job in looking after the disadvantaged. 'Strange to say,' he declared, 'but betting shops are actually a force for good in our society. They enhance social cohesion and a sense of community and they act as comfortable drop-in centres for pensioners, the unemployed and the homeless. In a way they have taken on the traditional role of the churches – except they are much more fun.' Perhaps I could get a three-year research grant to supplement his work on the racecourse: something along the lines of 'Barry Dennis: social menace or pastoral leader?'

Ownership

When I first began to follow racing as a teenager, the idea that I might ever become a racehorse owner on a journalist's salary was an impossible dream. Since then the democratisation of racing through the growth of syndicate group ownership has enabled thousands like me to enjoy the very special thrill that comes with watching a horse run in your colours, albeit shared with ten or a dozen others. In a couple of small, friendly syndicates, first with Simon Christian and then with Andy Turnell, I have enjoyed a heady whiff of the pleasures which I had imagined would remain confined to the Wildensteins and Niarchoses, the Sangsters and the Aga Khans. I have been able to knock around stable yards and cluster on the gallops watching my horses being prepared and to cheer them home on the racecourse.

I shall be very careful here saying just how much pleasure that has given me. Mick Fitzgerald's relationship with the lady he was with at the time he won the Grand National did not survive long after his breathless post-Grand National comment to interviewer Desmond Lynam that the experience had been 'better than sex'. But Mrs Oakley knows that she never gave me a better surprise present than the share she purchased for me to join the syndicate behind Sunday For Monday, initiated by my long-time *Times* colleague Richard Evans, who made the switch from politics to racing much more swiftly than I did.

Sunday For Monday, whose colours, appropriately for a bunch of newspapermen including *The Times* editor Charles Wilson, were black and white check with a red sash, gave us plenty of fun with a few placed efforts, trained firstly by Simon Christian and then by Ron Hodges. Unfortunately for me, when Richard got together a succeeding syndicate for a horse called Northern Saddler, also trained by Ron Hodges, I faced a choice. I could either continue stuffing fivers into a manger in the hope of a return or I could guarantee that my two children didn't go barefoot to university. I opted out. The canny

Richard took 100-1 from Ladbroke's against the horse winning three races in its first season. In fact Northern Saddler, a very useful two-miler with a bit of give in the track, won four of his first five and when he retired after winning, I believe, thirteen races in all, he had collected more than £60,000.

Partly because I was by then involved again in writing regularly about racing, I was much more involved in the Rhapsody in Blue syndicate headed by Malcolm Palmer, Ladbroke's courteous and ever-smiling PR presence on the racecourse. Rhapsody in Blue soon became Rhaps for short and I haven't forgotten the promise of his first time out at Kempton. This was how I greeted it at the time:

> Move over Robert Sangster. Eat your heart out Sheikh Mohammed. Well, perhaps not just yet. But as this fifteenth part of the Eternal Optimists syndicate managed by Coral's Malcolm Palmer joined the other proud owners huddling in the parade ring at Kempton evening meeting last week, my excitement was every bit as great as racing's superstars when they introduce an expensive new star to the racecourse. One of 24 two-year-olds contesting the six-furlong European Breeders Fund Median Auction Stakes, carrying a prize of £2,386 to the winner, Rhapsody in Blue (no, I wasn't responsible for the politically partial name) did not exactly earn rave previews on his racecourse debut.
>
> The *Racing Post* said ungenerously, '3,500 (Irish) gns foal from a stable hardly associated with first-time-out winners.' The racecard noted, tersely if accurately, 'This first outing will probably be required.' Indeed, this was intended as an educational experience, a first trip to the racecourse for our son of

Magical Strike (USA) out of Palace Blue (IRE) to learn what racing was all about.

Six-furlong sprints will not be Rhapsody's future. His canny trainer Andy Turnell, who had him looking a picture, told us he would almost certainly need further. He was the biggest horse in the parade ring at Kempton and jump jockeys who visit the East Hendred stable are already looking at his impressive frame and inquiring about the chances of getting a leg-up on him over timber in a couple of years. But he did everything right. Bright of eye, ears pricked, he strolled around the ring with athletic dignity, led by conditional jockey Colin Rae.

When he first arrived in the yard Rhapsody had been somewhat coltish, his mind rather less on the job of getting fit than on mounting anything from passing lasses to the visiting postman. But whether it had been his working regime or whether he had heard the rumours of an imminent trip to the vets to deprive him of his wedding tackle, Rhaps has turned into the perfect gent. At Kempton's Irish night he was not distracted in the slightest by the barbecue smoke, the strong whiff of Guinness on the breeze nor the ghetto-blasting rumpus of the energetic Irish band.

But what about the serious part of his evening? He went down comfortably to the start, entered the stalls without a fuss and set out more or less with the others under the coaxing hands of Nicky Adams, John Reid having initially decided he couldn't make it from York to Kempton in time – only to turn up riding the favourite in Rhapsody's race. All we cared about was that he returned safely from this first experience – it is surprising how protective you become. After the first furlong it looked as though that would be all there was to care about, with Rhapsody's yellow jacket, striped sleeves and blue epaulets showing clearly last of the 24 runners.

But as the charge up the centre of the Kempton track went on he began to realise why he was at the races. After two furlongs he began picking off the stragglers and, with his owners on collective tip-toe (no mean feat in some cases) suddenly he was steaming through the pack, having engaged another gear, to do all his best work at the business end of the race.

'Never near enough to challenge,' said the next day's *Sporting Life*, which had taken an unaccountable interest merely in the first eight home. But for fifteen proud owners and the delighted trainer a ninth place that could have been improved upon had his jockey been harder on him was the ideal introduction. 'Just what I would have hoped for, but you never know until you get them on a racecourse,' said Andy Turnell as Rhapsody, the treacly horse sweat rolling off his neck on the clammy evening, paraded comfortably before us with the air of a child who'd come home a plucky fourth in the egg-and-spoon race on Parents Day. He gave every sign of having enjoyed it too and when I spoke to Andy the next day it turned out that Rhapsody had dived into his dinner that night with relish and tucked away his breakfast with no bother. 'I couldn't be happier with his attitude.' So far, so good.

I won't take you through every race that Rhapsody ran. Life as a working journalist ensured that I did not see them all myself. He worked well, giving visiting jockeys a good feel. Still on the leggy side as a three-year-old, he looked good and was starting to fill out his big frame. Indeed there was a danger he might fill it out too well.

As an owner you need to learn how to translate the language of trainer-speak. 'He needs time' generally means 'He's as slow as a carthorse but please keep paying the bills until he confirms it on the racecourse next spring'. 'He won't want too far' means that he struggles to get five furlongs even in a horsebox. 'He's a bit of a lad' means that no human can enter his box without an armed escort and he has already killed the stable cat and maimed two lads.

Trainer Andy Turnell was and is no flanneller but when he noted that Rhaps was 'a good doer' that turned out to mean that he munched his way through his meals and then started on his bedding, even if it was crunched-up newspapers. So after mealtimes he was muzzled.

When Andy told us however that Rhaps 'does things slowly' that was not trainer speak for 'Actually he's a dud'. What he meant was that Rhaps was a long-striding animal who took time to wind up. His orders to jockey Nicky Carlisle in the Brighton parade ring in June 1998 were 'Pop him out and keep hold of him as long as you can'. The professional Carlisle, no doubt an indulgent parent too, replied, 'You mean get him organised as soon as possible but give him time to find himself?' He did precisely that and Rhaps lobbed along at the back, taking some time to find himself and rather longer to find the others in the race. Being the big fellow that he is, he did not handle the downhill track too well but once they reached the rising ground a couple of reminders from N. Carlisle saw him doing his best work at the end of the seven furlongs. 'I'd rather see them slow to start and running on than the other way around,' said our trainer, who does a very good encouraging smile but was having to make a lot of use of it, especially since he won the race that day with Academy at 33-1 and hadn't told us that he fancied that one a bit.

Jockeys with a view to future rides can be diplomats too and Nicky Carlisle was accentuating the positive as he dismounted: 'He's got a lovely long stride.' He agreed that Rhaps hadn't really been able to go the pace early on and that he had struggled down the hill but he said he was confident he would stay at least a mile and a quarter. We should certainly win a race with him, he declared, if we didn't aim too high.

Before the Brighton contest the *Racing Post* had summed up Rhaps's career so far as 'unfancied and soundly beaten in three maidens at 6–7f'. Afterwards the only comment was 'always behind'. But we had been given enough (it doesn't take much) to go on hoping.

The optimist sees the doughnut, the pessimist sees the hole, and plenty of the Eternal Optimists, who included the TV business editor Jeff Randall, were there at Lingfield in August when our pride and joy padded around the parade ring with six duck eggs in front of his name on the racecard. I had learned the previous week how to make twenty bitter enemies in half an hour: I had to pick the prize-winner from 21 entrants in a children's fancy dress parade at a village fête, with all their mothers present. The racecard compiler at Lingfield rapidly assumed a similar status in our group when we read his verdict on Rhapsody in Blue: 'Unplaced in all six starts. Well beaten when 11th of 13 on previous start over 1m 4f at Windsor. He races from 8lbs out of the handicap today. Ignore.'

The Eternal Optimists sniffed at such careless cruelty and looked for comfort amid the threatening drizzle. Doesn't he look well? Hadn't Andy had two winners in his last nine runners at the track? Hadn't our jockey Darren Williams ridden the winner of the race the year before … and wasn't there a subtle difference this time? Previously racecards had listed Rhapsody as B h Magical Strike

(USA)–Palace Blue (IRE). Now he was just a little lighter after a visit to the vet had turned him into B g Magical Strike–Palace Blue. The prospect of a glorious career at stud to follow his racing days might have disappeared but surely now he was going to concentrate harder on the job and rather less on any filly within sniffing distance.

Rhaps strode purposefully around the parade ring, his coat gleaming in its usual tribute to the Turnell stable team. Despite those six noughts on his record and the 50-1 available against him on the Tote, it was the loose-limbed walk of an athlete, not the self-conscious slouch of a no-hoper. True, the Lingfield hill might not suit him, but off his low handicap mark you had to take chances where you could find them. He looked ready to take on all comers. 'Try and put him in the race before it starts,' said Andy to the jockey. 'Don't hurt him, but be firm with him.' We headed off to take some of that 50-1.

Rhaps stood quietly before the start, broke well and went up on the outside of the field to take fourth or fifth. He looked comfortable, well able to take the pace and Darren Williams looked to be able to ride the race as instructed. Then, suddenly, calamity struck. One moment he was on the heels of the leaders ready to accelerate as they hit the rising ground, the next he was slipping back through the field like a Tour de France cyclist with a puncture: sixth, ninth ... thirteenth ... With all hope gone, Darren Williams didn't punish him and they trailed in last of all but for a horse which had lost its rider on the turn.

Like relatives at the bedside we gathered for the verdict as Rhapsody, blowing gently but entirely sound and showing no sign of distress, was unsaddled. There was no trainer-speak from Andy, no assertions that 'he needed the race' or that he 'has been held up in his preparation'. He didn't even offer Rhaps's recent loss of his cojones as an excuse, although I am sure it would have affected my performance. He was as mystified as the rest of us. 'He stopped as if he had been shot,' said his young rider. 'It was as if the lights went out or he'd run out of petrol.' With hindsight that probably was a fair description because it seems that Rhapsody was one of those horses who would suddenly and inexplicably 'swallow his tongue'.

Anyway, that was it for the Flat and Rhapsody's next experience on the racecourse was over hurdles at Worcester in October. You don't go to Worcester, I noted at the time, for champagne and caviar, more for the sustaining curry and chips available in the main betting hall. Indeed one was lucky to arrive at Worcester at all given the lack of signage around that lovely city's tortuous one-way system. At least the course itself was in sympathetic hands: clerk of the course Hugo Bevan could remember once turning into the straight on a chaser that was moving slower than the swans on the adjacent river.

Rhapsody having failed to secure a single place in his seven outings on the Flat, some of my fourteen owner colleagues had a different timescale for eternity: only five of the Eternal Optimists turned up for his National Hunt debut.

Once again the handsome Rhapsody looked a picture with his fine head, athletic carriage and easy temperament. In the saddling box Andy Turnell, in what looked much too good a suit for such an operation, sought to fit a mildly indignant Rhapsody with a strap to prevent him swallowing his tongue and so once more abruptly running out of gas, as he had at Lingfield. Fitting a tongue strap, in my observation, is about as easy as lining up jelly beans in order in a tub of Vaseline. They had to have another go at the start, only for that to prove equally impermanent. It can be done with ladies tights, but I didn't know any of the female company well enough to suggest the sacrifice. At least the racecard for once struck a note of optimism. After Lingfield's tart one-word summary for punters: 'Ignore', Worcester's compiler instead recorded: 'Well beaten behind Joli's Son when 13th of 14 on his latest outing on the Flat. Can only improve over hurdles.'

It had been a shock to find the morning papers suggesting Rhapsody in Blue's starting price might be 7-1. A more realistic 25-1 was available on course and I felt quids in when finding some 33-1. For a moment or two it looked as though we might be in the money. Rhaps took his hurdles easily and was clearly enjoying himself, and in the back straight jockey Luke Harvey moved him sweetly up to the leaders. But then once again disaster struck. As Luke put it afterwards, 'In a hundred yards he had gone.' Once again his breathing had seized up with a fearful noise. Almost certainly he had swallowed his tongue again and Rhaps's race was over. Only the fact that he was a natural jumper saw him beat a couple home. Luke's wise advice was a soft palate operation pronto rather than souring the horse by running him again with such a physical handicap. After all, the experience must have been even more of a shock for him than it was for us.

I had only recently learned from speaking to Newmarket vet Richard Greenwood that horses are obligatory nose-breathers. They don't breathe through their mouths and the palate is closed off from the mouth when they are galloping. Sometimes the soft palate becomes detached and flaps, causing turbulence and gurgling in the airway. Tongue strapping, if it holds, can work by pulling the larynx forward and anchoring the soft palate. If it does not then surgery is pretty well the only answer.

It looked like a few vet's bills would soon be coming: for me Rhaps was too promising not to give him that chance. I had felt truly excited as he surged down the back straight and Luke was impressed enough to express an interest in taking on the horse if the Eternal Optimists did not want to persevere.

One of Paddy Ashdown's fellow Lib Dem MPs once told me of an encounter with a man who had served with the restlessly energetic Paddy during his SBS career. 'Ah yes, Captain Ashdown,' he had mused. 'The men would follow him anywhere, if nothing else, out of a sense of sheer curiosity.' By March 1999 sheer curiosity was about the only thing left for those of us still following Rhapsody in Blue around Britain's racecourses. Nine duck eggs in nine races was not much of a record as he faced the starter at Newbury. To be honest, even I was becoming fainthearted. What would the explanation be this time for his failure to oblige? The wrong going? The wrong trip? The assistant starter's aftershave? Obliged to be at another racecourse that day, this was how I recorded what happened next.

No more need we suffer the slings and arrows of cynical friends with their unfeeling cracks about cat food and glue factories. We have a real racehorse. First of all the apologies. I must apologise first to those Warwick racegoers who at around 4.08 observed an apparently sober racegoer past the first flush of youth in front of a TV screen screaming 'Come on Rhaps you little beauty' and giving a passable imitation of a whirling dervish as from a course 50 miles away he attempted to assist Tony Dobbin with his finish. (The jockey was managing quite well without any support.) I must apologise to Andy Turnell for ever doubting that he would produce our strapping four-year-old at full race fitness after a five-month layoff since an operation and I must apologise to Rhapsody in Blue himself for ever suggesting that he might be destined for a permanent life among the also-rans.

So what did Rhapsody achieve at Newbury on Saturday? Had they switched the Dubai World Cup to Berkshire? Had he stormed home the winner of a big sponsored race? Not quite yet. What Rhapsody had done was to gallop his heart out round Newbury's two-mile hurdle track making a real race of it with the eventual winner Allgrit. So well was he going entering the straight that, having assured everyone from the friendly Warwick gatemen onwards that Rhaps was on no account to be backed, I feared for a moment I might have to be driven out of the course under a blanket. Only in the dying strides was Rhaps eased out of second place by Satwa Boulevard. He hadn't won but for the first time ever, and in only his second race over obstacles he had finished in the money. And since Rhapsody had cost us less than a tenth of the 47,000 guineas paid for Jim Old's winner Allgrit it was a truly promising run. His operation appeared to have been a success and at last it seemed we had a horse who could realise the potential we had all seen on the gallops. Yes, taking part is fun. But getting in the frame is a lot more fun.

After Newbury I had raided the superlatives cupboard and Andy Turnell too was chuffed. He reckoned that Rhaps remained in fine fettle and that we should strike while the iron was hot, so it was off to Uttoxeter two weeks later to see how the horse could improve on his Newbury showing. Racing, alas, rarely pulls you to your feet without following up with a blow to the solar plexus. The first time I saw Andy at Uttoxeter was in the hog roast queue and he wasn't looking at the quality of the meat, he was gazing nervously at the sky as the rain continued to fall.

With Richard Johnson riding, I went in heavily at 16-1. Andy told him to make the running if he could but they were never in contention from the fifth and trailed home tenth and last. Our horse had given him a lovely feel early on, said Dickie Johnson, but he had a daisy-cutter action with little knee lift and he simply couldn't handle ground that had become like a pudding. He had therefore left us some horse for another day.

For most of the syndicate that was it. Enough. Off Rhaps went to the sales. We had expected him to be bought as a potential hunter. Instead he was acquired, at a bargain price of about a quarter of what we had paid, for a small group of owners in Eric Cousins' old yard at Tarporley in Cheshire, now being run by Richard Ford, then husband of Carrie Ford, the leading woman rider.

Rhapsody in Blue was kitted out with an Australian-style tongue strap for his first run for Bricks Bills and Beer, a group comprising a builder, a publican and twenty Post Office workers from Liverpool. Their trainer advised the new owners to back him each way. He finished third of 23 at 25-1 and went on to win two or three races for his new connections before being retired to go hunting in the Morecambe Bay area, from where his new owner later contacted me to say that he was enjoying life. It was, I suppose, a typical life story for a jumper and one with a happier ending than some. Funds permitting I would do it again tomorrow.

Racing abroad

When travelling abroad for business with politicians or for pleasure with Mrs Oakley I have always seized any opportunity to extend my experience of racing in other countries. I have been racing in Australia and New Zealand, in Mauritius and Hong Kong, in France, in Ireland, in Dubai, in Cyprus and in Turkey, although one of my biggest regrets – to be rectified in semi-retirement – is that I have not yet attended a Breeders' Cup meeting in America or a Kentucky Derby.

Friends tell me to expect a whole new vocabulary wrapped around the sport when I do go racing in the USA, and Her Majesty the Queen and her advisers experienced that one year when she was privately visiting stud farms in Kentucky. One of her former press secretaries told me that when news of the trip became local knowledge he had drafted a small press release for the US media, which he headed 'Queen to visit studs in the USA'. After he was reminded by more earthy souls of how Britain and America are two nations divided by a common language, he rapidly redrafted it to read 'Her Majesty to visit US breeding establishments'.

New Zealand

It was thanks to the Queen that I once went racing at the Ellerslie Park track in Auckland during a Commonwealth Heads of Government meeting I was reporting there in 1995. She was to present the prize for a NZ$30,000 race named after her and I felt it my duty to miss some of the politics and follow her to the races to ensure no misfortune befell her.

Thanks to the Tote monopoly I found that NZ$2 (then rather less than £1) gave me entry to a nicely landscaped course, a pleasant though not luxurious grandstand and a ten-race card. Inside I learned that New Zealand then had some 80 mini jockey clubs running 60 different racecourses for the population of just three million. Maths was never my strong point but proportionately that would give us about 625 tracks in Britain rather than the 55 we have. Perhaps that embarrassment of riches had something to do with the fact that New Zealanders, as one Ellerslie Park punter told me, 'will bet on anything that moves. And if it doesn't move they will kick it and bet on it when it starts to move.'

They called the parade ring there 'the birdcage' and kept it uncluttered by owners and their hangers-on. The horses were then accompanied to the starting stalls by men in hunting pink. The first thing I noticed at that particular New Zealand track was that most of the jockeys were a lot prettier than those in Britain, largely because more than half of them were female. My written comments on that when back home were picked up and developed in the New Zealand media. I had reported:

> One race had ten lady riders in a 14-horse field. To the prejudiced who still believe that women do not have the strength to punch home in a tight finish I have to say that nearly all the races were hotly contested and seven were won by women riders. Despite the Jockey Club's planned lifting of the minimum weight at the end of this season from 7st 7lb to 7st 10lb, fewer jockeys in our well-nourished society are going to be able to do the lower weights without starving to danger level, taking pee pills and laxatives and driving to the races in sweat suits with the heater full on. Most jockeys riding today are six inches taller than their father's generation and unless minimum weights are raised regularly there will surely be more and more opportunities for women riders. My advice to the girls who hope to seize them is to head to New Zealand fast and acquire experience where there is so much less fuss about the gender beneath the silks.

New Zealanders certainly work their horses. The Queen was surprised to learn that the nine-year-old mare Brilliant Venture was having her 92nd outing on a racecourse. The unbeaten Derby winner Lammtarra only had four runs in his life, although admittedly they also included the King George VI and Queen Elizabeth Stakes and the Prix de l'Arc de Triomphe.

France

It isn't always easy finding what you want in France. The US film director Billy Wilder had been asked to bring home a bidet one time and he finished up sending a telegram: 'Unable to locate bidet. Suggest handstand in shower.' I was luckier with finding a French racetrack on a day off from reporting a presidential election campaign for CNN in April 2002.

It was the perfect spring morning in Paris. The rabbits on the Porte Maillot roundabout were safely back in their burrows. The sun was shining. Long-aproned waiters were washing down the pavements outside their brasseries, taxi drivers were warming up their horns, more out of habit than in expectation, and on my day off it was to be either the Louvre or racing at Maisons-Laffitte. Simple choice.

Unlike Londoners, racing-minded Parisians had it easy. In close range were Longchamp, Saint-Cloud, Auteuil and Vincennes. With a short hop on the Métro, a train from the Gare St Lazare and a taxi from the station I was within 50 minutes sitting at the *Pur Sang* ('Thoroughbred') restaurant just outside the Maisons-Laffitte Hippodrome gates sharing a table with a *gigot d'agneau* and an amiable half-bottle of Brouilly as the odour of stable drifted on the breeze and early race entries clopped their way across the tarmac from their horseboxes. I had long wanted not so much to attend a grand French racing day like the Arc as a journalist but to compare an average day's racing both sides of the Channel as a punter and to see if, handicapped as I was, I could actually find a winner or two.

The first handicap was language. After a week or two my French gets me by in politics or restaurants but I struggle with the more specialised vocabulary of the Turf. The second handicap was my lack of knowledge of Gallic form or of the less internationally minded French trainers and jockeys.

Inside the course I was initially impressed. Entry was less than £2.50. There were plenty of families in the small crowd, which confirmed that France can still supply central casting with enough perma-tanned males with elegant silk handkerchiefs and impossibly shined brogues, the sort who usually got the girl in Riviera romantic comedies starring Audrey Hepburn. The atmosphere was informal, the course and the paddock beautifully planted with limes, horse chestnuts, maples and even a splendid Cedris Atlantica Glaucia (I am showing off here – Mrs Oakley once planted one in our garden).

The loos were clean and plentiful, the grandstand was capacious and the Maisons-Laffitte track has an astonishing 1,800-metre straight. There were helpful notices explaining the functions of trainers, jockeys and lads, where and when to see the horses and how to make a bet. As for my wagering, travel clearly clarifies as well as broadening the mind: I finished up with three winners in seven races and it would have been four in eight if a confused French punter had not spent so long arguing about his bet in front of me that I missed the off for the sixth. It wasn't quite Waterloo but by my standards it wasn't far short of it.

My good fortune was thanks largely to Olivier Peslier

and the prodigy Christophe Soumillon, both well respected this side of the Channel. I took a particular interest in anything either was riding and looked out where I could for early-season condition in the paddock. Where the two coincided I plunged. In the day's biggest race, the 41,000 Prix Matchem, Peslier brought Thattinger with a devastating burst, paying €17.80 to a single Euro and €5.30 for a place. I liked Peslier's in the next too but he finished down the field. Pity I didn't switch to Soumillon, whose mount came home at 24-1.

The fifth was an amateur race for 'Cavalières et Gentlemen-riders' as the racecard put it (we do help them out a bit with the language). Feminists look away at this point. I decided shamelessly to accept my ignorance by backing the prettiest *cavalière* riding for a top stable. My selection, the diminutive Mademoiselle Blanche de Granvilliers brought Manchester with a great run through the last furlong but just failed to catch the winner Montfalgoux. Her smile in the unsaddling enclosure would have brought instant forgiveness from any disappointed punter. Red-blooded males wanted to vault the barrier and carry her saddle back for her.

The sixth race was ruined for me by the disgruntled French punter. But in the seventh, playing by now with pari-mutuel money, I backed both Peslier's and Soumillon's mounts each way and cheered them home first and second with Peslier an easy winner on the 6.8-1 Barangay. When I had a word with him afterwards he grinned and said, 'It was just like an English race.' I think he meant that it was run at an easy pace early on, enabling him gradually to wind up the tempo in front, rather than the fact that it was conducted during the day's only shower. After the late swoop on Thattinger it really showcased Peslier's talents. He clearly enjoyed his day and I won enough for a decent meal even in a Paris restaurant.

So why, despite the technical excellence of what was on offer (bar the scrappy single-sheet racecard with no display of the jockey's colours) will I not be rushing back to race in France? Sadly there was a total lack of atmosphere. Tote monopolies may make for good facilities and better rewards to owners but without the bookies the off-track scene definitely lacks colour. It wasn't, well, racy enough. It was utterly disengaged. There were no paddock interviews with the jockeys and trainers, no presentations to the winners. The announcer might have been listing departures at King's Cross rather than a thrilling lifetime's best for a participant. It all worked like clockwork but it sounded as soulless as clockwork too. At least the English look as though they are enjoying their racing.

Hong Kong

Two places in the world lived up to my imagination when I finally arrived there: Venice and Hong Kong. I love the buzz and bustle of Hong Kong, a city state which does not need a national flag or flower. It has instead a national sound, the near-permanent clatter of the pneumatic drill as Hong Kong strives constantly to better itself with still swankier hotels, yet taller office blocks. Hong Kong has one more advantage. A land with a betting mad public who wager one in seven of the dollars they earn truly can claim horseracing to be its national sport.

A gushing hostess once asked Bernard Shaw as he left her party if he had enjoyed himself. 'Yes madam, and it was the only thing I did enjoy,' he replied. Going racing at Sha Tin in Derby week 1997 was an object lesson in the different ways people do enjoy themselves.

Sha Tin had wonderful electronic gadgetry, marvellous viewing facilities and a buffet dinner in the air-conditioned restaurant at £20 a head offered the rarest of rare beef, excellent curries and puddings which any French pâtissier would have been proud to claim as his own. Races started to time, horses which played up in the stall were rapidly ruled out and jockeys' dropped whips, steering problems and bumps in running were meticulously detailed in stewards' reports as the swallows wheeled in and out under the floodlights. I was, I admit, short of the Cantonese for 'Go on my son' or 'Stick in there Majestic Conqueror' as the crowd seemed to cheer their favourites home. But there were no bookies as on English tracks and something was lacking in the atmosphere, something made plain to me by old Red Socks. There he was, respectably dressed and sitting on the ground near the lifts as I went up for the first race. There he was five races later as I came down again. All that had changed was the heavy underscoring on his folded up newspaper and the pile of betting slips beside him. With a TV monitor close by he had never moved further than the 25 yards to the Tote windows. On the course too there were no excited post-race clusters within the winners' enclosure. There was no sense of involvement. I suppose that like Bernard Shaw, old Red Socks had enjoyed himself. But I was so pleased to be back at Epsom that Saturday amid a crowd straining to get close enough to see the sweat on Benny The Dip's coat and raucously cheering jockey Willie Ryan, the honest understudy who was enjoying his fifteen minutes of fame on a horse his trainer had run only for the place money. Involvement was the word, whether you were wearing a topper or a kiss-me-quick. British racing may lack the big money but it has the character to make you care.

I did though want to give Hong Kong another try and

when the BBC gave me, as a parting present for eight years' service as Political Editor, the right to choose my own venue to present a holiday programme, I opted for Hong Kong at International Race Day time in December 2000.

There were downsides. For another part of the travelogue they had me do a fashion shoot at Shanghai Tang which involved my dressing in what kind friends tactfully called a kimono but which felt uncomfortably like a dress – and I am definitely not Kate Moss. But this time the racing was sublime.

In the Hong Kong Mile the long-time local hero Fairy King Prawn, trained by Ivan Allen, was being blown home by the crowd as he failed by a short head to catch Sunline, a tough New Zealand race mare, after giving her a five-lengths lead into the straight. The locals made Cheltenham on Gold Cup day sound like a mere tune-up. I have rarely heard a racecourse din like it.

Familiarity with British form fortunately proved no hindrance. Having been bought by Hong Kong property millionaire Robert Ng Chee Siong to join Ivan Allen's string, Daliapour was running his final race for Sir Michael Stoute and he showed all his class in taking the Hong Kong Vase by a comfortable four lengths. It was Fantastic Light though, trained by Saeed bin Suroor, who did me a real favour. When I interviewed Frankie Dettori before the race he was so bullish about his chances that I urged all the camera team to back his mount. Frankie delivered in style, coming home a length and a bit clear of the Stoute-trained Greek Dance. Just as well for me as the next day we were filming an item on Chinese medicine, which involved my imbibing what looked like a concoction of flaked dried lizard skin and pickled sea slug. Had my tipping skills failed I suspect it might have been a case of 'We'll need another take on that one Robin ... and another ...'

The $40 million International Race Day staged by the Hong Kong Jockey Club and watched by a billion people worldwide was a real eye-opener. When I spoke to racing director Winfried Engelbrecht-Bresges he outlined a simple philosophy: top-class racing, top-class information to the betting public and top-class integrity. He put the meeting's growing international status down to Hong Kong's readiness to stump up top prize money and to offer the best hospitality for owners and trainers. They certainly provide that and the racecard was an object lesson too. So was the scrupulous cleanliness of the premises. The cameraman recording my frustration over a narrow loser had his next shot planned as I tore up my betting slip but he could not execute it: even before my shredded ticket had reached the ground an eager cleaning lady had dashed forward with scoop and broom.

We saw winners on the day from Britain, Australia, New Zealand, the United Arab Emirates and Hong Kong. The Anglo-Italian Frankie Dettori's win on Fantastic Light clinched victory for the pair in the Emirates World Series. Ireland's Johnny Murtagh won on Daliapour, New Zealand's Sunline was partnered by Australian Greg Childs and South Africa's Basil Marcus rode a double in two of the domestic races. You really can't get any more international than Hong Kong.

Chief executive Lawrence Wong explained proudly that they had 23 Group One winners from ten countries on the card. There were, he said, 80,000 spectators at Sha Tin and their sister course Happy Valley, where the track is surrounded by high-rise apartments. Their punting and the efforts of 4,000 telephone staff saw the issue of 100 million betting tickets on the day (the Hong Kong population is just short of seven million people) and with $12 billion of an $84 billion a year turnover the HKJC provides 11 per cent of the Hong Kong government's entire tax take. No wonder the Hong Kong authorities share the British government's alarm at the growth of offshore internet betting.

Cyprus

Racing in Cyprus on a holiday there was different again. That November day in 2002 Mrs Oakley had unaccountably decided that she preferred being wrapped in seaweed derivatives and sipping cool white wine on the hotel terrace near Polis to six hours driving there and back across the mountains and crawling round Limassol to the Nicosia Race Club's track. But for me it was worth it.

With a ten-race card twice a week on Wednesdays and Saturdays and entry an amazingly cheap 50p there was plenty of reason for locals leaving work to head off to the pretty little sandtrack with its pineapple palms, neatly manicured trees, oleander hedges and beguiling odour of freshly roasting kebabs behind the grandstand. They could still catch the second half of proceedings which had begun at 2.00pm, aided after sundown by floodlighting.

How enduring a political legacy Britain has left around the world is disputed. But in most places locals seem grateful for the racing traditions we handed down. In Cyprus, said Panayiotis Kazamias, the Race Club's general manager, racing started after the British takeover in the 1870s when moustachioed cavalry officers in baggy jodhpurs took each other on for sidestakes. The Nicosia Race Club was legalised in 1936. Most of the thoroughbred stallions are imported from England, the Cyprus Turf Club rules were modelled on those of the Jockey Club and the urine samples taken from winners and others were sent to Newmarket for testing, which was then costing £124,000 a year.

There were differences of course. You would not find punters in the Members Bar on English tracks with plates of figs and black olives in front of them. There were no winners' enclosure ceremonies and no triumphal interviews with winning trainers. After a perfunctory photo the jockeys disappeared and the horses were led back to the racecourse stables. The racing was well organised, the camera patrols and photo-finish equipment were state of the art and the Tote computers system was formidable, but I would have liked a little more ceremony.

The riders, by British standards, were not particularly well-rewarded. The monthly salary for jockeys was 273 Cyprus pounds, the equivalent of about £321. Riding fees were CYP22 a race and the 29 jockeys employed at the track divided CYP183,000 between them as their 5 per cent share of prize money last year.

Some things of course are the same the world over. The commentary was, alas, all Greek to me but by the end of the afternoon I could do a passable imitation of 'Go on my son' in the noble tongue. I had a pretty good idea of what 'That shifty little bastard never tried a yard' sounded like in Greek as well.

The informality was relaxing. I don't think I saw a tie in the parade ring all afternoon and when the stalls handlers in their yellow T-shirts were brought back from the 1,600 metre start to the 1,200 metre jump-off they all piled into a little white shack on wheels that reminded me of student games trying to see how many people you could squeeze into a telephone box.

Finding winners proved easier than expected. The form, as far as I could read it, made the favourite Only

Olivers a cert in the first. I was slightly disconcerted to see that he was ridden by one Chr. Pavlou, a piratical-looking figure with a goatee beard, a single gold earring and a ponytail. But Mr Pavlou rode a copybook race, jumping his mount into an early lead, giving him a breather before the final turn and keeping a bit in hand to beat off his single challenger. In the second, for two-year-old maidens, I was so taken with the appearance of Amathus Desire, a gorgeous chestnut filly, that I looked no further. Despite some unfortunate racing colours that made her jockey look like a giant Neapolitan ice cream, the further they went, the further she was ahead. I went for a coincidence bet in the third on Lovely Christy because a woman, a total stranger, once asked me to inscribe that in one of my books and then walked away without paying for it. I felt that Lovely Christy owed me one but alas sixth was all she could manage.

I struck once more in the fifth race, backing the local champion jockey Nicos Nikolau on Asygritos. He stepped up the pace nicely from the front and won looking around. The nattiest thing on the course by far, with his extra-elegant riding boots, immaculate breeches and trendy goggles, Nikolau looked the local equivalent of Frankie Dettori. Good thing he didn't try a flying dismount though. Try that in the chute through to the weighing room where most dismounted and you could stun yourself on the roof. Never mind: three winners in five races I will settle for any day.

Dubai

There are many places in the world where I still yearn to race, many where I would like to be a regular for the big occasions. Nowhere does that apply more than Dubai,

where I went for the *Financial Times* one year to discover
how Sheikh Mohammed has used horseracing to brand
and publicise his country as the ultimate sportsman's
destination:

> It is three hours before the start of the 2009 Dubai
> World Cup, the richest race meeting in the world
> (total prize money $21.5m [£14.2m]) and the cli-
> max of the Arab emirate's annual two-month racing
> carnival. At the Nad Al Sheba racetrack thousands
> of people are already installed and in the free pub-
> lic enclosures people are shedding their shoes and
> spreading small carpets on any spare patch of con-
> crete terrace or grass.
>
> Women in black abayas, some wearing veils which
> cover all but their eyes, dish out family picnics of
> curry and flatbread. Groups of men in white dishda-
> shas squat down to pore over newspaper form sheets.
> Others, in rope-circled kefiyehs, stride up and down
> the concourse discussing the prospects of local train-
> ers and riders against the invaders from the US and
> Britain, from Hong Kong and South Africa, from
> Australia and Japan.
>
> Along the track at the 300-metre mark, the atmos-
> phere among paying customers at what is regarded
> as Dubai's social event of the year is a cross between
> Royal Ascot and Cheltenham. In the 'Irish Village'
> young male expats enjoy a Guinness or three while in
> the 'Bubble Lounge' girls in floaty mini-dresses and
> high heels drink champagne before teetering off for
> a photoshoot with *Ahlan!*, a *Hello*-style magazine.
>
> If, as economic commentators have suggested,
> Dubai's bubble has burst then there is little sign of
> it here – not unless you feel restricted by a choice
> between Bollinger, Taittinger and five other types of
> champagne.

In the coveted reserved seats of the main stand, a fluttering of white robes in mini-Mexican waves reflects the movements of Dubai's ruler Sheikh Mohammed bin Rashid Al Maktoum, clad in the blue that is the livery of his worldwide racing operation Godolphin. When he stands, everyone stands. When he sits, everyone sits. When he moves down to the parade ring to inspect the horses, to brief a jockey or congratulate a winner, a gently rustling phalanx of 20 or 30 accompanies him.

Racing folk around the world refer to the meet, with its lavish laser-light shows, horse acrobatics and fireworks, as 'Sheikh Mo's desert party'. And this time there is plenty for him to celebrate. Godolphin enjoys a one-two in a couple of early races. But the best is saved for last and the final three races on the card.

The successful rider in the first two is the apprentice Ahmad Ajtebi, a former camel rider and protégé of Sheikh Mohammed. Leading from the front on Gladiatorus and swooping in the last stride on Eastern Anthem, he becomes the first Emirati jockey in the event's 14-year history to win a race on World Cup night. Both horses are locally trained by first-season handler Mubarak bin Shafya and each runs in the colours of one of Sheikh Mohammed's sons.

In Europe I had been counselled that the Arab racing scene, with alcohol restricted and on-track betting banned, lacked atmosphere. Not at Nad Al Sheba. The triumphant apprentice milks the crowd, rising in his stirrups, pointing to his chest, waving his whip and raising both hands aloft. Frankie Dettori, the top jockey in Sheikh Mohammed's worldwide operation, couldn't have done it better and the whistling, cheering response is delirious, louder even than when the American horse Well Armed streaks home to win the final $6m World Cup race.

British-based jockey John Egan, who rides in Dubai for prominent owner Dr James Hay, has also experienced the Dubai race fans' passion: 'They'll be going 'E-gan, E-gan, E-gan', whether you are riding a 50-1 shot or a 6-4 favourite,' he tells me. 'Perhaps they've backed you before on one that's won. I often see the same people cheering me.' Hay, whose wife Fitri has three runners in her pink and green colours on World Cup night, adds, 'They kind of adopt horses. It's almost like a football team.'

Despite the lack of on-course betting, financial allegiances are not entirely absent from the proceedings. Although I was barred access to a betting website from my hotel room computer, there was no such problem phoning a UK bookmaker and, somehow, I don't think all the racegoers I saw with mobile phones to their ears five minutes before the off were calling their wives to inquire if they should drop in for a takeaway on the way home.

For locals without recourse to out-of-country betting, there are free-to-enter competitions – no money hazarded – requiring them to select the first three horses home in each of two races or the 'Pick Seven', in which they must find the winner of every race. The odds against doing so are forbidding but the rewards if they succeed are life-transforming. To a low-wage construction worker on a Dubai skyscraper, £20,000 is a fortune beyond belief.

On World Cup night there was a surprising amount of intermittent rain, but nothing could spoil the party. Ajtebi's victories and the fact that this was the last Dubai World Cup to be held at Nad Al Sheba – next year it will move to a venue currently under construction at nearby Meydan – gave the occasion a landmark feel. It also marked a new stage in Dubai's strategy of using a horse race to market a country, a concept which has, in the past decade and a half, rewritten the international racing calendar and boosted the fortunes of previously overlooked racing countries.

Why horses? Partly, it's because the 'boss', as those who work for Sheikh Mohammed refer to him, has a passion for them and for racing. Last week, amid the serenity of the Godolphin yard, I spoke to Simon Crisford, the former journalist who has been Godolphin's racing manager since the early 1990s. The boss, now the wrong side of 60, was elsewhere – out riding in a 120km endurance race.

Crisford says of a man said to be able to distinguish his own camel's tracks from those of a hundred others in the desert sands, 'Sheikh Mohammed is as close to nature as anyone you could ever meet. That's what fascinates him about this sport. He wouldn't get the same attraction from looking at cars or football players.' The Sheikh's favourite horse, Dubai Millennium, could be a brute with some people. But his owner would spend hours in Dubai Millenium's box. He would fondle the horse's tongue, and the horse would rest his head under the Sheikh's arm.

Passion is matched by pragmatism. Sheikh Mohammed, who shuttles a hundred horses to Newmarket around this time of year for the British season, based Godolphin in Dubai because he wanted his horses near him and because the climate aided their preparation. He founded the World Cup both to foster true international competition and because he planned a future for Dubai as a sporting and tourist destination when the oil runs out. The first chairman of the Dubai World Cup committee, back in 1996, was instructed, 'You are here to market Dubai as a tourist destination. We've got to fill all these five-star hotels.'

Dubai has few historic panoramas to attract the tourist so the Maktoums chose another way to make its mark. They determined that it would epitomise the culture of being biggest, best and first. This is why the tiny emirate now boasts the tallest building in the world, the still-growing Burj Dubai; the biggest man-made island in the world, Palm Jumeirah; and a 400-metre ski run in a shopping mall. The fact that the thoroughbred originated in his part of the world also convinced Sheikh Mohammed to put horses at the centre of Dubai's appeal.

First there were international jockey competitions. Then, 14 years ago, came the first World Cup. Logistically there were hurdles. For the inaugural event Dubai wanted to entice Allan Paulson, the boss of Gulfstream and owner of Cigar, then the best horse in the world. Paulson wouldn't come without his dogs accompanying him, so quarantine rules were waived for him to bring them on his executive jet. There are advantages sometimes in being a principality.

The presence of a champion like Cigar was seen as crucial. Sheikh Mohammed wanted his horses to be the best. But that involved racing them against the best and, as Crisford explains, 'Americans then had a fear of coming to Dubai. "Why travel so far to run in the desert?" But Paulson did.' Having arrived, he marvelled that Sheikh Mohammed, as Paulson enviously put it, had been able to sell a race, a city and a country to the world for the cost of one night's prize money.

Others quickly followed Paulson's example and so a meeting which started as a curiosity, a one-off desert party before the real racing season began, became a key fixture in the international racing calendar. Then, five years ago, the first Dubai Carnival of Racing was held. Running from January to mid-March it subsidises international owners to encourage them to bring their best horses. Why run for £3,000 on the all-weather track at Lingfield in February when you can be competing for £100,000 at normally sunny Nad Al Sheba?

A decade ago, the world knew little of racehorses from South Africa or South America. But Invasor, who won the 2007 World Cup for Sheikh Mohammed's brother Sheikh Hamdan Al Maktoum, was bred in Argentina and originally trained in Uruguay. Of the World Cup field on Saturday night, four horses had begun their careers in Argentina and two more in Brazil. Herman Brown, a South African trainer, says, 'Dubai has given us a venue and become a showcase for our horses. You cannot believe what has been done for our breeding industry.'

Until this year, 659 horses from 25 countries had run in the Dubai carnivals. Visitors had won more than half the races contested and taken home more than $103m in prize money. Construction magnate Jim Hay, whose racing career began amid warm beer and soggy pies backing handicappers on Scottish tracks, says that the carnival is like Royal Ascot, only longer: 'You get the opportunity to compete with the absolute crème de la crème. What drives owners is partly the prize money but also the sheer colour.' This is a common view and generally the only grumble you hear from the owners is that the Maktoums' bottomless purses, perhaps being drawn a little tighter now, have inflated bloodstock prices to levels few can afford.

On the back of its international racing and other sporting showcases Dubai has built up its tourism from 50,000 a year in 1996 to more than 5m currently. It has hosted golf's Desert Classic since 1989, and has redrawn the game's map to the extent that what used to be the European Tour of Merit is being replaced by the 'Race to Dubai'. It also stages world-class tennis tournaments, and the Sports City project, due to be finished in 2010, includes a 25,000-capacity cricket stadium which might offer an alternative venue for international teams driven out of the Indian subcontinent by terrorism.

Dubai authorities have made some adjustments to the world scene: they realised they had to swallow hard and accept betting-related television deals in other countries to get the Carnival fixtures shown across the world. But others have had to change their calendars. Clive Brittain, a British trainer who has been coming to Dubai since the racing started, says, 'We are having to adjust our season to cope with an early spring.'

Crisford argues that Godolphin, which has become a kind of Dubai national team around the world's racetracks, has with the World Cup helped make Dubai the sporting capital of the Middle East. 'In any one week during the winter you might have Frankie Dettori, the Williams sisters, Tiger Woods and Michael Schumacher all here at the same time,' he says. 'Sport out here is massive and the people love it.'

In 2000, before Dubai Millennium won the World Cup (the horse was boldly named with that target in mind), Sheikh Mohammed said, 'You can't just do your job and sit at home. We must strive together, we must go forward, we must invent something – even from nothing. That's what Godolphin is about, that's what Dubai is about, that's what me and my brothers are about.'

But can the development continue at the rate it has? A year ago Dubai was keeping busy a third of the cranes in the world. The pace of new building was such that taxi drivers needed monthly refresher courses in finding their way round. But, like anywhere else that has expanded fast on borrowed money, Dubai is hurting. Local employers are shedding labour and projects have been mothballed.

Some in the racing community have fretted that the new course at Meydan, where Sheikh Mohammed has promised to increase the purse for the World Cup race alone from $6m to $10m, could find itself among them. But Simon Crisford insists there is no need to worry: 'I don't know where that fear is coming from. It's absolute nonsense. Things may be slowing down a bit but Meydan's not slowing down.' Nad Al Sheba regulars such as Clive Brittain are also optimistic. 'If Sheikh Mohammed says it will happen, it will,' he says.

Sure enough, when last weekend's racing was finished, the next morning bulldozers moved into Nad Al Sheba to pull down its Maktoum and Millennium grandstands, facilities which many British tracks would be proud to offer. At nearby Meydan, meanwhile, the shell of a one-kilometre long 'landscraper' grandstand has started to take shape. It has, of course, become the biggest in the world.

Mauritius

Wherever I have been in the world, following prime ministers and presidents in the day job or simply on holiday, the first thing to go into my hand baggage has always been my binoculars. One of the most pleasurable holiday surprises was going racing in Mauritus back in 1998.

Before last Saturday's Colonel Baker Cup, runners from the 'Epsom' and 'Ascot' stables paraded along with those from Ecurie Fok and Ecurie Gujadhur. But this was Port Louis, Mauritius, not Newbury or Goodwood. Overshadowing the parade ring was a majestic banyan tree. In corrugated iron and canvas shacks in the centre of the course the cheap enclosure crowd parked their crash helmets with an enterprising stallholder, ate fish and rice from steaming vats and gambled incessantly between races at pique, throwing darts onto chequered number boards. Crowds thronged around (win only) bookies with takeaway curry names like Yeung Kim Fat, Foo Kune and Herve Wong Leung Ki. The 'Epsom' and 'Ascot' stables clustered among monkey puzzle trees on a hillside of elegant villas behind the Champ de Mars racecourse: on the other side were mountain crests known as the Lion, the Thumb and the Frog. The beach that day could offer little competition.

Mauritius is an island where Hindu, Tamil, Muslim, Franco-Mauritians, Chinese and Creoles seem to co-exist happily in a tension-free jumble of inter-married races, languages and religions, and appropriately racing began there as a means of creating unity. Shortly after the British ousted the French colonial power, the good Colonel Draper decided that Franco-British relations could best be improved by turning the old army manoeuvres ground into the second-oldest racecourse in the southern hemisphere. And if the English won the original power struggle, the French seem to have had the best of it in recent years on the racecourse. Serge Henry was that year heading for his third successive trainers' championship.

Racing and betting have thrived in Mauritius since that 1812 inception and the Mauritius Turf Club conducts weekly meetings from May through to November. Eight recognised stables provide the bulk of the handicappers in six divisions who contest events from 1,365 metres to 2,400, with seven free-lance trainers responsible for the rest of the 350 horses trained on the island.

Punters certainly get some assistance. As many as 300 people turn up to watch morning work on the track from 5.30am. Each horse has to exercise bearing its name and every walk, canter and 'spurt' is meticulously recorded and made available when Saturday declarations are announced. Security is tight. Horses due to run the next Saturday have to be produced the Sunday before, They are then secured in stables which can only be opened by double lock, with one key held by stable staff and the other by the security team. Officials follow each horse to and from its morning exercise.

Copious racecard information (British racetracks please copy) enabled even this ignorant visitor to find three winners on the eight-race card and contests were conducted with military precision. Saddling up and 'Horses away' commands are swiftly obeyed. No sooner are the contestants on their way to the start than red-shirted attendants are hand-whisking loose straw back into the saddling boxes.

I watched a couple of races with Khalid Rawat, the generously welcoming and needle-sharp clerk of the course. Before each race he checked every jockey's colours, sending back Australian Gavin Howes to change. In the parade ring he was noting that not only blinkers, visors and bandages were as declared but even which kind of bit each horse had fitted. We watched from the judges' box with its distinctive odour of film developer. Then it was swiftly down to the weighing room to tape-record the comments of the jockeys as they came in. Not only would the stewards hear them, they would be published for all to see.

In Mauritius jockeys, not trainers, saddle up the

horses. A wise precaution, said Khalid, with such intense betting interest. No jockey will willingly risk a slipping saddle. Should such an accident occur, no one can point a finger of suspicion at the yard.

Sadly for Mauritians, most winners are ridden not by locals who lack apprentice schools or even an electric horse but by imports from South Africa or Australia who have not quite made the top grade at home, grizzled veterans on the downward slope or youngsters seeking to broaden their experience. One in the latter category, the film-star blond Piet Botha, argued that if you can ride winners in Mauritius you can ride them anywhere: 'It's a tight track with a lot of tactical riding. You need a lot in your favour to win, a decent draw, a reasonable weight and plenty of luck.' You could say he has had that. Botha had only ridden two winners this year to add to his 120 in South Africa but they included two of the four Mauritian Classics.

It really is a tough school. Five jockeys have already been sacked by their trainers this season: 'There's too much money involved for people to be patient. One moment you are a hero to the crowd, the next they are calling you names.'

The victories of Dancing Sherpa, Dempsta and Volcano Lover did little more than pay for a round of rum punches in my hotel but my raceday in Mauritius won't easily be forgotten. It is fast, fun and friendly. As I passed Serge Henry's stable yard on the way out, the sun was gleaming on the flanks of a contestant being hosed down after his race. Mynah birds called above. But in my mind was the soulful gaze of a young Mauritian, peering through the slats of the weighing-room blinds at an incoming winner and clearly wondering if he would ever have the chance of such a mount himself. How about a British Horseracing Board scholarship or two?

Racing issues

The all-weather

One of the biggest changes to racing in my lifetime has been the development of the all-weather tracks, first Lingfield, then Southwell and Wolverhampton, then, as part of an £18 million redevelopment, Kempton Park Even Newbury has flirted with the idea. To many they are just there to provide low-grade betting-shop fodder, making sure that bookies have enough races to keep punters coming through their doors even when the elements have made racing on turf tracks impossible through frost, snow or flooding. Never mind the quality, feel the each-way opportunities. In early days of low attendances they used to joke that the natural order of things was reversed on the all-weather: instead of jockey changes being announced to the crowd they used to announce crowd changes to the jockeys huddled for warmth in the weighing room.

I wrote a pretty sour piece about a day at Lingfield in January 2001:

> I don't know how many others were like me at Lingfield for the all-weather racing on Saturday because the jumping meetings at Sandown and Huntingdon had failed to survive the weather. But I doubt if many of them will be rushing back. I like a bet when I go racing, but I don't go just for the betting. I go racing too for sport, spectacle and excitement. I go for colour, character and camaraderie. But although four of the six races ended with the leaders separated by three-quarters of a length or less, there was about as much excitement about the proceedings as you would find in an undertaker's car park.

This was racing for those who bet on numbers or colours as much as they do on measuring the respective qualities of horses, riders and trainers.

Where was the nobility of the equine athlete, the glamour of sporting excellence? Hot Pants, winner of the five-furlong sprint, did the business but looked like something from an attic where the moths had taken over. No self-respecting tramp would have worn her coat.

Of course even low-grade racing can be fun with the right presentation but it doesn't do much to enrich the entertainment or inform the punter when the scratchy racecard doesn't even include a colour illustration of the jockeys' silks. There is no excuse for that: we are in the 21st century. The trainers didn't do a lot to help either. Six stables had winners; in five cases the winning trainers – Mick Channon, Richard Hannon, Stan Moore, David Chapman and Ken Ivory (who admittedly was on holiday in Malaga) – did not show their faces at Lingfield.

OK, so the horses they race on the all-weather aren't usually their stars. Trainers running mega-horsepower yards can't be at every meeting. But none of those winning Lingfield trainers had runners over the jumps at Uttoxeter or Haydock, and they too are part of an entertainment business. People want to be able to nudge each other and spot the racing personalities, even to exchange a brief word with them. The one winning trainer who was there, Hugh Collingridge, took the richest race of the day with the consistent Admiral's Place and promptly re-stirred a controversy from a fortnight before.

On that day, racing at Lingfield was abandoned. But it was not abandoned after a morning inspection, saving people a fruitless journey, it was abandoned just before the first race because the stalls handlers pointed out to jockeys arriving at the start that there was just a thin veneer of sand over the frozen surface. The stewards called off the meeting. Owners, trainers and racegoers let Lingfield's owners Arena Leisure know exactly what they thought of such cack-handed management.

Trainer Nick Littmoden said 'a blind man with his stick would have known it was rock-solid frozen' and Collingridge and others quite naturally demanded compensation for their costs. That Saturday Collingridge called for the track, which had clearly deteriorated over the eleven years since it was laid, to be dug up and have new drainage installed. Having been training since 1974, he pointed out, he was in on the ground floor of all-weather racing. 'I love coming here. Lingfield is a super track, but the only course is to take it up and employ some modern technology.'

That, of course, raised the question of who was to pay for works that would cost at least £1.5 million: Arena Leisure or the soon-to-expire Levy Board? Somehow between them the Levy Board and Arena had to make sure that the tracks which had become crucial to bookmaking revenue, and through that to the continued existence of the sport, once more became what their name implied, true all-weather tracks.

Nine years later, Lingfield having installed a new Polytrack surface, I was singing a slightly different tune. In January 2010 I wrote:

Where would we be without 'all-weather' racing on artificial surfaces? With Sandown's jumping card frosted off last Saturday I wasn't the only one who scuttled across Surrey to Lingfield's Polytrack, where

Betdaq had sponsored an extra day to keep the cash tills rolling and the internet wires humming with the bets that help to sustain our sport.

All-weather racing began here only twenty years ago, just before the Berlin Wall fell. But with an ear-nipping chill and snow still visible on the grandstand roof, we still enjoyed a seven-race card. Gone are the days when you went to Lingfield just to watch the little guys of the sport kicking sand in each other's faces in front of crowds no bigger than a bus queue. These days top trainers too send their horses to the artificial tracks: Ghanaati won last year's 1,000 Guineas on her turf debut after two prep runs on Kempton's all-weather.

Top jockeys have found they can boost their careers by staying put at Wolverhampton, Southwell, Lingfield and Kempton rather than heading off to the sun in India or Dubai. Punters relish the greater predictability of results on the all-weather. Trainers too had been converted. Noel Chance tended to put any invalid jumpers on the all-weather before going back over fences. Andy Turnell told me at Lingfield that he was quite a fan: 'None of them comes back with "a leg" after racing on this surface', and George Margarson cut to the quick: 'There are so many all-weather races now you've got no choice but to come.'

In between, in January 2003 I had noted how the all-weather was improving life too for busy lightweights like Jimmy Quinn:

If Jimmy Quinn rode horses as fast as he talks, the rest of them would never catch up with him. He is a 7st 10lb ginger-haired bundle of energy who never stops. Last year he rode more than 1,100 horses in races in Britain and scored 101 victories. On top of that he had more than 100 rides in Germany. He rode in Ireland, in Italy, even in Istanbul and was second in the Swiss Derby. He reckons he had just three Sundays off in the calendar year.

I could only catch him for a quick word on Saturday at Lingfield as he took a quick drag on a cigarette after the fourth race: the fifth was the only contest on the eight-race card in which he didn't have a mount. For lightweights like Jimmy Quinn the steady build-up of the all-weather tracks at Lingfield, Southwell and Wolverhampton has been a boon, increasing both the size and the steadiness of their incomes.

You won't see Kieren Fallon, Richard Hughes, Kevin Darley or Frankie Dettori blowing on their mittened fingers in February before a seven-furlong seller at Southwell, although Pat Eddery, eager to clock his normal century of British winners, did take all-weather rides in December (he finished on a frustrating 99). But for the next rank of jockeys the all-weather tracks have become a godsend, as they have for smaller trainers who won't be getting much of a look-in when the big yards are in full swing. Epsom yards could hardly exist without their regular victories at conveniently close-by Lingfield and Kempton. Trainer Jim Boyle told me that the all-weather tracks make planning a campaign for a horse much easier: 'So often you have a horse lined up for a turf race and then the ground goes.' The all-weather tracks too are kinder to problem horses: 'They don't always come back so well off the turf.'

Jimmy Quinn has become one of the stars of the all-weather tracks, along with Ian Mongan and Eddie Ahern, who scored a treble on Saturday's Lingfield card.

In the bad old days at Lingfield, say the jockeys,

there wasn't much finesse about it. There was so much kick-back from the sand that your only realistic hope was to dash into the lead and stay there as long as you could. But since the excellent new Polytrack surface was laid it has been much more like turf racing, with a variety of tactics applied.

Jimmy Quinn says, 'It's a nice track to ride now, but you have to use your head. It's hard to ride here now from in front. You need a horse which can travel, there can be a lot of traffic coming into the straight.' The key to many races, he says, is coming down the hill between the three- and two-furlong markers, and there his fellow Irishman Eddie Ahern has perfected what has become known as the 'slingshot technique', a long, smooth acceleration through that furlong, building momentum for the swing around the turn into the straight.

All-weather racing still lacks something in atmosphere but spice is sensibly being added in the Bet Direct All-Weather Jockeys Championship, running from November to March. At least at Kempton, I noted one day, the runners make a good silhouette as they turn into the back straight and you see them silhouetted against the in-course lake. 'That's fine,' said former jockey John Lowe, 'providing you're not on a horse that's hanging left round the bend and, like me, you can't swim.'

Winter Flat racing has improved steadily in quality with yards like those of Barry Hills and Brian Meehan spotting the improved prize money and up-and-coming trainers like Andrew Balding taking the chance to get his name on the winners' lists after taking over from his father Ian. At least they hadn't had to waste too much on the horses' rugs in the changeover, merely unpicking the 'I' from the previous I.A.B.

Emerging jockey talent too was there to be spotted on the all-weather. That winter I picked out in my *Spectator* column a certain Tom Queally, later to be Frankel's partner through his glorious career. I wrote:

> A claimer who showed that you don't have to be an old sweat to master the Lingfield tactics was young Tom Queally, a former Irish champion apprentice who is attached to the Aidan O'Brien yard and who was on a working holiday with David Elsworth. He timed his run coolly on old Indian Blaze in the seller. We all have to start somewhere …

The whip controversy

Trainer Sir Mark Prescott once noted that the greyhound races for the anticipated pleasure of sinking its teeth into a fluffy white bunny tail ahead. The human athlete races for the hope of fame and riches. But what's in it, he asked, for the horse?

One thing that *has* been in it for the racehorse has been the coercion of the whip, the fear that if it doesn't do its utmost, a wallop or two will follow, the hope that if it does stick its head down and go all out, that little demon on top will stop belting away.

It wasn't a reasoning that worked particularly well for me at boarding school. The masters and matrons who wielded cane or slipper, in some cases with obvious relish, only made me stroppier. But racing folk have clung to the old theories. What used to be euphemistically termed the 'persuader' or the 'attitude adjuster' was defended as an essential. Some even claim the whipping of horses in races as part of some mystical, noble ritual.

It is an issue no racing writer can really avoid and I

became involved for the first time after the 2,000 Guineas of 1996. That year three horses drove to the line together with Mark of Esteem prevailing by a head from Even Top with Bijou d'Inde only another head away. All three jockeys, Frankie Dettori, Philip Robinson and Jason Weaver gave all they had. All three whipped their horses into giving all they had. And the stewards suspended the three for eight, four and two days respectively. The penalties were set to reflect the respective severity of the offences, the amount of times the jockeys used their whips, whether or not they had applied excessive force and whether or not they had hit the colts out of rhythm with their strides.

I wrote then that in most sports if you break the rules you are disqualified. Horses do generally respond to the whip. If you make excessive use of the whip and so break the rules to give your horse an advantage then the difference between that and feeding it some prohibited substance to make it go faster is only a qualitative one. But doping would have you disqualified and banned.

And yet if any of the three horses had been disqualified there would have been an outcry. Racing is all about winning. To have handed the race to the fourth horse home Alhaarth would have been absurd. The action of the stewards was realistic. And yet a niggle remained. If by whipping his horse another ten times and harder still, Jason Weaver could have improved his place from third to first, would that have been considered within the bounds as well? Where does trying to win end and cruelty begin?

In a thrilling St Leger that year, Dettori got up Shantou by a neck from Eddery on Dushyantor. But again both he and Eddery were given two-day suspensions for using the whip with unreasonable frequency. That time I wrote:

The two riders are ultimate professionals, one the champion jockey the other ten times the champion before him. Rules are rules and you cannot blame the stewards for implementing them. But as Eddery says it surely cannot go on like this. Not only does the intensity of the occasion make it likely that every time there is a close finish to a Classic all the jockeys involved are going to be collecting whip bans. It ensures too that on the occasions when the sport receives maximum attention from the media and non-regular racegoers, the question of potential cruelty becomes the major focus.

What adds intensity from the jockeys' point of view is the 'totting up' procedure which nowadays applies. After you have received twelve days' worth of bans for similar offences, any further transgression triggers a reference to the Jockey Club's disciplinary committee with an automatic extra 14-day ban to follow. Frankie Dettori is now on the 12-day mark, Pat Eddery on ten and both will have to take extra care on future mounts, a fact which could be seen as a penalty on the trainers and owners who put them up from now on this season.

Frequent examples highlighted the dilemma. There have been few more thrilling racecourse duels than the battle to the line in Sandown's Coral-Eclipse in the year 2000 between Giant's Causeway and Kalanisi. But George Duffield had hit Giant's Causeway more than fifteen times with the whip in the straight and Pat Eddery had given his mount a similar number of reminders. Both jockeys were referred to the Jockey Club for 'excessive use' and were stood down for ten days as a result, a blow to their earning capacity in high season and for Eddery a penalty that could have affected his chances of retaining the jockeys' championship.

Admitting that he broke the rules and would have to pay the price, Duffield said, 'It was a true championship race, the kind that people come to see.' He would, he added, do it again if that was what was needed to win the race. An upset Eddery added, 'Bans are ruining the game. We are doing our best for everyone. It was exciting for the public and we have to suffer for it.'

I had mixed feelings. Neither horse appeared damaged or distressed after the race. Both responded gamely to their jockeys' urgings and continued to do so in races later that season. We did, after all, expect the authorities to come down hard on jockeys in other races who did not make enough effort to win.

But I noted at the time that Pat Eddery, Kieren Fallon and Frankie Dettori had all been penalised too for 'excessive use' after the 1998 Juddmonte International, one of the best races for years, with Pat punished for hitting One So Wonderful 23 times. There do have to be limits in the interests of horse welfare and it was interesting that the introduction of automatic ten-day bans for excessive use of the whip in Group One races, where the financial rewards for victory involve the strongest temptation to overdo the use of the 'persuader', did result temporarily in a sharp decline in the number of such offences. George Duffield's comments at the time suggested that there was in racing as well as football a concept of the 'professional foul'.

As a townie for most of my life rather than a countryman, and with little riding experience I feel that my right to pronounce on the whip issue is limited. But there are genuine experts like Sir Peter O'Sullevan who have campaigned for more restrictions on whip use and I cannot condone anything which amounts to cruelty. In the autumn of 2011 therefore I welcomed a new set of rules on whip use from the racing authorities, particularly as they appeared to have the backing of some top racing professionals.

The new British Horseracing Authority rules, I wrote, marked a new era:

It is racing's final acknowledgment that while the whip may be used for occasional correction, it is no longer appropriate beyond a very clearly defined point for coercion. Under new rules the number of times a jockey's whip can be used during a race has been nearly halved to seven times on the Flat and eight times over jumps, with a maximum of five strikes in the last furlong or after the last obstacle. Jockeys breaking the rules will face automatic suspension. They will lose riding fees and prize money percentages, and it will be an offence for owners or trainers to encourage wrongdoing by recompensing riders for what they have lost.

Things came to a head after Ballabriggs' victory in the Grand National. Jason Maguire, by no means a whip-happy jockey, was suspended for five days for hitting his mount seventeen times although, under the old rules, he didn't lose his £40,000 share of the prize money. Frankie Dettori's thrilling Ascot victory on Rewilding over So You Think also came under scrutiny because he hit his mount 24 times, earning him a nine-day compulsory holiday.

It simply could not go on, the most eye-catching events in racing's calendar constantly clouded by cruelty issues. Desperate for a greater share of the leisure dollar, the industry has accepted that.

Old-school jockeys used to insist that they could make horses go faster with use of the whip and true horsemen like Peter Scudamore, sensitive enough to determine how horses were responding, did just that.

Too often though we also saw tired horses flogged home unnecessarily by clumsy riders in a way which demeaned the sport.

Talking to great riders like Dessie Hughes and Richard Dunwoody, as I did for my history of the Cheltenham Festival, I found they are now regretful about how the customs of the time allowed and even encouraged them to belt away at horses like Monksfield and Viking Spirit. Now with Dettori, jumps champion AP McCoy and champion trainer Paul Nicholls lining up in support of the new law's clarity, we have the chance to turn a page.

The key phrase Paul used was 'the time has come'. Traditions have their attractions but if we never accepted the need to reflect the mood of a new age we would still have ponies down pits, children up chimneys and landowners helping themselves to rosy-cheeked peasant girls. The people we want to see thronging Britain's racetracks don't see the care and attention lavished on racehorses in stable yards by devoted staff: racing's image is determined for them by what they observe at the business end of races on track.

But if the BHA has done well in setting such clear new limits, it has done well too in refusing to be panicked into getting rid of the whip altogether. You can't sit a horse on the naughty step or stop its pocket money: whips are needed to control wayward behaviour, to aid steering and balance and to prevent injury to the animal and others. Some wanted horses disqualified from their victories where riders have committed whip offences. For me that is a step too far, punishing owners, trainers and punters for a rider's misdemeanour, although racing might note that if the new regulations don't work it may be all we have left to try.

Some riders are muttering. What, they ask, if you've used up your 'hits allowance' and a horse starts drifting dangerously across the course? Seamie Heffernan fears that owners will say 'You gave him five smacks and he just got beat, why didn't you give him the other two?' Johnny Murtagh grumbles that owners of lazy horses will be penalised and wonders how pleased punters will be to see him put down his stick when a horse is responding well to vigorous urging but a limit has been reached. The answer is: we'll learn to live with it. This is a threatened sport and it doesn't any longer live in a world of its own.

I had been abroad when the new rules were published and I returned to find massive controversy, with many jockeys pronouncing the scheme unworkable. Returning to the subject I wrote:

> From Canadian waters, noting that jockeys like Frankie Dettori and Tony McCoy had backed the reforms, I welcomed them too. I still back reform. Racing needs public approval and bigger crowds and the public response to whip use has to be heeded. But in the way they introduced the rules and the punishments they decreed for those found contravening the new rules, the British Horseracing Authority formed a circular firing squad.
>
> October 15, the first Champions Day at Ascot, was planned as Britain's richest and most exciting day's racing ever, featuring the wondrous Frankel. So it was, but because the BHA chose to introduce the rule changes that week, sporting headlines were dominated for a fortnight not by Champions Day but by endless stories about jockeys being found in breach of the new whip regulations.
>
> Ascot's attempts to cement its position as a hub of

international racing suffered a huge setback when the amazed Christophe Soumillon, the Belgian who is one of Europe's leading riders, lost his £50,000 share of the Champion Stakes prize money for giving his horse one smack more than the newly permitted five in the final furlong.

Dettori and McCoy, it turns out, had effectively been suckered into their public support. Richard Hughes, probably the best jockey in Britain, refused to ride again until the rules were changed and riders both on the Flat and over jumps were incensed both at the complexity of the new rules and the scale of the penalties. A jockeys' strike was threatened.

It was a public relations disaster. Jockeys involved in frantic finishes found it impossible in many cases to count whether they had used their stick the permitted five times or an extra one which brought automatic and condign punishment. What they had done in most cases was to infringe a technicality: what the public absorbed from the headlines was that large numbers of jockeys were daily being found guilty of cruelty to their mounts.

In their eagerness to demonstrate the smack of firm government, the BHA have inflicted severe damage on the sport they are supposed to succour and protect. They are trying to change the behaviour of professionals who in many cases have been riding under one system for twenty years, and who are criticised and penalised if they don't go all out to win.

The sensible way of proceeding would have been to announce the new rules but run a trial period with no penalties for the first two months. Jockeys who transgressed could have been called in and cautioned each time, and warned of the penalties they would have suffered if the new laws had come into force while they adapted.

There were other concerns. Taking away a jockey's riding fee as well as his or her share of the prize after a whip transgression was unfair, especially for those at the bottom end whose fee may largely be swallowed up anyway by travel costs.

Not surprisingly the BHA has been forced to backtrack, while huffing and puffing that it is for regulators not participants to regulate and that 'regulation is not a negotiation'. Overall limits on the number of whip strokes remain, rightly. But the unworkable specific limits in the last furlong or after the last obstacle have now been removed and penalties scaled down. M. Soumillon keeps his cash.

Slowly we are edging towards a workable reform. I haven't met any jockey or trainer who opposes reform in principle. But plenty of problems remain to be addressed. What can you do with lazy horses? Will international jockeys like Soumillon continue to race in Britain given the risks of suspensions which apply at home too? What about riders like Ruby Walsh who ride regularly both in Britain and Ireland? After an Aintree race earned him a five-day ban from the saddle for exceeding the prescribed number of strikes he declared, 'I don't want to be coming over here and getting bans in small races and missing big rides for Willie Mullins back home.' Is it realistic to restrict riders to virtually the same number of strokes in a five-furlong sprint and a three-mile steeplechase? What about the safety issue when a rider who has used his 'strike allowance' finds his mount veering across the track, endangering others?

As I write, incensed riders are still threatening strike action until there are further revisions to the reforms. I hope they don't push their luck. Racing has suffered enough damage already. All we need now to turn a disaster into a debacle is tabloid headlines declaring 'Jockeys strike for the right to thrash their horses harder', which is how it would be presented.

Since then, mercifully, things have quietened down, thanks to a few more tweaks of the rules, the building in of a little more discretion and some personnel changes at the BHA. Some reform has been achieved.

Women jockeys

Most women seem to enjoy racing – the dressing up, the chance of a flutter. Mrs Oakley, fun to be with on any other occasion, just cannot get the racing bug, however hard I try. I have even found her in the racecourse car park devouring the latest well-reviewed novel rather than cheering on my fancy in the fifth. But racing simply cannot manage any longer without those of the female gender, and that is why I have long campaigned for a better deal for women riders. It has been a long, long time coming.

At first, of course, by decree of the Jockey Club, women weren't allowed to be trainers. Not until 1966 did Florence Nagle become the first woman licence-holder, although of course she had trained since 1938 with her head lad Bill Stickley nominally holding the licence, the subterfuge several redoubtable ladies had to adopt. The subsequent successes of the likes of Monica Dickinson, Mary Reveley, Jenny Pitman and Venetia Williams exposed that for the stuffed-shirt nonsense that it was.

Tim Neligan, former managing director of United Racecourses, told me how Flo Nagle had once berated him for the lack of race-riding opportunities for girls.

She wrote him a cheque on the spot to sponsor a race at Kempton and left funds in her will for its continuance. The race was first run in 1986 and John Lawrence wrote in the *Daily Telegraph* that Mrs Nagle was no doubt looking down from her celestial cloud with approval. She politely wrote in to tell him that she was still happily on this planet, but that when she moved on she was expecting to land up somewhere hotter than Heaven – and there to meet most of her racing friends!

Mrs Nagle, as ever, was well ahead of her time and in 1999 I was complaining as loudly as I could that there had not been a single woman in the top 50 riders on the Flat or over jumps the previous season. Having observed before the Whitbread Gold Cup that spring that twelve of the seventeen contestants were led round the parade ring by lasses, I argued that most yards would grind to a halt without female staff. That is even more true today. In the age of McDonalds, Kentucky Fried Chicken and pizza parlours, trainers have been delighted to have some lighter-weight girls to put up on the gallops. And yet a prejudice has persisted in many quarters about using women riders on the racecourse.

Women have been riding winners in Britain since the 1970s but it is a sad comment on racing's conservatism that when her husband David 'Dandy' Nicholls gave her a leg-up on Portuguese Lil in 1996, Alex Greaves was the first woman ever to ride in the Derby. Not until Hayley Turner was given a no-hoper to ride in the 2012 Derby was the phenomenon repeated. Gay Kelleway, first amateur and then professional ladies champion, was for many years the only woman to have been given a ride at Royal Ascot. Yet in 1996 when I watched an average day's racing in Auckland, New Zealand, seven of the ten races were won by women jockeys. In the United States when Julie

Krone proved herself as good as the men on the way to her 3,700 winners she was hired for plenty of rides in top races to reflect that. In 2011 Tammi Piermarini became the fifth female in US racing history to register 2,000 winners. But in Britain it has been a long, hard struggle for the women.

When I spoke to Alex Greaves back in 1996 she was philosophical. The hierarchy had been stuffy in the past, she said, but people could not help the way they were brought up and the younger generation were more liberal-minded. 'There will always be some prejudice. Some people won't use lightweights and that's it.' But, she added, the stuffy ones would be the losers for it. 'Take the strike rate of winners to rides and people like me and Emma [O'Gorman] and Kim [Tinkler] would be pretty high on the list. But most people say "Women jockeys haven't got the experience" and if they don't give us the rides we're not going to get the experience.'

Alex Greaves and Kim Tinkler, another female rider with more than 100 wins accumulated at that time, were both married to trainers. Emma O'Gorman, another prominent rider then, had a trainer father. But Diane Clay and Lorna Vincent, two capable riders in their time, were never given a fair chance over jumps. As Diane Clay said, 'If you haven't got connections it's a waste of time. This is the only sport in which women compete with men on equal terms but you have to be better than a man to get the opportunity to prove it.' Interestingly, women who made the breakthrough as trainers like Gold Cup winners Jenny Pitman and Henrietta Knight weren't known for putting up women riders. Henrietta Knight actually said she hoped never to put up a woman because she didn't believe the female form was made to take falls at racing pace. I hesitate ever to question my friend Hen, but were male bodies any better designed to do so?

In recent years, thank Heaven, the penny has dropped with most trainers both on the Flat and over jumps. Hayley Turner is top class and Newmarket trainer Michael Bell has given her the chance to prove it. Knocking down the targets like ninepins, she shared the champion apprentice title in 2005 with Saleem Golam and in 2008 became the first woman to ride 100 winners in a season. In 2011 she became the first woman to ride a Group One winner in her own right (Alex Greaves once dead-heated in one), taking both the July Cup on Dream Ahead and the Nunthorpe on Margot Did. Perhaps just as importantly, the year Hayley rode her first 100, Kirsty Milczarek rode 70 winners, just to show Hayley was no freak. In the 2012 season Amy Scott was champion apprentice in her own right and Cathy Gannon too has grafted herself into popularity with English trainers after coming over from Ireland.

The lovely thing about Hayley Turner is the girl-next-door naturalness she retains despite her achievements, but when you talk to her there is, too, a steady gaze which reflects the inner confidence she has needed to mix it with the boys. Although the no-nonsense Hayley, much happier riding horses than letting the media try to mould her into a PR personality and fashion icon, has had a couple of seasons disrupted by a head injury and a broken ankle, she is back at the top of her game and is now in contention with half a dozen good girl riders.

Over jumps Lucy Alexander became the first woman to win the conditional riders championship in 2012/13. But that does not mean we should be complacent. Like some of those who paved the way before her, Lucy Alexander has a trainer father and the Irish duo Katie Walsh and Nina Carberry come from families steeped in racing.

And while a few top names have come through, the talented South African Lisa Jones, who was hailed as a breakthrough model herself when riding 47 winners back in 2004, was forced to go abroad to Macau and India because of the lack of opportunities and bookings in Britain once she lost her claim.

Progress has been made, but we will only really know that we have arrived at a sensible position when we in the media have stopped greeting every female-ridden Group winner as a newsworthy item in itself. We need to abandon the fenced-off category of 'woman rider' altogether. Just like their male equivalents they are jockeys – bad, indifferent, or in the cases of riders like Hayley Turner and Cathy Gannon, top-class, tactically intelligent and instinctively resourceful.

I guess though that we will never completely get away from the sex factor. I haven't forgotten one bookie's reaction to the finish of the gruelling four-mile National Hunt Chase for amateurs at the Cheltenham Festival in 2010. In a desperate, flailing finish Katie Walsh and Nina Carberry both earned bans for over-use of 'the persuader'. 'Birds first and second,' he rasped. 'And what about the way they used those whips?' 'Oh yes, oh yes,' said a gent in a camel-hair coat standing next to me, dreamily turning an excited shade of pink. It takes all sorts, even in a racing crowd.

It has to be said, incidentally, that some women trainers do add to our pleasures by the way they turn themselves out, as well as their horses. One day at Kempton in March 2005 I noted:

One of the pleasures of seeing Venetia Williams's horses triumph is anticipating what racing's best-turned-out trainer will be wearing in the winners' enclosure. After Clear Thinking's triumph at

Newbury the other day it was a brown suede crea-
tion with black tassels. Elegant tassels, I hasten to
add, not tassels of the twirling kind. When Limerick
Boy came smoothly home at Kempton to capture the
Favourites Racing Pendil Novices Chase, the trainer
arrived to greet him in a coat that was not so much
something to keep the cold out as a piece of modern art with buttons. Mrs Oakley, and my credit-card
company, would no doubt have been able to name
the designer. I can only describe it as a snowstorm
in a coalmine or a soot-blast in an ice-cream factory.
White on black or black on white, it was quite literally
dazzling. So much so that, biro poised and jaw dropping, I only narrowly escaped a kick from Limerick
Boy which would have removed my right kneecap.
Perhaps he preferred the brown suede.

While we are on the subject of the disadvantaged, I do
have another sympathy in racing: what happens to those
top-class young riders when they lose the right to claim
those few pounds off which make them good value in a
shrewd trainer's eyes. The Mauritius-born Salcem Golam,
who shared that apprentice title with Hayley Turner, has
not found life easy since. At unfashionable Folkestone
in September 2008 he was riding a couple for Stuart
Williams, who agreed, 'It's very hard when young riders
lose their allowance and it depends very much on whether
those who have helped to make them a success while they
had it stick with them like Michael Bell has done with
Hayley Turner.'

Too much racing?

It was the master of Warren Place who began it all in August
1996. Henry Cecil, from a stable where you suspected most

of the horses, given half a chance, would wear Gucci racing plates and Hermes head collars, complained that there was too much racing in Britain and that it was breeding mediocrity, weakening and bringing down the racing industry. Rod Fabricius, clerk of the course at Goodwood, intensified the argument by objecting that the fixture list had swollen excessively in the past decade and that racing was spreading its product too thin. He pointed out that during Goodwood's five-day festival meeting ten years before, there had been 22 other meetings, with just two in the same catchment area. That year there were 29 other meetings, six of them in places competing for customers.

Nudged along by the *Sporting Life* with rather more than hands and heels, the 'too much racing' debate has proceeded in stable yards, parade rings and racecourse bars up and down the land. For the most part, the responses have depended on whether you are in a yard where the owners drink Bellinis and holiday in Mustique or whether your stable familiars bury their heads in a Guinness glass and take their leisure on the Costa Brava.

Many races are restricted to horses within a particular range of handicap ratings and so the top trainers, with yards full of equine Porsches, ask 'Where on earth do I find a race for all the horses I have rated at 90-plus?' They mutter that if they had a yard full of very moderate nags rated at 40–50 they could find opportunities to race them three afternoons a week and in the evenings and on some Sundays as well. They want less racing with bigger prizes.

'All very well for them,' say the smaller fry. 'But our owners can only afford moderate horses and there must be moderate races for them to win. If there were not lots of moderate horses swelling the racecards, what would happen to the volume of betting and the rake-off from it, however skimpy, on which everybody in racing depends?'.

Both camps have a point. You can sympathise with Luca Cumani's complaint from one of the best addresses in Newmarket that three-quarters of the racing calendar is made up of races which his horses are too good to enter and that it is bad for racing's image for it to appear as a mediocre sport. In a world of increasing leisure opportunities, racing has to compete with a number of glamorous inducements for the punter to part with their spending money, and if they acquire the impression that racing is second rate then they will go hang-gliding, play golf or save up for the next 'final' tour by the Rolling Stones instead.

But smaller trainers say that if a race produces plenty of runners and a good finish, most people are not too bothered about the calibre of the racing. If there is a cutback in the racing programme, they say, then the number of opportunities for small owners will decline and that cannot be good. As Derek Haydn Jones put it, 'There are a lot of mediocre horses in training owned by people who love racing but simply cannot afford anything better.' That includes me.

The extra meetings have come about partly because courses press for more: they can only generate so much revenue from non-racing days staging mini-golf or antique fairs. Bookmakers too called for more racing to increase their turnover at slacker times and were accommodated by racing authorities keen to increase levy income. The present structure which the bigger trainers resent came about partly because they were not content to leave the cheaper maiden races on the less fashionable tracks to the smaller yards but sent their higher-grade horses along to boost their win totals.

There is now too much racing. For evidence, just look at the whey-faced jockeys on the weighing-room steps as they head off, barrel-bags slung over their shoulders for another motorway slog to the next meeting. It has become impossible for anybody outside a small group of full-time professionals to keep up with the form book. And part of the problem is that nearly half the races run on Britain's tracks are handicaps. It is a system that forces good horses, which have demonstrated their ability, to carry lumps of weight to struggle against indifferent animals. It is a system that encourages manipulation, with trainers seeking to produce well-handicapped horses rather than top-quality horses. It is a system that, at its worst, encourages jockeys to make mistakes that are costly to punters because trainers don't want their horses to win by too much to the detriment of their handicap rating. And it is a system that drives equine talent abroad. Horses good enough to be forced to carry big weights in handicaps but not quite good enough to run in non-handicap Pattern and Listed races tend to be exported, thinning the talent pool in Britain. Mark Johnston, always a voice to be heeded in racing's debates, insists there must be reform. Racing, he argues, 'is not some politically correct version of non-competitive primary school sports where everyone can expect a prize'.

I have much sympathy for the fixture-framers at the British Horseracing Board who have to balance the conflicting interests, and I remain resistant to the calls for much less racing. For racing to mean anything it must be a spectator sport, not a private club, and I fear that an early victim of the 'too much racing' lobby would be the Sunday and evening meetings that are bringing in a new kind of spectator. We might lose too some of the smaller tracks and if young people have no racecourse in their area then they will never develop the habit of going racing. But adjustments could be made. Although a jumping enthusiast, I would shed no tears over the end of summer jumping. There should be fewer Flat races in July and August on baking ground and more in early autumn and perhaps a bigger differential between the prizes for winning a 0–60 handicap and those for winning better-class races.

Perhaps the answer in the end will be some kind of premier league, with top courses staging prestige racing getting extra dollops of levy money and smaller courses left largely to survive on their own, offering sparser facilities but extra fun. I won't expect Ascot when I go to Brighton or to Catterick, but I shall still go. In the meantime, racing should stop squabbling about who gets which slice of prize money and concentrate on baking a bigger cake.

INDEX

INDEX

Dylan Thomas, 67, 196

Easby Abbey, 91
East Molesey, 5, 254
Easterby, Peter, 91–2
Easterby, Tim, 146–7
Ebor, the, *see* York
Eclipse Stakes, *see* Sandown
Eclipse, 151
Eddery, Pat, 140–6, 152, 170, 203,
    221, 305, 309–10
Eddery, Robert 127
Edredon Bleu, 85–6
Edward VII, 116
Egan, John, 292
Ellerslie Park, 278–9
Elliott, Curtis, 221–2
Elsworth, David, 43, 84, 166, 210,
    237, 307
Elves, Tony, 162
Empery, 59, 73
Engelbrecht-Bresges, Winfried, 286
Epsom, 14, 37–8, 40–3, 47–55,
    58–9, 62–7, 70, 73–4, 167,
    198, 213, 284, 297–8, 305
    Coronation Cup, 132, 251
    Derby, the, 14, 41, 54, 59–75,
        86, 93, 106, 130–1, 143, 146,
        152–3, 158, 199–202, 207,
        221, 226, 249, 317
    Derby Day, 14, 60–1, 75, 198
    Oaks, the 59, 63, 79, 162, 245
    Race Committee, 59
    Tattenham Corner, 61–2, 67,
        73, 200
    Tattenham Hill, 61
    Training and Development
        Fund, 53–4
Epsom Downs, 36, 39, 52–6
E.P. Taylor Stakes, *see* Woodbine
Esha Ness, 31
Evans, Richard, 266
Even Top, 308
Excelebration, 240

Fabre, André, 65, 71–3
Fabricius, Rod, 117, 322
Fairy King Prawn, 285
Falbrav, 236, 250, 261

Fallon, Kieren, 64–6, 121–2, 134–5,
    143, 146, 152, 154–62, 170,
    195–202, 235–7, 305, 310
Falmouth Stakes, 221, 245
Fanshawe, James, 194
Fantasia, 244–5
Fantastic Light, 133–4, 250, 285–6
Faringdon Place, 215, 217, 227
Farrell, Paddy, 16
Feltham Novices Chase, 114
Fifinella, 63
Financial Times, 290
Findlay, Harry, 239, 246–7
Finglas council estate, 187
Fitzgerald, Jimmy, 73
Fitzgerald, Mick, 2, 103, 170–3,
    177, 180–2, 266
Flagship Uberalles, 85
Foinavon fence, *see* Aintree
Fontwell Park, 250
Ford, Carrie, 27, 32–3, 277
Ford, Richard, 277
Forest Gunner, 28, 32
Forgive 'n Forget, 73
Francis, Dick, 24, 165, 176, 208
Francome, John, 52, 93, 228
Frankel, 133, 166, 231, 238–41,
    307, 313
Frankincense, 224–5, 255
Freemason Lodge, 161
Freud, Sir Clement, 259
Frozen Fire, 150
Fruits of Love, 131
Fujiyama Crest, 138–41

Galbreath, John, 60
Galileo, 61, 64, 68–9, 75, 133–4
Gallagher, Dean, 190–5
Gannon, Cathy, 319–20
Gare St Lazare, 280
Gay Trip, 31
Geezer, The, 148
George Washington, 66
Geraghty, Barry, 178
Ghanaati, 245, 304
Giant's Causeway, 70, 117, 144–5,
    152–3, 232, 309
Gifford, Josh, 25, 31
Gillespie, Edward, 60, 79–80

Hills, Michael, 122, 215, 233
Hills, Richard, 223
Hindu Kush, 150, 298
Hodges, Ron, 266
Holman, William, 89
Honey End, 31
Hong Kong, 44, 130, 172, 216, 250,
    278, 283–7, 290
    Jockey Club, 286
Hors La Loi II, 194
Hot Weld, 180
Howard, Michael, 258
Howes, Gavin, 299
Howling, Paul, 201
Hughes, Dessie, 92, 184, 192, 312
Hughes, Richard, 45–6, 62, 121–2,
    169, 172, 184, 188–90, 305,
    314
Humdoleila, 106
Humorist, 63
Hurricane Run, 202
Hurst Park racecourse, 5–8

I Cried For You, 169
Imperial Commander, 249
Independent, 17
India, 320
Indian Haven, 237
Ingram, Roger, 48, 50, 167
Injured Jockeys Fund, 16, 214
Irish Champion Stakes, 64, 86, 114,
    149, 249
Irish Derby, 57, 69, 148–50
Irish Grand National, 89, 233
Iron Stand Club, *see* Ascot
Ivory, Ken, 302

Jackdaw's Castle, 76
Jacob, Daryl, 88
James, David, 56–8
Japan, 250
Japan Cup, 60, 133, 179, 218, 252
Jardine's Lookout, 119
Jarvis, Michael, 67
Jarvis, William 208, 215
Jay Trump, 82
Jeans, Sir Alick, 9
Jibber the Kibber, 254
Jibe, 162

Jockey Club, 22, 48, 73, 153, 161,
    163, 166, 177, 198, 279,
    286–7, 309, 316
Joe 'n Jack, 49–50
Johnson, David, 78, 186
Johnson, Dickie, 178, 277
Johnson, Frank, 38
Johnson, Richard, 179, 277
Johnston, Mark, 123, 152, 190, 205,
    324
Jones, Lisa, 320
Jones, Peter, 122
Jones, Tom, 225
Jordan, Frank, 49
Juddmonte International, *see* York

Kafue Bridge, 5
Kakatosi, 154–5
Kalanisi, 152–3, 309
Katie Cecil, 197
Kauto Star, 2, 114, 231, 246–9
Kavanagh, John, 103, 177
Kazamias, Panayiotis, 287
Kelleway, Gay, 317
Kelleway, Paul, 90
Kempton Park, 11, 23, 43, 112–15,
    206, 233, 267–9, 301, 304–6,
    317, 320–1
    Great Jubilee Handicap, 11
    King George VI Chase, 85,
    113–14, 232–3
Kentucky Derby, 75, 218, 278
Killiney, 82
Kinane, Mick, 47, 69, 132–4, 152,
    158
Kinane, Tommy, 92
King George VI Chase, *see*
    Kempton Park
King George VI and Queen
    Elizabeth Stakes, *see* Ascot
King Of The Refs, 179
King, Annabel, 168–9
King's Glory, 37
Kingmambo, 235–7
Kinnegad Kid, 49
Knavesmire racetrack, *see* York
Knight, Henrietta, 85, 206, 232,
    318
Kong, 148

INDEX

INDEX

INDEX

INDEX